D1561340

HEMI

First published in 2009 by Motorbooks, an imprint of Quarto Publishing Group USA Inc., 400 First Avenue North, Suite 400, Minneapolis, MN 55401 USA

Editor: Chris Endres
Designer: LK Design, Inc., Laura Rades
Cover designed by: Simon Larkin

On the front cover: Bold graphics on a Ramcharger hood call out the 1971 Dodge Super Bee's underhood prowess. *Mike Mueller*

On the back cover , left to right: 1969 Charger R/T, 426 street Hemi, 1970 Special Edition Challenger hardtop. *Mike Mueller*

On the frontispiece: Very few muscle cars can match the prodigious smoke show possible with a Hemi Road Runner. *Mike Mueller*

On the title pages: If a '71 Hemi 'Cuda convertible doesn't quicken your pulse, you probably drive a Prius. *Mike Mueller*

Printed in China

10 9 8 7 6 5 4

Library of Congress Cataloging-in-Publication Data

Mueller, Mike, 1959-
The complete book of classic Dodge and Plymouth muscle / by Mike Mueller.
p. cm.
Rev. ed. of: The complete book of Dodge and Plymouth muscle / Mike Mueller. 2009.
Summary: "The complete book of Dodge and Plymouth muscle collects and showcases the beauty and history of some of America's most iconic muscle cars of the late 20th century: from the Road Runner and Superbee to the Daytona Charger and more, the personalities, quirks, challenges and triumphs are all presented in detailed, explicit prose and beautiful original photography"-Provided by publisher.
ISBN 978-0-7603-4477-4 (flexibound sc)
1. Dodge automobile. 2. Plymouth automobile. 3. Muscle cars. I. Title.
TL215.D6M84 2013
629.222'2--dc23

2012048198

THE COMPLETE BOOK OF

DODGE AND PLYMOUTH MUSCLE

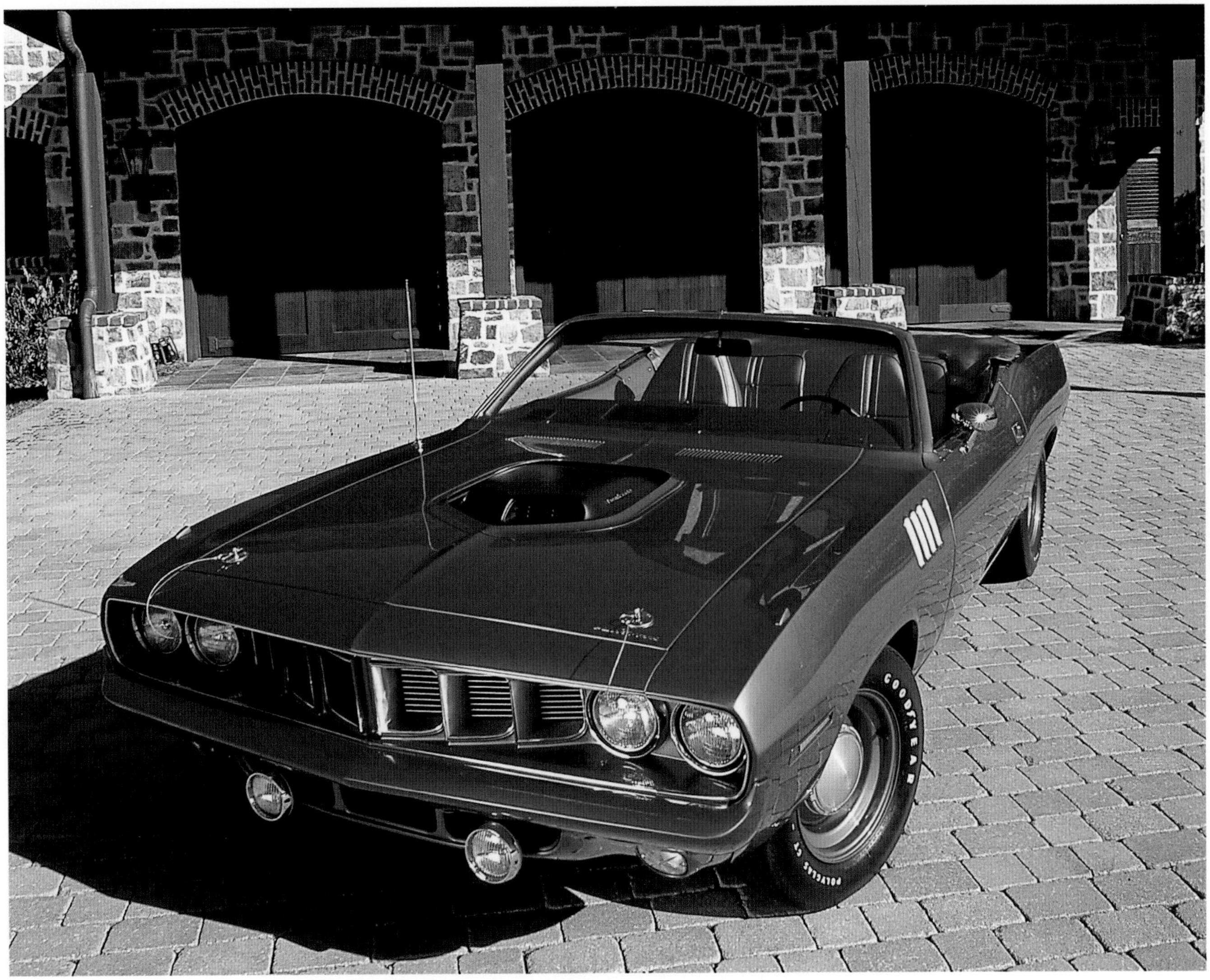

Contents

Acknowledgments

A lot goes into a book this size, and I'm not just speaking of pages, nor words and photos. Like every author out there, I would never have been able to hammer out the following text if not for the kind assistance of so many others, in this case knowledgeable Mopar muscle fanatics who can't ever seem to get enough of the cars featured within these covers. So many were willing to drop everything to answer my technical questions, and if they couldn't set me straight, they were ready, willing, and able to point me toward someone who could. Most of these people also were a great help when it came time to photograph all the Dodge and Plymouth factory hot rods you'll see on the pages to follow. And still others were there simply when I needed a little push, or shove, to help get this hefty epic into print.

Among that last group were Zack Miller and Chris Endres, two of MBI Publishing's finest. Zack has put up with my antics for as long as I've been doing this—nearly 20 years—and he amazingly shows no sign of closing the book on me, at least not yet. My editor on two MBI project so far, Chris too has demonstrated an ability to withstand "working with Mueller," and he's probably got the receding hair line to prove it. I promise, guys, I will make it up to you both someday, if only by including you in my will. What'll it be, my empty beer bottle collection or my Pocket Fisherman?

Additional priceless support came from my new best friend, Robin Connell, who calls Miami home and also calls up here to Atlanta's far north suburbs as often as she can—a notable feat considering her work keeps her buried even deeper than mine does me. Unlimited local and long-distance calling, what a concept, right, Robin? Now if I'd only buy a cell phone, then perhaps we could get to know each other even better.

Various family members back home in the Champaign, Illinois, area also continued to lend helping hands whenever I needed free labor during various photo sessions, just as they have for . . . has it really been almost 20 years now? My parents, Jim and Nancy Mueller, again allowed me to use their home as a remote office, and my brother-in-law, Frank Young, was his usual amusing self on a shoot or two. Yes, Frank, the check is in the mail. Should I use your new address or the one you left behind three years ago? As for you, Ma, great tacos! Brothers Dave and Jim Mueller Jr. also did more than their fair share and thus will also receive more than their fair share—of hearty thanks.

Many thanks also go out to Brandt Rosenbusch and Phyllis McClintock at Chrysler's Corporate Historical Collection for all the times they jumped through hoops whenever I called in search of vintage photographical support. This tends to be a full-time job for Brandt, who has been there when I've needed him many times over the last 10 years or so.

Another longtime comrade, *Musclecar Enthusiast* magazine editor and tall Texan Steven Statham, once again stepped up to help out in last-second fashion, just as he has always done dating back to our days together in Florida working for Dobbs Publishing (*Mopar Muscle*, *Musclecar Review*, etc.) back in the early nineties. Former Dobbs man and *Musclecar Review* editor Paul Zazarine deserves a handshake too, if only for answering my e-mails a few times. Fellow Motorbooks author Jim Schild did even more, picking up the phone at all hours of the night to hear my pleas. Paul knows better, but Jim apparently still has a lot to learn.

Additional tips of the hat go to various other friends, both old and new: Roger Gibson at Roger Gibson Restorations in Kelso, Missouri; Floyd Garrett and Bob Hancock at the Floyd Garrett Muscle Car Museum in Sevierville, Tennessee; Ted Bernstein at the RPM Collection in Fishers, Indiana; Ken Mosier at the Finer Details in Danville, Indiana; Ted Stephens at Stephens Performance in Rogersville, Alabama; John Gastman and his crew at Roanoke Dodge in Roanoke, Illinois; Don Garlits, T. C. Lemons, Tommy Kennedy, Dennis Youngs, and Peggy Hunnewell down at the Garlits Museum of Drag Racing near Ocala, Florida; and Ryan Patton at Patton's Upholstery in Champaign, Illinois.

Various club people and avid collectors also made major contributions, including Roy Gobczynski, Boris Bonutti, and all the Mopar crazies in and around Effingham, Illinois. Calling these men (and women) "car guys" is an understatement. Calling them "great guys" (and gals) is only the right thing to do after they basically handed me the key to their town.

Kervyn Mach, at the Plymouth Barracuda/'Cuda Owners Club, was a joy to work with, and without his help I would never have met Norm VerHage (Holland, Michigan) and Brian Eberhart (Mishawaka, Indiana), two more avid Mopar men whom I hope I'll be calling good friends for many years to come. The same goes for John Bober, the man behind the Dodge Super Bee registry, based down in Viera, Florida.

Last but certainly not least, I can't close without mentioning all the men and women who took the time to share their pride-and-joys with me and my Hasselblad—yes, I also do not own a digital camera. Space constraints keep me from thanking each of you individually here, what with so many fabulous Dodge and Plymouth muscle cars finding their way onto the following pages. But you know who you are and certainly so do I. You will not be forgotten, nor will you be rid of me easily.

Here's to y'all. Just remember to screen your calls the next time.

—*Mike Mueller*

Introduction
A Loud, Proud Legacy

Some things old often can be new again: just as Hemi power was the hottest thing going in Detroit 40 years ago, it is again in 2008. Both of these Mopar muscle cars feature 425 horses supplied by Hemi V-8s. The vintage Road Runner at right is fitted with Plymouth's optional 426-cubic-inch street Hemi, an option in 1968. A 6.1-liter Hemi is standard for Dodge's latest Super Bee. *Mike Mueller*

About 100 miles separate Chicago and the small Illinois town of Roanoke, located a little west of I-39 among the rolling cornfields downstate of the Windy City. Head out of this quiet burg toward Peoria on County Road 117, and you'll find Roanoke Dodge, a long-standing dealership run by John Gastman, a Mopar man through and through. Or perhaps it's a time machine Gastman operates. In some ways, his showroom sometimes reminds visitors of another day at another place, this one once found at the corner of west Grand and north Spaulding avenues in Chi-town. Take a gander at all the hot cars (not to mention trucks) and parts commonly found at Gastman's place today, and you might think you'd jumped those 100 clicks north, as well as 40 years back, to Mr. Norm's Grand-Spaulding Dodge.

Founded in October 1962 by Norman and Lenny Kraus, Grand-Spaulding was *the* place to go during the sixties and early seventies if going fast in a Mopar muscle car was your goal. Mr. Norm's men not only sold the factory hot rods, they also created and marketed their own brand of Dodge performance, identified most prominently over the years by the dealership's legendary "GSS" badges. And if you took your own hot wheels in, the Grand-Spaulding guys could warm them up even further. Beating the other brands severely about the head and shoulders, both on the street and at the track, was what Mr. Norm's was all about.

Among Grand-Spaulding's many happy customers back in the day was John Gastman. A regular at local eighth-mile strips almost as soon as he himself became street legal, Gastman preferred Mopars from the start. "Everyone else wanted Chevys or Fords to win," he recalled with a chuckle in 2008. "But I've always been kind of a maverick; I wanted the other guys to win." His first weapon of

Above:
Dodge showrooms today are commonly loaded with hot cars, what with so much Hemi power now being offered. But John Gastman's Roanoke Dodge, in Roanoke, Illinois, often reminds visitors of just how long Chrysler has been building some of Detroit's meanest machines, thanks to an occasional display from his personal collection. Beneath this 1968 Road Runner's hood is an original street Hemi V-8. *Mike Mueller*

Right:
During the 1960s and early 1970s, Mr. Norm's Grand-Spaulding Dodge, located on Chicago's west side, was the hub of the Mopar muscle universe. Young drag racers like John Gastman flocked to Norm Kraus' dealership forty years back to have their cars maxed out.

choice at the drags was a 1962 Sport Fury convertible, "a real ugly car" (his words) that he replaced with a 1967 GTX, then a 1969 383 Road Runner. All his Mopars made the trip northeast up to Grand-Spaulding to experience some of Mr. Norm's winning touch, in turn making young Gastman a winner almost everywhere he went.

Gastman went to work at Roanoke Dodge in 1964, paid his dues, then bought into the business 20 years later. He already was an enthusiastic Mopar muscle collector by then, and a 1970 Challenger T/A that he acquired in 1973 remains one of his pride-and-joys 35 years later. If you're lucky, Gastman just might have one or two of his vintage machines on display in his showroom when you drop by.

Along with his 40-year-old iron, he's also equally proud of his Vipers, a collection that grew naturally as Gastman's business rolled on. From 1995 to 2000, Roanoke Dodge was this country's number one Viper dealer, hands down, and the firm has claimed that annual honor various times since. All told, no other dealership nationwide has delivered more of these V-10 monsters from 1992 to 2008 than Roanoke Dodge, basically because Gastman truly loves to play with Mopar muscle.

"We do quite well with these cars," he said. "I enjoy selling them. It's good to put a little excitement in driving. These automobiles are just fun. When you look out in your garage and say that's mine, it doesn't get much better. When you get out of a car with a smile on your face, you've had a great day."

And he wasn't just talking about Vipers. Dodge officials, too, have been doing more than their fair share of time-tripping in recent years. Witness the return of so many great high-performance nameplates of yore, not to mention the Hemi V-8. Charger, Challenger, R/T, Super Bee—these fun machines are also plentiful at Roanoke Dodge, as are all of Chrysler's Street and Racing Technology vehicles, be it SRT-4, -6, -8, or -10.

That so much Mopar muscle has become available in recent years is the direct result of Chrysler Corporation's many decades of experience in the field, and we're not just talking about what went on during the sixties and seventies. Consider Dodge's born-again Hemi V-8. This legacy alone dates back more than a half century, at least from a Mopar perspective. Hemispherical combustion chambers certainly were nothing new when Chrysler rolled out its award-winning Firepower V-8 in 1951, but no one had mass-marketed them with so much success up to that point. Nor has anyone done it better since. Even before Dodge engineers dusted off the design for their Ram-tough trucks in 2002, any mention of the term Hemi automatically brought Chrysler to mind.

What makes this particular engine so swwwweet? Hemi-head advantages are many, beginning with those symmetrical, domed combustion chambers and their centrally located spark plugs. This layout not only makes for superb volumetric efficiency, the physical nature of those rounded chambers allows more room for bigger valves compared

Left:
Chrysler's new-for-1951 model not only was honored with *Motor Trend's* Car of the Year award, it also was picked as the prestigious pace car for that year's Indianapolis 500. Its impressive Firepower V-8 was the key to its success. *Chrysler LLC Corporate Historical Collection*

Below:
Hemi-head engines became the toast of organized drag racing in 1957, and pioneering hot rodders simply couldn't resist both the muscle and eye-appeal of Chrysler's big Firepower V-8. When creative builder Aaron Grote opted to pay homage to his early 1960s forerunners, he chose a 1958 392 Hemi for his "Atomic Punk" retro-rod. Talk about a blast from the past. *Mike Mueller*

to conventional "wedge-head" designs. Hemi valves are also inclined in opposite directions to match the shape of the chambers, and this means less restriction for both intake and exhaust flow. In with the good air, out with the bad is simply a breeze for the free-breathing Hemi.

Downsides to Chrysler original design included its relatively complex valvetrain and definitely its excessive weight. Twin rocker shafts were needed to locate the inclined valves atop those hemispherical chambers, meaning the heads had to be big and wide. This, in turn, made for a tight fit between any fenders, big car or small. And those hefty chunks of cast-iron weighed as much as 25 percent more than comparable wedge heads. This weight penalty, coupled with all the fuss and muss required to engineer and manufacture Hemi heads, had helped convince Chrysler officials to give up on the idea the first time around. The Firepower V-8's short, happy career ended in 1958.

Firepower roots dated back to development work originally considered in 1935. Putting Hemi-head technology into regular production 16 years later then helped Chrysler dramatically unseat Cadillac atop Detroit's rapidly developing horsepower race. At 180 horsepower, the 331-cubic-inch Firepower V-8 was 20 horses hotter than Cadillac's history-making overhead-valve engine, making Chrysler the talk of the town in 1951.

"The tremendous power of this V-8 is enough in itself to be a strong selling point for the Chrysler," claimed a *Road & Track* review. "Regardless of the rest of the car's advantages or disadvantages, when you touch that throttle, you know something mighty impressive is happening under the hood." *Motor Trend*'s staff was so impressed, they awarded their "Car of the Year" trophy to the 1951 Firepower Chrysler. According to *Motor Trend*'s Griffith Borgeson, the Hemi-head Chrysler represented "a major step ahead in American automotive history."

Hemi heads found their way beneath DeSoto hoods in 1952, then migrated into Dodge ranks the following year. Plymouth never did benefit from the design during the fifties, but its so-called "poly-head" V-8, introduced to its own raves in 1955, represented ample improvement to drivers who'd only had six cylinders to play with up until then. Even bigger news that year involved Chrysler's release of Detroit's first modern 300-horsepower engine, a Firepower V-8 that was showcased in the C-300, the milestone machine some Mopar mavens still talk about whenever someone asks which car actually kicked off Detroit's original muscle car era.

In 1956, Chrysler's second-edition "letter car," the 300B, became the first member of Detroit's one-horsepower-per-cubic-inch fraternity. No, the 1957 Corvette's 283-horsepower, 283-cubic-inch, fuel-injected small-block wasn't the founding member. The 300B's

Three Hemi-powered machines set drag racing speed records in 1957, with Emory Cook's Cook-Bedwell rail (middle) becoming the first into the 160-mile-per-hour range in February. The *Speed Sport Special* (top) did 169 miles per hour in October with Red Greth at the wheel. Then Don Garlits blew everyone away the next month with his *Swamp Rat* (bottom) after turning 176-mile-per-hour in Brooksville, Florida. *Swamp Rat* appears here as it did in 1959. *Mike Mueller*

Chrysler's 426 street Hemi probably needs no introduction. About 11,000 of these monsters, conservatively rated at 425 horsepower, were installed in Dodge and Plymouth muscle cars from 1966 to 1971. *Mike Mueller*

optional Firepower V-8, enlarged to 354 cubic inches, was advertised at 355 horsepower the year before. Take that, General Motors promotional people, who to this day still make that false claim concerning Chevrolet's first "fuelie" Corvette.

By 1957 Chrysler's Firepower V-8 was displacing 392 cubic inches and making 390 horsepower. So much muscle certainly was hard to miss, especially by drag racing pioneers like Florida's Don Garlits. National Hot Rod Association quarter-mile speed records seemingly fell left and right in 1957, in each case thanks to Chrysler V-8s. Emory Cook's 354-powered rail was the first to run 160 miles per hour in February, a feat many experts had deemed impossible. His 166.97-miles-per-hour clocking was then bested in October by another 354 Chrysler, the *Speed Sport Special*, which managed a smoking 169.11 miles per hour. Garlits then blew everyone away after trading his 354 for the big 392. In November 1957 his *Swamp Rat I* ran an amazing 176.40 miles per hour at Brooksville, Florida.

More than one critic cried foul, claiming the timers were faulty or Garlits had benefited from a "home-field advantage" of sorts. But most naysayers were quickly quieted after he continued putting up big numbers on the way to becoming the newborn sport's greatest name. "The less-than-nine-seconds it took Garlits to cover the quarter-mile that day changed him from a small-town dragster pilot into one of the fastest and most controversial figures in U.S. drag racing," wrote *Car Craft* magazine's Bob Behme two years later, this after "Big Daddy" had hiked the bar even higher to 183.66 miles per hour.

Garlits and Chrysler power went together like orange shorts and Hooters girls for decades to come. Big Daddy was still piloting a Hemi-powered Top Fueler after turning 70 in 2002. To say he helped make NHRA competition what it is today is an understatement, and the same also might be said about the engine he remained devoted to all those years. Dropping the name "Hemi" during the sixties and seventies left most gearheads primarily thinking "Garlits." And vice versa.

Racing involvement was what inspired Chrysler to bring the Hemi back the first time in 1964. Displacement that year was 426 cubic inches, the official output label a laughable 425 maximum horsepower for an engine meant only for competition use. Race Hemis fitted with dual four-barrel carburetors took drag strips by storm, while single-carb versions appeared on NASCAR speedways, where they were banned by big Bill France and the boys in 1965—because they weren't regular-production options. Chrysler officials then righted this apparent wrong by introducing the 426-cube "street Hemi" as a Dodge and Plymouth option in 1966.

The output label again read 425 horsepower, which, as engineer Tom Hoover later explained, "was purely an advertising number." "Most of the street Hemis would make 500 horsepower or better," he continued. In his opinion, using the 425-horse rating "was purely a matter of everybody being in fear that they would be called to Washington to testify before some committee that would say, 'you dirty dogs are out there making more power for cars and that's the un-American thing to do.' We were really worried about that as far back as the early sixties. We were scared to death."

Mid sized B-body models made up the bulk of the Mopar muscle lineup during the 1960s. Dodge's 1967 Coronet R/T (at right) helped kick off Chrysler's response to Pontiac's GTO, the car that got the whole muscle car race rolling in 1964. Plymouth's Road Runner joined the fun in 1968. A 1969 Road Runner, powered by the breed's base 383-cubic-inch big-block V-8, is at left. *Mike Mueller*

Detroit's original muscle car reached its zenith in 1970 before tightening safety and emissions standards, coupled with rising fuel and insurance costs, put an end to the fun, albeit temporarily. Among Chrysler Corporation's strongest offerings that year was Plymouth's 440-powered GTX (left) and Dodge's new Challenger R/T, fitted in this case with the optional 440 Six Pack V-8. *Mike Mueller*

On the other hand, so was the competition. Hemi-powered Dodge and Plymouth muscle cars hit the ground running in 1966 and remained among Detroit's hottest machines up through 1971. An expensive option, yes, but that didn't stop the 426 Hemi from squeezing its way between the fenders of nearly everything the two Chrysler divisions built during those years. Most went into midsized B-body models, which had introduced unit-body construction to Dodge and Plymouth lines in 1960. Dodge's Coronet and Charger and Plymouth's Belvedere and Satellite were the first to receive optional Hemi power in 1966. Sexier wrappings then appeared the following year when Dodge introduced its R/T renditions of the Coronet and Charger and Plymouth rolled out a gussied-up Belvedere called GTX. Two more hopped-up B-bodies, Plymouth's Road Runner and Dodge's Super Bee, debuted for 1968, and they, too, listed the 426 Hemi as an available option.

Hemi A-body installations also happened in 1968. The compact Valiant, introduced for 1960, was Chrysler's first A-body, and an upsized version of this little Plymouth was joined by a downsized Dart running mate from Dodge in 1963. A Valiant hardtop was then morphed into Plymouth's sloped-back Barracuda the following year. The A-body was redesigned for 1967 resulting in a bigger, better Barracuda and Dart, and allowing for the installation of optional big-block power. This, in turn, allowed engineers to stuff a handful of 426-cube race Hemis into super-stock Dodge and Plymouth A-bodies in 1968.

Perhaps the supreme home for the Hemi, at least from an everyday transport point of view, arrived in 1970, the year Chrysler introduced its compact E-body platform, used as a foundation for both Plymouth's latest, greatest Barracuda and Dodge's totally new Challenger. In their day, Hemi-powered E-bodies were among the fastest things you'd ever see sitting at a stoplight on Main Street U.S.A. Today these rare machines are seven-digit auction fodder.

With all the attention it has received over the years, it's almost hard to believe that the street Hemi was so damned few and far between in its day. Only about 10,500 race and street versions were released between 1964 and 1971. Often overshadowed, then and now, were the other performance powerplants offered by Dodge and Plymouth in much greater numbers during that span. Various big- and small-block V-8s played major roles in the Mopar muscle story too, including a hefty 440-cubic-inch monster that offered much of the Hemi's might at a portion of its cost.

The 440's roots run back to the 392 Firepower's retirement in 1958. DeSoto and Dodge had dropped their smaller Hemi-head V-8s the previous year, replacing them with a lighter, far less complex B-series V-8 that featured a typical inline valve layout and conventional wedge-shaped combustion chambers. All B engines from then up through the bloodline's demise in 1978 relied on the same stroke—3.375 inches—and matching that crank with a 4.060-inch bore resulted in the 350-cubic-inch wedge-head V-8 that both DeSoto and Plymouth unveiled for 1958. Increasing the B-series block's bore to 4.125 inches produced the 361 wedge, which DeSoto also used that year along with Dodge.

Chrysler Division, meanwhile, turned to an even larger B-series variant for 1959 to replace the Hemi-head 392 in its upscale ranks. Known as an "RB," or "tall-deck" V-8, this new powerplant was

Continued on page 14

The 300

Chrysler designers in 1955 combined Imperial luxury and style with maximized Hemi-head performance, resulting in the C-300, what some old-timers call Detroit's first muscle car. *Mike Mueller*

The C-300 got at least part of its name from its standard horsepower count: its 331-cubic-inch Firepower V-8 produced 300 horses. Two four-barrel carbs fed this little Hemi and continued to be found on all letter cars up through 1963. An available single-carb engine appeared in 1964. *Mike Mueller*

Some old-timers will argue that the great American muscle car wasn't born in 1964 and Pontiac didn't handle conception. They claim Mopar men did the honors and that 1955 was the correct date of birth. New that year was chief engineer Bob Rodger's C-300, the first of Chrysler's legendary "letter cars." Combining various lavish Imperial features with the division's hot 331 Firepower Hemi, the original letter car was named for its historic output rating—discounting the very rare, very expensive Duesenbergs built before World War II, this modern milestone was Detroit's first to offer 300 horsepower in standard form. As for that "C" designation, it reportedly was in honor of Briggs Cunningham's various Hemi-powered Le Mans racers of 1951–1954, all of which also wore a C prefix. Actually the letter in the 1955 300's case was simply short for "Chrysler." Apparently the incorrect assumption about the Cunningham connection was accepted as fact early on after it was initially insinuated, rather casually, by veteran *Mechanix Illustrated* road tester Tom McCahill in 1955.

Any questions about the actual origins of the initial name fell by the wayside after a second rendition appeared for 1956 wearing a "300B" tag. An alphabetical progression followed from there, hence the "letter-car" reference. The 300B was followed by the 300C and so on up through the last of the legacy, the 300L, built for 1965. Chrysler officials opted to skip the letter I—which should have predictably showed up for 1963—to avoid confusion with the Roman numeral "I."

Styling guru Virgil Exner already had spent $100 million or so restyling Chrysler's 1955 line when Rodger approached him and division manager Ed Quinn about the possibility of combining the Hemi-head muscle he'd helped create with a heaping helping of posh prestige. Exner loved the idea, and Quinn gave the go-ahead, leaving Rodger to team up with Cliff Voss, head of the Imperial design studio, and Production chief Tom Piorier to build a true postwar classic.

Though Rodger and Voss saved mucho money by relying on existing pieces, Chrysler's letter car still came off looking, and performing, like nothing seen before. Based on a New Yorker hardtop body shell, the C-300 featured an attractive egg-crate Imperial grille, a leather interior, power brakes, and heavy-duty suspension. Rodger's contribution was the 300-horsepower, 331-cubic-inch Hemi with its twin Carter carbs.

Debuting in January 1955, the C-300 was, in Chrysler's words, "America's greatest performing motor car, with the speed of the wind, the maneuverability of a polo pony, the power to pass on the road safely, an all-around performance quite unlike anything you will find available here in America or abroad." According to McCahill, it was "the most powerful sedan in the world, and the fastest, teamed up with rock-crushing Suspension and a competition Engine capable of yanking Bob Fulton's steamboat over the George Washington Bridge."

Chrysler's early letter cars also took to racing like Fulton did to inventing. After setting speed records on the beach at Daytona, the C-300 went on to dominate stock-car competition in 1955 and 1956, thanks to the factory-backed efforts of Carl Kiekhaefer's Mercury Outboards team.

Off the track, the 4,300-pound C-300 was an able match for Chevrolet's much lighter V-8 Corvette, at least on the straight and narrow. Chevy's

After the C-300 came the 300B, 300C, and so on up through 300L—hence the letter-car label. At left is a 1957 300C, at right is a 1959 300E, and in back is a 1960 300F. *Mike Mueller*

fiberglass-bodied two-seater could do the 0–60 run in 9.0 seconds, the quarter-mile in 17.2 seconds at 81.5 miles per hour. The palatial C-300 ran the quarter in 17.6 seconds (at 82 miles per hour) and roared from rest to 60 miles per hour in 9.5 seconds.

Although the 300's racing career came to a close after 1956, it continued running strong into the sixties, inspiring automotive journalist Karl Ludvigsen to christen it "the Beautiful Brute." Eleven model runs ended a bit tamely with the 300L, but all previous models lived up to the standards established in 1955.

Highlights during this run included a little history made in 1956. New that year was an optional 355-horsepower, 354-cubic-inch Hemi, Detroit's first engine to breech the one-horsepower-per-cubic-inch "barrier." No, Chevrolet wasn't the first to reach this plateau with its 283/283 "fuelie" Corvette in 1957, as is still often reported today. Maximum output for the letter car came in 1960 in the form of an optional 400-horsepower, 413-cubic-inch V-8.

A rare fuel injection option was offered in 1958, the last year for Chrysler's original Hemi-head technology. The 392-cubic-inch Firepower V-8 was replaced by a 413-cubic-inch wedge in 1959, and the following year this RB big-block was topped by Chrysler's intriguing ram-induction hardware with its dual Carter four-barrels hung outside the valve covers on long, tubular manifolds. Ram induction was standard up through 1963, optional in 1964, the year a single four-barrel carburetor appeared for the first time atop a letter car's V-8. A single-carb 413 was the only engine offered for the 300L in 1965.

It technically wasn't a letter car, but Plymouth promotional people still couldn't help but make the connection when they rolled out their 300H in 1970. Specially customized by Hurst, this full-sized flyer featured a domed hood, rear spoiler, and exclusive gold-accented paint. *Chrysler LLC Corporate Historical Collection*

All letter cars built for 1955 and 1956 were hardtops. A convertible joined the lineup in 1957 and stuck around up to the end. That the 300 made its last stand in 1965 was the result of various factors, not the least of which involved the appearance of Pontiac's ground breaking GTO in 1964. Full-sized performance lost much of its flavor once midsized muscle cars began flooding the market. And working in concert with this thoroughly modern trend was Chrysler's dilution of a once-proud nameplate. A "non-letter" 300 line debuted for 1962, and this "300 Sport Series" was nothing (at least in standard form) compared to its 300H counterpart. Due to the comparatively plain 300's arrival, many witnesses, including those in the Milestone Car Society, have long called the 300G of 1961 the last great letter car. Calling Chrysler's lettered 300s Detroit's first muscle car is up to you.

Less expensive than the Hemi yet nearly as potent, a triple-carb 440 wedge first appeared as a race-ready option for special Super Bee and Road Runner models midyear in 1969. Dodge's 440 Six Pack and Plymouth's 440 Six Barrel (shown here) then became available for B- and E-body applications the following year. Those three Holley two-barrel carbs helped make 390 horsepower. *Mike Mueller*

simply a B engine with a raised (thus the "R") cylinder block deck, a casting modification made to increase displacement potential by allowing for a longer stroke. The measurement from deck surface to crank centerline within a "low-deck" B engine was 9.980 inches; the distance in the RB block was 10.725 inches. This extra deck height made room for a 3.750-inch stroke, which also remained constant during the RB's run up through 1978. In 1959 this stroke was paired with a 4.180-inch bore to displace 413 cubic inches. Another RB, a little-known 383-cubic-inch rendition, also appeared briefly for 1959 and 1960 (with a 4.030-inch bore) and shouldn't be confused with the much more popular low-deck 383-cube B engine that debuted in 1961. The bore in the B-series 383 was 4.250 inches.

Though primarily a quiet giant meant mostly for luxury liner applications, the 413 V-8 did work well as the heart of Chrysler's letter-car line from 1959 to 1965, maxing out at 405 horsepower as an option for the 300H in 1962. That same year both Dodge and Plymouth began offering the meanest, nastiest 413 ever, the so-called "Max Wedge" with its cross-ram, dual-carb intake and high-flying, header-like exhaust manifolds. Clearly meant for competition only, the Max Wedge V-8 was enlarged to 426 cubic inches in 1963 thanks to a bore increase to 4.250 inches. The 426 Max Wedge was then replaced early in 1964 by the awesome 426 race Hemi.

A civilized version of the 426 wedge debuted in 1964, though few seemingly noticed this 365-horsepower RB big-block. Both Dodge and Plymouth offered this relatively strong, rarely seen performance option into 1965. Then along came the 426 street Hemi the following year to change all the rules.

But, as mentioned, this expensive option wasn't for everyone. At the time, Plymouth's GTX and Dodge's Coronet R/T were waiting in the wings for 1967, and each were counted on to find far more buyers than the high-priced Hemi cars initially did in 1966. Hemi power was optional for both, but a new standard power source was needed if costs were to be kept down and excitement up. That new mill was the 440.

Created in 1966 by increasing the RB block's bore to a hefty 4.320 inches, Chrysler's "440 TNT" big-block was at first intended only for full-sized C-body luxury car applications. But transforming this 350-horsepower gentle giant into a 375-horse beast was as easy as adding better-breathing open-chamber heads, freer-flowing exhaust manifolds, a big Carter four-barrel carb, and a more aggressive hydraulic cam. Introduced for 1967, this high-performance package was called the 440 Magnum by Dodge, the 440 Super Commando by Plymouth.

While compression (10.1:1) was the same for the TNT and its 375-horse alter ego, that latter RB V-8 was topped off with a low-restriction, dual-snorkel air cleaner to help its Carter carb suck like nobody's business. Modifications also included a revised valvetrain better suited to handle the lumpier cam's reciprocating demands. High-load valve springs helped resist valve float, and those springs incorporated surge dampers to limit unwanted harmonics. At 2.08 inches, intake valve size carried over from the TNT, but exhaust diameter was enlarged from 1.60 inches to 1.74 for the Magnum/Super Commando. The Magnum was the 1967 Coronet R/T's standard power source, and the Super Commando was the new GTX's.

While some R/T and GTX customers did choose the optional Hemi, the majority stuck with the 375-horse 440, losing little in the deal, face or otherwise. What the 440 lacked in horsepower, it made up for in overall ease of use compared to its cantankerous solid-lifter cousin, not to mention cost.

The 440 initially wasn't offered as an option for Plymouth's Road Runner and Dodge's Super Bee, which both came standard with a 383-cubic-inch B-series big-block that used some RB components to help it make 335 horsepower. But that situation changed in 1969. New that summer were two special models, the 440 Six Pack Super Bee and its 440 Six Barrel Road Runner running mate, both outfitted identically to go right from the dealer's lot to the drag strip. The heart of these two wild animals was a triple-carb 440 rated at 390 horsepower. A similar 390-horse 440 returned as a B-body option for 1970, and this top-dog RB also appeared in E-body ranks that year. But like the Hemi, it was cancelled at year's end in 1971.

"LA" was the code for small-block Mopar muscle during the sixties and seventies. Some over the years have called these little V-8s "A" engines, but this misnomer only helps confuse casual witnesses not familiar with Chrysler's engine family ties. Plymouth's poly-head V-8, introduced for 1955, first officially used the same designation. Various bore and stroke combinations were used in poly-head engines, with a 3.31-inch crank going into a 3.91-inch block in 1957 to produce the largest A-series V-8, a 318-cubic-incher that remained in production up through 1966.

Chrysler Corporation's LA V-8 was born in 1964 and stuck around until 1992. Initial displacement was 273 cubic inches, thanks to a 3.63-inch bore and 3.31-inch stroke. Fitted with a two-barrel carburetor, the 273 LA initially made 180 horsepower, but this figure was pumped up to 235 the following year thanks primarily to a switch to a four-barrel carb. A four-barrel 273 was the hottest engine available for Plymouth's Barracuda and Dodge's Dart GT prior to 1967, when an optional 383 big-block appeared for both.

Attractive dress-up was standard for a high-performance version of Dodge and Plymouth's 273-cubic-inch LA small-block V-8, introduced for Dart GTs and Barracudas in 1965. Output was 235 horsepower. *Chrysler LLC Corporate Historical Collection*

Also new for 1967 was an enlarged small-block, a second 318-cubic-inch V-8 created by increasing the LA block's bore to 3.91 inches. With its larger physical dimensions, the retired A-series V-8 soon became known as the "wide-block 318" to hopefully help avoid even more confusion between these distinctly different engine families. As for the LA 318, it never was used in performance applications, and a two-barrel was the norm during its career.

A third LA, on the other hand, was built only for high-performance duty. Created in 1968 by boring the block again to 4.04 inches, the hot little 340 never featured anything other than dual exhausts and a four-barrel carburetor. Its heads incorporated big valves: 2.02-inch intakes and 1.60-inch exhausts, compared to 1.78/1.50 for the 318 and 273. It was rated at 275 horsepower, but those in the know doubted this figure. All anyone had to do was get behind the wheel of a 340-powered Barracuda or Dart Swinger to get a feel for the truth.

The biggest LA, the 360, appeared for 1971 after bore and stroke was increased to 4.00 and 3.58 inches, respectively. The 360's heads used a smaller (1.88-inch) intake valve, and these less preferable hunks of iron were bolted atop the 340 small-block in 1972, demonstrating that the end also was in sight for the small-block Mopar muscle legacy. Indeed, the 340 was dropped after 1973 in favor of the 360 as an option for performance-oriented B- and A-bodies. It just wasn't the same.

Both the Challenger and 'Cuda retired after 1974 too, leaving nothing else in the way of sporty cars from Dodge and Plymouth, though the former did rev things up a little in 1978 with a hot rod pickup, the Li'l Red Express Truck, powered by a reasonably warm 360 small-block. It was rough going from there, however, and a handful of turbocharged four-cylinder models did little to revive the feeling during the eighties.

Then along came Dodge's Viper in 1992. First seen in prototype form as the Indianapolis 500 pace car in May 1991, this sexy snake featured a V-10 engine that displaced 488 cubic inches and made 400 horsepower—and just like that it was 1970 all over again. Viper output topped 500 horses when the SRT-10 version was introduced for 2003, and the figure soared to 600 horsepower in 2008. Dodge even began offering a 500-horsepower, Viper-powered Ram truck in 2004 to let a few utility-vehicle buyers into the fun too.

Now we also have Hemi-powered Super Bees, Charger R/Ts, and Challengers, but for how much longer is anyone's guess. Word has it as these pages go to press that the Viper isn't long for this world, we can only wonder what implications 2008's soaring fuel prices and economic woes have for the future of four-wheeled toys, certainly those featuring V-8 muscle. As it surely was back in 1970, the best advice at present is probably "enjoy all this while you can."

Without a doubt Roanoke Dodge's John Gastman definitely will. "I hope I'll still be doing this in 10 years," was his reply in September 2008 when asked what awaits his dealership around the next corner. You go, John.

01

lights
dome panel
REVERSE ● NEUTRAL ● DRIVE ● SECOND ● FIRST

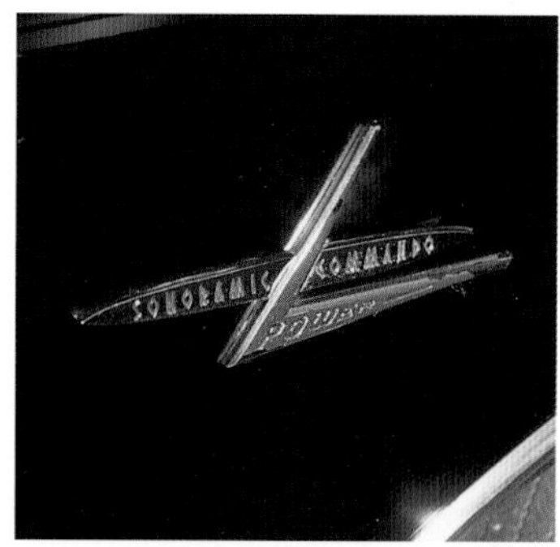
SONORAMIC COMMANDO

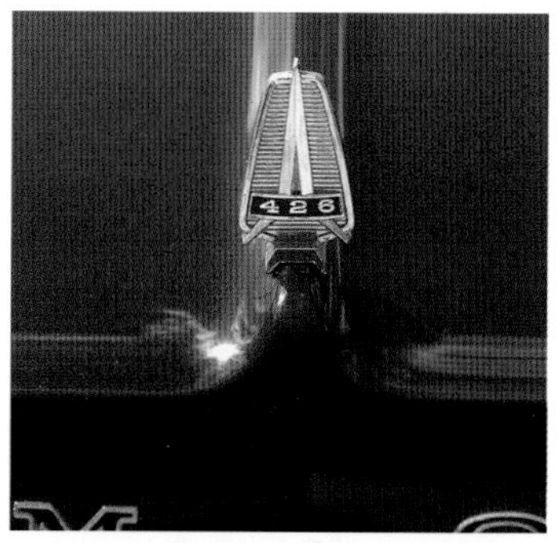
426

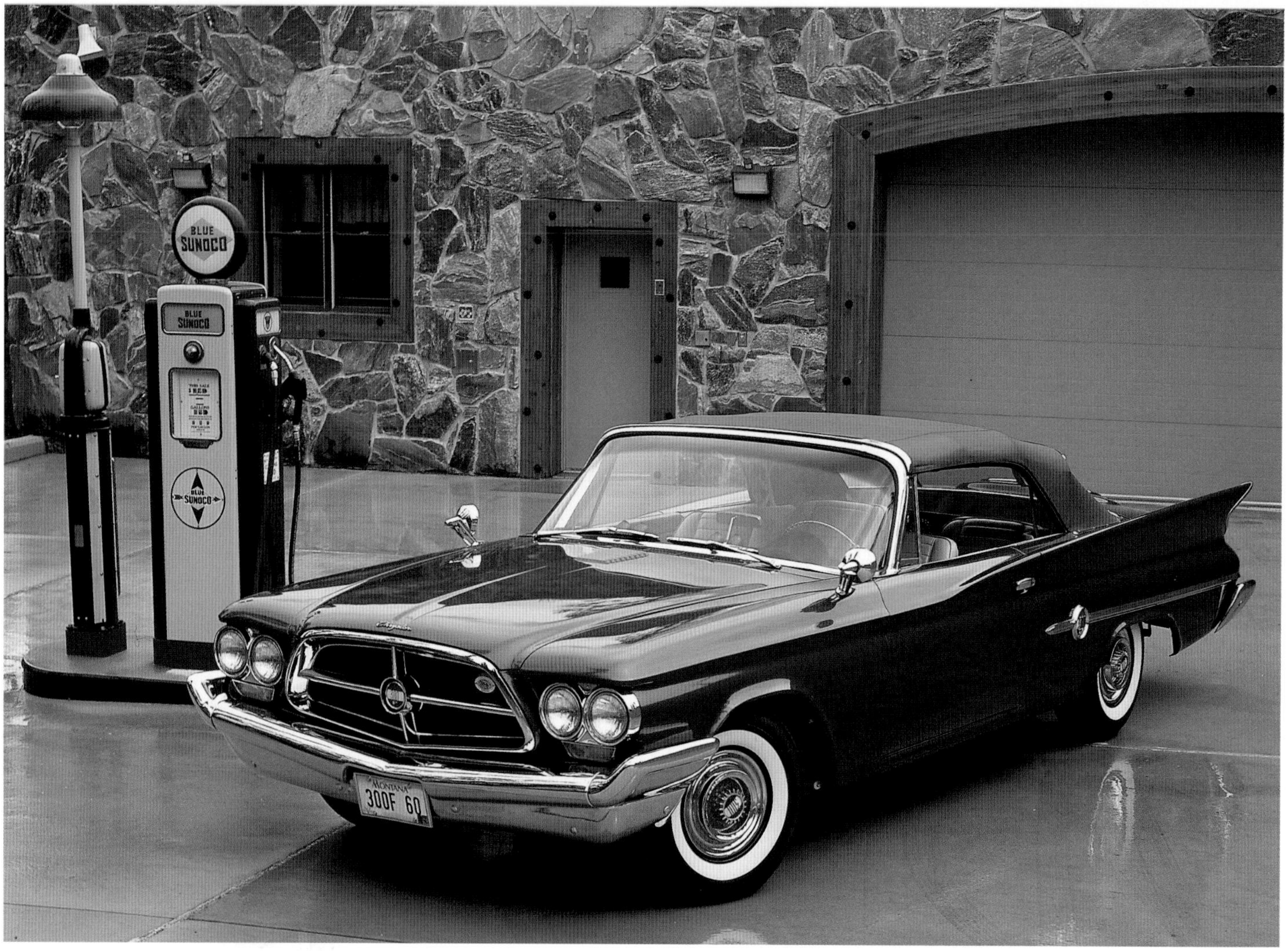

Muscular Mopars 1960–1967

Off the Line

Detroit's horsepower race sure was a dilly during the fifties. Chrysler Corporation's cars continually stood tall as annual favorites due, of course, to the company's exceptional Hemi-head engines. But who knows how competitive things would've become between Chrysler, General Motors, and Ford Motor Company late in the decade had the Automobile Manufacturers Association not put the kibosh on factory racing involvement in the summer of 1957. Up until then, all three had been busy as hell promoting their products' performance by winning races, and all also were damned proud of these achievements. Not so after the infamous AMA "ban," a paper tiger meant to chew apart the ties between engineering departments in Michigan and the roundy-round speedways primarily found in southeastern states.

In truth the AMA edict was more or less toothless, yet it still made an historic impact. Ford officials, by preferred choice, definitely reined their horses in hard after its enactment, and all companies toned down their approaches, if only to appease any stuffed shirts who just might be watching. But GM simply went underground as Chevrolet, Pontiac, and, to a lesser degree, Oldsmobile all quietly continued delivering hot parts to pro racers, primarily those on the NASCAR circuit. Mopar men, too, laughed off AMA killjoys. Sure, the days of Carl Kiefhaefer's fully factory-backed dominance on the NASCAR circuit were over, but Chrysler engineers by no means were ready to take their ponies out back and shoot 'em.

Indeed, horsepower continued to be a strong selling point as the fifties wound down. And when yet another opportunity to show off all that strength in front of crowds of potential customers appeared, Chrysler officials wasted little time jumping on it. Drag racing was the sport this time, while the sanctioning body was the California-based National Hot Rod Association, founded in 1951 by *Hot Rod* magazine editor Wally Parks. Primarily a West Coast phenomenon early on, organized quarter-mile competition swept the nation by storm once Parks started turning young Americans onto it using the pages of his burgeoning publication, itself first seen in 1948. It was no coincidence that NHRA officials opted for America's heartland—Great Bend, Kansas—as a site for its first U.S. Nationals meet in 1955; involving as

Opposite:
Chrysler's big 300 letter car was still the corporation's top performance machine as the sixties began. As had been the case since 1957, the 300F was offered in both hardtop and convertible forms for 1960.
Mike Mueller

Left:
It was two carburetors or none at all for Chrysler's letter cars from 1955 to 1963. Up through 1960, these twin Carter four-barrels were mounted in conventional inline fashion, as demonstrated by the 413-cubic-inch 1959 300E V-8 shown here. *Mike Mueller*

Opposite:
New beneath the 300F's enormous hood in 1960 was a standard ram-induction V-8, easily one of the coolest-looking powerplants created during the sixties. Output for the 300F's base 413-cubic-inch V-8 was 375 horsepower. *Mike Mueller*

many enthusiasts as possible from all corners of the country was the goal. The rest is alcohol burning, tire-melting, ear-splitting history.

This legendary tale didn't gain real momentum, however, until the factory guys were enticed into the game, which didn't start happening until the NHRA Nats were moved to Motown in 1959. "What was undoubtedly the best selling job ever done in behalf of the hot rod sport was accomplished at Detroit this year when members of the National Hot Rod Association presented the 5th annual National Championship Drag Races there," wrote Parks in his November 1959 *Hot Rod* column. "Among the 80,000 or so who attended were hundreds of representatives from the various auto manufacturing companies."

"Detroit and the automobile industries got their first real look at drag racing à la NHRA, and judging from all appearances, they like it," added *Hot Rod*'s Bob Pendergrast. According to Parks, Chrysler head Tex Colbert and Chevrolet chief Ed Cole stood by betting on whose cars would win, and after proverbial pushes were followed by so-called shoves, their companies found themselves in the drag car business. First came hotter and hotter parts for the garden-variety vehicles that competed in NHRA stock-class racing, but these soon were followed by complete packages, full-fledged factory machines meant to escalate the battle even further.

It all had been so simple at Great Bend in 1955, since only four classes existed for completely stock Detroit iron. But by 1968, NHRA rules books listed 34 Stock and 12 Super/Stock categories. Automatic cars had gained their own classifications in 1962, and Optional Super/Stock had appeared the previous year. Meant to pick up where S/S limitations left off, the OS/S class was created to make a home for so-called stock factory hardware that didn't quite qualify as being available to the general public.

OS/S formation was inspired by Pontiac, which in 1961 rolled out its race-ready 389 Super Duty Catalinas, purpose-built vehicles that, among other things, featured weight-saving aluminum bumpers. Ford and Chevrolet then announced their own lightweight drag cars in 1962 to help stretch the definition of factory stock to its limits. NHRA officials, in turn, responded with their new Factory Experimental (F/X) class, a category that struggled to contain a collection of truly uncivilized Detroit-built ground-pounders up through 1966. From there it was the unrestricted Funny Car genre that took over.

But well before all that fiberglass and aluminum started showing up, before interiors were gutted and wheelbases altered, it was engines that first were tricked out specially to do battle in the factory super-stock wars. And, after making so many rompin', stompin' horses

during the fifties, it was Mopar engineers who had the advantage early on as a new decade rolled around.

Looking way too cool at the drags, wedged between Dodge and Plymouth fenders in 1960, was the same ram-induction setup that came standard that year beneath the hood of Chrysler's full-sized 300F. A "poorman's supercharger," if you will, this equipment consisted of 30-inch-long tubular manifolds that helped boost output by 10 percent compared to the conventional inline dual-carb design used in 1959. How'd those spidery intakes do it?

First off, inertia created as the fuel charge accelerated over the tube's length helped ram the mixture home once the intake valve opened. Additional assistance stuffing as much fuel/air as possible into the combustion chamber was supplied by natural reverberations that occurred as the intake valve slammed shut. Every time one of these closed, it initiated a rapid resonance wave through the pressurized mixture column in the manifold tube. The trick was to make that wave rebound back down that tube just as the intake valve reopened, thus enhancing the ramcharging effect even further. Furthermore, engineers could produce a desired power range by choosing a preferred tube length: the longer the tube, the lower the revs needed to reach a maximum powerband. Adjusting that band by modifying tube length was called "tuning."

Tuned induction system experiments dated back to 1946 at Chrysler. In 1952 a 331-cubic-inch Hemi intended for Indy 500 competition and topped by Hilborn fuel injectors on tuned intake stacks made 447 horsepower. Engineering research head James Zeder's group discovered the optimum length for those stacks after experimenting with special adjustable intake tubes. When

1960

Chrysler 300F

Specifications

Model availability	two-door hardtop, two-door convertible
Wheelbase	126 inches
Length	216.6 inches
Width	79.4 inches
Height	55.1 inches (hardtop); 55.5 inches (convertible)
Weight	4,270 pounds (hardtop); 4,310 pounds (convertible)
Base Price	$5,411 (hardtop); $5,841 (convertible)
Track (front/rear, in inches)	61.2/60.0
Wheels	9×14
Tires	Goodyear Blue Streak
Construction	unitized body/frame with bolt-on front subframe
Suspension	long-arm/short-arm with longitudinal torsion bars in front; longitudinal leaf springs in back
Steering	rack and sector with power assist standard
Brakes	four-wheel drums with power assist standard
Engine	375-horsepower, 413-cubic-inch Golden Lion V-8
Bore and stroke	4.19×3.75 inches
Compression	10.1:1
Fuel delivery	two Carter four-barrel carburetors on ram-induction intakes
Transmission	three-speed Torqueflite automatic
Axle ratio	3.31:1, standard
Production	964 hardtops, 248 convertibles

Above:
Performance-conscious Plymouth engineers didn't necessarily focus all their attention on V-8s during the early sixties. Their hot "Hyper-Pak" option was offered for the compact Valiant's slant-six engine in 1960 and 1961. High compression (10.5:1), a hot cam, a header-type exhaust manifold, and a four-barrel carburetor on a long-ram intake helped the 170-cubic-inch Hyper-Pak six make 148 horsepower. *Chrysler LLC Corporate Historical Collection*

Opposite, top:
The D500 option was available on all Dodge models in 1960 from the big (122-inch-wheelbase) Polaras and Matadors to the shorter (118-inch-wheelbase) Darts. Three models made up the Dart line: Seneca, Pioneer, and Phoenix (shown here). *Mike Mueller*

Opposite, below:
The D500 package initially was available only for the top-of-the-line Dart, the Phoenix, in 1960. It became a Seneca and Pioneer option not long after Dodge's new models were introduced that year. *Mike Mueller*

dynamometer tests achieved desired peaks, the tube lengths were set. In this application, meant to make mucho power at sky-high revs, the tubes were quite short.

But the situation was completely different for street cars. Making usable power at about 2,500–3,000 revolutions required ram tube lengths of at least 2.5 feet, and fitting such tubes between regular-production fenders was, as expected, no simple task. Nor was it cheap.

"Chrysler people admit they're way out on a limb on costs with this setup," explained *Hot Rod* magazine's Roger Huntington. "But they felt the performance boost in the usable rpm range would be a good enough sales gimmick to make it pay off." Chrysler folks also felt ram induction enhanced performance enough on its own to justify dropping their proven hemispherical heads after 1959 in favor of lighter, easier-to-engineer wedge-head V-8s.

Ram induction became a performance option for Dodge, Plymouth, and terminally ill DeSoto in 1960. Dodge customers discovered a ram-induction V-8 in that year's D500 package, offered for both the division's full-sized models and its new downsized Darts. Big D500 Dodges got a 330-horsepower, 383-cubic-inch ram motor, while the smaller Darts were fitted with a 361-cubic-inch ram-induction engine rated at 310 horsepower. Apparently it was possible to mix and match things because some 383-equipped D500 Darts were built. The D500 package also was available for all models, including four-doors and station wagons.

A little-known option in 1960 dealt with the tuning issue. Available over dealer counters was a short-ram setup that looked identical to the standard long-tube equipment. Inside those siamesed pairs of intake runners, however, the short-ram manifolds incorporated cut-down "walls" that effectively reduced tuned internal tube

Phoenix

This unobtrusive deck lid badge represented the only outward clue to a D500 Dodge's presence in 1960. The D500 option cost $413 in Dart Phoenix ranks that year. *Mike Mueller*

Dodge offered two D500 V-8s in 1960, a 383-cubic-inch version for Polaras and Matadors, and a 361-cubic-inch version for the smaller Darts. Some 383 V-8s, however, did find their way into Dart models. The 383 ram-induction engine produced 330 horsepower; its 361 running mate (shown here) was rated at 310 horses. *Mike Mueller*

Above:
Customized a half-century ago by its original owner, NASCAR driver Buddy Arrington, this 1960 Plymouth is adorned with both Belvedere and Fury trim pieces. Arrington also ordered ram-induction power for his chrome-encrusted sedan. *Mike Mueller*

Right:
Plymouth used the "Sonoramic Commando" label for its ram-induction V-8s. Like its counterpart from Dodge, the Sonoramic Commando was available in two sizes: 361 and 383 cubic inches. *Mike Mueller*

Again like their Dodge counterparts, Plymouth's 361 and 383 ram-induction V-8s were rated at 310 and 330 horsepower, respectively. Compression was 10:1 in both cases. *Mike Mueller*

1960

Plymouth Sonoramic Commando V-8

Specifications	
Model availability	various models and body styles
Wheelbase	118 inches
Length	209.4 inches
Width	78.6 inches
Height	54.5 inches
Weight	not available
Price	$4,030, approximate
Track (front/rear, in inches)	60.9/59.7
Wheels	not available
Tires	7.5×14.0
Construction	unitized body/frame with bolt-on front subframe
Suspension	long-arm/short-arm with longitudinal torsion bars in front; longitudinal leaf springs in back
Steering	not available
Brakes	four-wheel drums
Engine	310-horsepower, 361-cubic-inch V-8; 330-horsepower, 383-cubic-inch V-8
Bore and stroke	4.12×3.38 inches, 361 V-8; 4.25×3.38 inches, 383 V-8
Compression	10:1 for both
Fuel delivery	two Carter four-barrel carburetors on ram-induction intakes
Transmission	Torqueflite automatic
Axle ratio	3.31:1
Production	not available

length from about 28 inches to 18. Both types of ram-induction intakes were available for the 1960 300F, with the long-ram engine rated at 375 horsepower, its short-ram running mate at 400. As a dealer installation on Dodge's 383, the short-ram manifolds upped maximum output to 340 horsepower.

According to *Motor Trend* a 383-powered Dart D500 could make the time-honored 0–60 run in 8.5 seconds, while 16.3 clicks went by as it lunged over a quarter-mile. Driving a 361-powered D500 Dart, *Sports Car Illustrated* recorded quarter-mile times in the 16.5-second range. But numbers only told part of the story. "The response when both carburetors cut in is instantaneous," explained *Motor Trend*'s Walt Woron. "It comes on with a roar, pushing you back in your seat, and the car leaps ahead like a ram rushing to butt a challenger to his supremacy over his flock."

Dodge continued offering both the optional ram-induction setup and D500 package in 1961, although the two were no longer necessarily one in the same, since the basic D500 package included an engine sporting a single carburetor. Available for 1961 Darts was the aptly named "Dart D-500" V-8, a 305-horse 361 fed by a Carter four-barrel. For the longer Polara there was—you guessed it—the "Polara D-500" V-8, a 325-horse 383 also crowned by one Carter four-barrel. The 413-cubic-inch RB-series V-8 appeared midyear for 1961, and it, too, received D500 treatment. Rated at 350 horsepower, the Super D-500 413 featured a single four-barrel, while its Super Ram Induction D-500 big brother produced 375 horses.

Ram induction also carried over into Plymouth ranks in 1960 with appropriately different names: "Sonoramic Commando" for the 330-horsepower 383, simply "Sonoramic" for its 310-horse 361 sibling. Each was basically identical featuring 10:1 compression, hydraulic lifters, the same two Carter AFBs, and all the excitement offered by Dodge's renditions. In Plymouth's words, "the first ram induction engine in a production car [offers] supercharged results without stealing

Space was tight beneath a Sonoramic Commando Plymouth's hood. Adding optional power brakes meant this system's boosted master cylinder had to be mounted parallel to the firewall. *Mike Mueller*

power . . . and puts out greater torque than 400 cu. in. mills!" *Hot Rod*'s Ray Brock managed a 15.6-second quarter-mile pass at 90 miles per hour in a 310-horse 1960 Fury.

Sounded like fun. But living with ram induction wasn't necessarily child's play. Changing spark plugs predictably was a major pain, and tinkering with the Carter carbs was no joy, either. At least designers graciously added removable access panels inside each front wheelwell, features that, by the way, represent one of the easiest ways to detect a legitimate Sonoramic Plymouth. Inherent space constraints also mandated the unconventional mounting—parallel to the firewall instead of perpendicular—of the optional power brake booster and master cylinder.

Plymouth officials furthermore chose to limit both their ram-induction V-8s to automatic transmission applications, fearing a wave of over-revved warranty work. No worries, though; Chrysler's renowned Torqueflite was more than capable of handling whatever a Sonoramic Commando put out.

"The three-speed Torqueflite automatic transmission is undoubtedly the best unit offered by any American manufacturer today when it comes to being punished by high horsepower," bragged Brock. In ram-induction installations, Plymouth's pushbutton-controlled Torqueflite was upgraded throughout, included beefed servo springs and increased oil pressure. Sure, strong shifts during hard acceleration resulted, as did unshakable, durable operation under even the harshest use.

Like Dodge, Plymouth also offered ram-induction equipment atop 361, 383, and 413 V-8s in 1961 before moving on to even more serious super-stock fodder, and just in the nick of time. When 1962 began, Pontiac's 421 Super Duty V-8, Chevrolet's famous 409, and

Big Daddy Don Garlits' men weren't the only ones to pilot this Max Wedge Dodge in 1962, so did Don's wife, Pat—at "powder puff" competitions in the Tampa, Florida, area. Jim Kaylor drove the car on the national stage. Notice the non-stock 1963 hood scoop. *Mike Mueller*

In the words of *Motor Trend*'s Roger Huntington, the 1962 Max Wedge offered "more performance per dollar than any other factory-assembled car in America." The price for the 410-horsepower, 413-cubic-inch V-8 was about $375. *Mike Mueller*

1960
Dodge D-500

Specifications	
Model availability	various models and body styles
Wheelbase	118 inches
Length	208.6 inches
Width	78 inches
Height	54.5 inches
Weight	not available
Price	D-500 option cost $332 to $383 depending on model application
Track (front/rear, in inches)	61.5/60.2
Wheels	not available
Tires	7.5×14.0
Construction	unitized body/frame with bolt-on front subframe
Suspension	long-arm/short-arm with longitudinal torsion bars in front; longitudinal leaf springs in back
Steering	not available
Brakes	four-wheel drums
Engine	310-horsepower, 361-cubic-inch V-8; 330-horsepower, 383-cubic-inch V-8
Bore and stroke	4.12×3.38 inches, 361 V-8; 4.25×3.38 inches, 383 V-8
Compression	10:1 for both
Fuel delivery	two Carter four-barrel carburetors on ram-induction intakes
Transmission	Torqueflite automatic
Axle ratio	3.31:1
Production	not available

Chrysler's exceptional Torqueflite transmission, controlled by pushbuttons in 1962, helped that year's Max Wedge cars dominate drag racing's Super/Stock Automatic classes. *Mike Mueller*

Ford's FE-series 406 were the kings of the quarter-mile. Chrysler's two divisions started that year well off the pace, but not for long. Newly appointed corporate president Lynn Townsend had put part-time racer, full-time engineer Tom Hoover in charge of his company's competition programs in October 1961, and Hoover proved to be just the man to put Mopars back into the race.

Hoover's retaliation came in the form of the 413-cubic-inch "Max Wedge" V-8, a quarter-mile legend that appeared in May 1962. Max Wedge actually was street slang, with "Max" coming from the "Maximum Performance" designation used in brochures, and "Wedge" referring to the engine's conventional wedge-shaped combustion chambers. Dodge's version was officially named the "Ramcharger 413," while Plymouth's wore a "Super Stock 413" label.

Whatever the name, this super-hot super-stock V-8 was offered at two output levels, 410 and 420 horsepower, depending on compression: 11:1 for the former, 13.5:1 for the latter. The 420-horse Max Wedge came from the factory with explicit instructions: "A final word of warning, the 13.5:1 engine must never be run at top speeds for more than 15 seconds at a time." That amount represented about three seconds longer than needed for one of these machines to reach the far end of a quarter-mile.

Built under precise conditions by Chrysler's Marine and Industrial Division, the 413 Max Wedge was especially lethal once installed in newly downsized Dodges and Plymouths, unit-body automobiles based on 116-inch wheelbases, two clicks shorter than 1961's foundation. These new models weighed a few hundred pounds less than their full-sized rivals from GM and Ford and thus didn't need any weight-saving modifications to go racing successfully. No fragile, costly fenders, bumpers, or hoods were offered in 1962.

Right:
The term "Max Wedge" was actually a street slang reference. The engine's correct name, in Dodge parlance, was "Ramcharger 413." Plymouth's rendition was called "Super Stock 413." *Mike Mueller*

Below:
Weight-saving aluminum body parts appeared for the Max Wedge super-stocks in 1963. A functional scoop also was added to the aluminum hood. *Mike Mueller*

1962
"Max Wedge" 413 Dodge Polara

Specifications	
Model availability	two-door hardtop
Wheelbase	116 inches
Length	202 inches
Width	76.5 inches
Height	not available
Weight	3,450 pounds (approximate)
Price	Ramcharger 413 V-8 option cost $374.40
Track (front/rear, in inches)	59.4/57.5
Wheels	14.0×5.5 inches; 6.5-inch-wide rear wheels, optional
Tires	7.5×14.0 Tyrex-cord, standard; 9.0×14.0 rear tires optional
Construction	unitized body/frame with front subframe
Suspension	long-arm/short-arm with longitudinal torsion bars in front; longitudinal heavy-duty leaf springs in back
Steering	not available
Brakes	four-wheel drums
Engine	410-horsepower, 413-cubic-inch Ramcharger V-8
Bore and stroke	4.19×3.75 inches
Compression	11:1
Fuel delivery	two Carter four-barrel carburetors on cross-ram intake
Transmission	Borg-Warner T-85 three-speed manual (Torqueflite automatic, optional)
Axle ratio	3.91:1 with Sure-Grip differential
Production	not available

Although initial plans called for building 200 Max Wedge Plymouths and Dodges that year, but the final tally apparently included about 50 more. The Max Wedge V-8 was available in various Plymouth and Dodge models, including station wagons, but most showed up in bare-bones sedans. According to Dodge ads, these stripped-down monsters featured "about the best power–weight ratio ever offered on a production car—now up to one horse for every 8.4 pounds." The car's amazing price, too, made headlines. "Dodge's new 'Ramcharger 413' package gives more performance per dollar than any other factory-assembled car in America," wrote *Motor Trend* contributor Roger Huntington. Dodge's 410-horse option cost $374.40.

For this rather tidy price, a Max Wedge customer got a truly purposeful powerplant. The block was about the only carryover from the standard 413, and those chosen for this application were reportedly inspected for main-bearing toughness. A forged-steel crank with hardened journals and high-load tri-metal bearings was bolted in, as were magnafluxed forged-steel rods and lightweight aluminum pistons. Underneath was a deep-sump oil pan incorporating anti-slosh baffles. On top, cylinder bores were notched to provide clearance for really big exhaust valves.

While intake valve size (2.08 inches) carried over from the basic 413, their 1.88-inch exhaust counterparts were nearly a quarter-inch larger than stock. Along with improved flow, the heads also were beefed to help prevent high-compression-induced gasket failure. Remaining valvetrain pieces included solid lifters, hardened 3/8-inch pushrods, adjustable cast-iron rocker arms, and high-pressure dual valve springs with spiral steel dampers sandwiched between them to prevent harmful harmonics at high rpm. Those dual springs made it impossible to install oil seals on the valve stems, making the Max Wedge a major oil-burner. Wide-clearance piston rings contributed to this condition too.

Shooting the juice on top were two Carter AFB carbs mounted diagonally on a cast-aluminum cross-ram intake that didn't feature a traditional heat crossover passage in the best interests of maximizing volumetric efficiency. Remember, a cooler fuel/air mixture is a denser mixture. On the exhaust end was equipment that Huntington described as "a work of art—far and away the most efficient [system] ever put on an American car." These high-flying, free-flowing cast-iron manifolds featured large two-inch individual passages that fed into three-inch collectors.

Following up those manifolds were three-inch-diameter head pipes that incorporated cutouts with bolt-on covers, which stayed on for relatively quiet running on the street, since spent gases were routed conventionally into two-inch tailpipes and a pair of Chrysler New Yorker mufflers. At the track the covers could've been yanked off for unrestricted, eardrum-bashing operation.

Transmission choices behind the Max Wedge numbered two: a heavy-duty Borg-Warner T-85 three-speed manual (with a 10.5-inch clutch) and the impressive A-727 Torqueflite three-speed automatic. With the durable Torqueflite, Max Wedge Mopars instantly became favorites in drag racing's Super Stock/Automatic class. Back on Main Street U.S.A., a completely stock automatic Max Wedge could run the quarter-mile in 14.40 seconds at 101 miles per hour, according to Huntington's *Motor Trend* test. With those cutouts unbolted and more rubber bolted on in back, the same car posted a 13.84/108.21 time slip, and further tinkering dropped those figures to 13.44/109.76. Racing slicks obviously would have induced even faster times, as pro racers demonstrated.

On July 15, 1962, Tom Grove's "Melrose Missile" Plymouth became the first "production stock passenger car with a factory option engine" to bust into the 11s, running 11.93 seconds at 118.57 miles

Max Wedge displacement increased to 426 cubic inches in 1963 thanks to a bore increase from 4.19 inches to 4.25. Maximum compression for the meanest 426 Maxie was a whopping 13.5:1. *Mike Mueller*

1963

"Max Wedge" 426 Dodge 330

Specifications	
Model availability	two-door sedan
Wheelbase	119 inches
Length	208.1 inches
Width	76.5 inches
Height	54.1 inches
Weight	3,300 pounds
Price	not available
Track (front/rear, in inches)	59.5/57.5
Wheels	14.0×5.5 inches, standard; 6.5-inch-wide rear wheels, optional
Tires	7.5×14.0Tyrex-cord, standard; 9.0×14.0 rear tires, optional
Construction	unitized body/frame with front subframe
Suspension	long-arm/short-arm with longitudinal torsion bars in front; longitudinal heavy-duty leaf springs in back
Steering	not available
Brakes	four-wheel drums
Engine	415-horsepower, 426-cubic-inch Ramcharger V-8
Bore and stroke	4.25×3.75 inches
Compression	11:1
Fuel delivery	two Carter four-barrel carburetors on cross-ram intake
Transmission	Borg-Warner T-85 three-speed manual (Torqueflite automatic, optional)
Axle ratio	3.91:1 with Sure-Grip differential
Production	not available

per hour at Fremont Drag Strip in California. In Grove's opinion, the Max Wedge 413 offered "the strongest potential in the super-stock field—more horsepower and less car weight per cubic inch than any of the competition. The engine is a beauty—none better." None, at least, until 1963.

An even more intimidating Max Wedge appeared that year, an overbored, 426-cubic-inch RB known as the "Stage II." Output this time was 415 and 425 horsepower, with the former featuring 11.0:1 compression, the latter an unheard of 13.5:1. Almost everything else carried over from the 413 rendition, and a single-carb version also was built to compete on the NASCAR circuit, where multiple carburetors, superchargers, and fuel injection had been illegal since 1957.

Modifications made early in 1963 resulted in an improved Stage III Max Wedge that featured larger carbs, massaged heads with bigger ports, and a more radical cam. Output ratings, meanwhile, stayed the same, even though the top-of-the-heap 426's compression was lowered to 12.5:1. As it was, engineers had pretty much maxed out the Max Wedge by then.

Hoover's engineers had begun working on another brand of super-stock V-8 in December 1962, opting in this case to bring back an old friend—the hemispherical combustion chamber. Based on the same RB foundation used by the 426 Stage III wedge, but sharing very few parts, Chrysler's 426 race Hemi was, as its name implied, built solely for the track. Its head-cracking compression alone—the same squeeze as the Stage III's—made that reality plainly apparent, as did its battleship-tough constitution. Bolting up those free-breathing

01

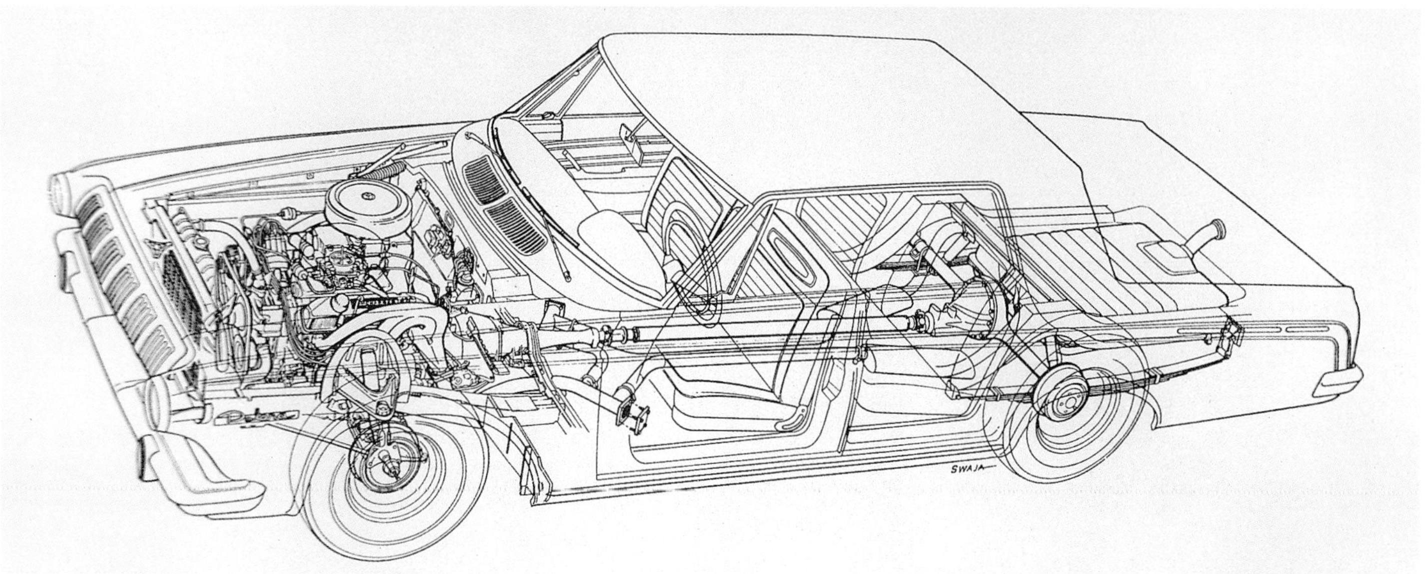

Oppsite, top:
This 1963 Dodge Max Wedge ghost view shows the unique exhaust system included in the package. Notice the driver-side cutout (unbolted and opened here) lined out below the steering wheel. With that cover in place, spent gases were routed through a conventional dual-exhaust system. *Chrysler LLC Corporate Historical Collection*

Oposite, bottom:
Founded in 1958, the famed "Ramchargers Maximum Performance Corporation" was not your typical car club. Led by Jim Thornton, the Ramchargers were made up of Chrysler engineers who couldn't stand to see Chevys beating their products at the drags. The original group campaigned some of Chrysler's hottest hardware—including the 1963 Max Wedge Dodges shown here—up through 1967. *Chrysler LLC Corporate Historical Collection*

Right:
Two race Hemi V-8s were initially released for drag racing in February 1964, a 415-horsepower version with two Carter four-barrels and the top-dog 425-horse variety (shown here), sporting two Holley carbs. Compression was 11.0:1 for the former, 12.5:1 for the latter. *Chrysler LLC Corporate Historical Collection*

Below, right:
Chrysler Engineering Vice President Paul Ackerman was more than proud of Chrysler's race Hemi V-8 in 1964. Shown here is the NASCAR version with its single four-barrel carburetor and cowl-induction air cleaner. *Chrysler LLC Corporate Historical Collection*

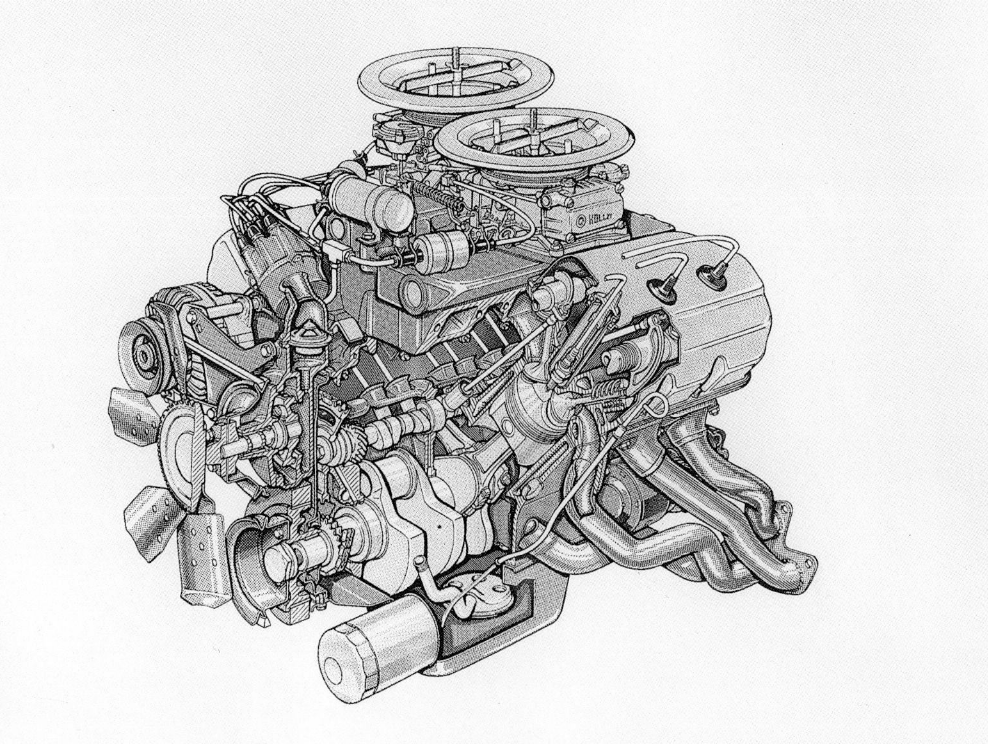

heads required various cylinder block modifications to guarantee sufficient oiling. Additional confidence was supplied by cross-bolted main bearing caps on the bottom end.

Two Carter four-barrels on a cross-ram intake also topped this beast, while steel-tube headers sent spent gases on their way in a hurry. Race Hemi valves, at 2.25 and 1.94 inches for intake and exhaust, respectively, dwarfed even the Stage III's big units. The Hemi was officially rated the same as the hotter Stage III, a joke that remained just as comical. Actual output surely was more like 550 or even 600 horsepower.

Hoover's group put together the race Hemi just in time for the 1964 Daytona 500. Hemi cars finished 1-2-3 there, with Richard Petty's winning Plymouth leading 5 other Mopars in the top 10. Petty eventually grabbed the NASCAR championship that season by a wide margin, so wide that big Bill France and his boys decided to cage this wild animal because it didn't qualify as a "regular-production engine." Chrysler's initial response involved boycotting the 1965 season. Twin-carb Hemis, meanwhile, continued to make big names for themselves in drag racing.

Altering wheelbases, a trick aimed at aiding weight transfer to the rear wheels during hard launches, became the latest trend in 1964, with noted Dodge drag racer Dick Landy leading the way. Landy also took the altered thing a bit further, using a solid front axle and a raised rear suspension. *Mike Mueller*

In May 1964, the dual-carb 426 Hemi replaced the Stage III wedge in Chrysler's super-stock lineup. Production figures are not complete, but it is known that at least 11 Dodges and 24 Plymouths were released with race Hemi V-8s after May 18 that year. Others surely followed that summer, though it remains unproven whether or not Chrysler's two divisions met the NHRA's minimum production requirement of 50 cars. Both the new A-833 four-speed manual and Torqueflite automatic were installed behind the race Hemi.

Various weight-saving touches also began appearing in 1964 for race Hemis. Both Plymouth and Dodge that year introduced optional "Y9" packages that traded steel for aluminum as far as the hood, fenders, radiator, and front bumper brackets were concerned. The aluminum hood also incorporated a large scoop. In Plymouth's case, steel bumpers were acid-dipped to cut additional weight, while Dodge's bumpers were aluminum. Aluminum door panels, Lexan windows, and stripped-down interiors with A-100 Dodge van bucket seats also became part of the super-stock deal in 1964, as did a battery relocated to the trunk to aid weight transfer.

Enhancing that transfer further were modifications made to four (two Dodges, two Plymouths) race Hemi cars during the summer of 1964. Moving more weight to the rear could be accomplished by simply relocating all four wheels forward, and such shenanigans were initially condoned by NHRA rules moguls, but only if they didn't differ from stock specifications by more than 2 percent. The resulting "2 percent" cars didn't appear all that different at a glance. But when posed next to a stock model there clearly was something funny going on. Get it—a funny car?

Both Dodge and Plymouth offered a "Y9" package for 1969. Along with various lightweight body parts, the Y9 option also included bucket seats borrowed from Dodge's A-100 van. The back seat was simply deleted. *Mike Mueller*

1965
Plymouth Satellite 426S

Specifications	
Model availability	two-door hardtop, two-door convertible
Wheelbase	116 inches
Length	203.4 inches
Width	not available
Height	not available
Weight	3,350 pounds, approximate
Price	not available
Track (front/rear, in inches)	59.5/58.5
Wheels	14×5 inches
Tires	7.35×14.00 bias-ply
Suspension	long-arm/short-arm with longitudinal torsion bars in front; longitudinal leaf springs in back
Steering	recirculating ball
Brakes	four-wheel drums
Engine	365-horsepower, 426-cubic-inch wedge-head V-8
Bore and stroke	4.25×3.75 inches
Compression	10.3:1
Fuel delivery	single Carter four-barrel carburetor
Transmission	three-speed manual, standard; four-speed manual and Torqueflite automatic, optional
Axle ratio	3.23:1, standard
Production	not available

This nickname immediately evolved into an accepted reference for an entirely new breed of so-called super-stock, a machine that still looked like a street car but smoked the quarter-mile like a true dragster. Pioneering funny cars quickly started leaving super-stocks and F/X models behind in 1965 and were off in a class all their own within a few more years.

Mildly humorous-looking modifications made in the 2 percent Mopar's case in 1964 included relocating the front K-member three inches forward, a change that translated into an equal move for the front wheels. This work in turn mandated lengthened torsion bars and redone upper control arms. In back, repositioned spring perches produced a four-inch forward shift for the rear axle, meaning the wheel wells, too, had to be relocated five inches forward. Rear body panels then, of course, had to be refashioned, with each wheel opening lip section moved up to match the wheels and a patch panel welded in behind to fill the gap. All this work happened at the Alexander Brothers Custom Shop in Detroit, but the 2 percent cars still were considered "factory" offerings and hence qualified for NHRA's A/FX class.

How much difference did the 2 percent trick make on the quarter-mile? A conventional lightweight Hemi super-stock ran in the 11.50s at 120-plus miles per hour in 1964. Dave Strickler's altered-wheelbase A/FX Dodge's best run was 10.66 ticks at 131 miles per hour. Such performance was too much to resist, leading other Mopar drivers to make similar conversions. Some tried even larger percentages.

Among these was "Dandy" Dick Landy, who first went drag racing, with a Ford, at age 19 in 1956. By 1962 he was driving a Plymouth and getting direct factory support from Ronnie Householder, Chrysler's competition projects chief. He then jumped over to Dodge two years later and stayed with that brand until finally retiring in 1981.

Left:
New for 1964 was Chrysler's race Hemi, a 426-cubic-inch monster crowned by two Carter four-barrels on a cross-ram intake. Token rated at 425 horsepower, the reborn Hemi put out more like 550 or 600 horses in top tune. *Mike Mueller*

Below:
Tom Grove's 1965 *Melrose Missile* demonstrates the so-called "2 percent" idea. NHRA rules at that point limited wheelbase alterations to no more than 2 percent of stock specifications. Notice the front and rear wheels, both relocated forward by relatively small margins. *Chrysler LLC Corporate Historical Collection*

Opposite:
Building the 2 percent cars inspired more than one drag racer to go more than one step beyond. Witness Dick Landy's radically altered 1965 Dodge, an outrageous machine capable of bursting into the 9-second bracket for the quarter-mile. *Chrysler LLC Corporate Historical Collection*

Landy's factory-direct connections supplied him with an early lightweight Hemi Dodge in 1964, and he competed this automatic-equipped, plain-Jane 330 sedan in NHRA S/SA racing until that year's U.S. Nationals, held on Labor Day weekend in Indianapolis. There Landy witnessed what a 2 percent Mopar could do, convincing him to do try a few chassis experiments himself. His end results looked even funnier.

For starters, the car sat up much higher due to the leaf-spring solid axle installed up front—the rear suspension, of course, was "jacked up" to match. Even more queer-looking, though, was its altered wheelbase. Front wheels were relocated forward about six inches, while the rears moved up eight inches. These major modifications made crowd-pleasing wheel stands as easy as pie, but they did little to endear the car to safety-conscious NHRA officials, who immediately banned Landy's radical Dodge, leaving it to compete in AHRA match-racing and other exhibitions.

Hot on the heels of Landy's altered 1964 Dodge came a new wave of Chrysler's own far-out machines. These extreme altered-wheelbase cars featured acid-dipped bodies, fiberglass fenders, and wheels relocated 10 inches in front, 15 in back. Eleven were built (six Dodges, five Plymouths), all also featuring front bumpers, hoods, doors, and dashboards made of fiberglass. Weighing roughly 3,000 pounds, they could run in the low 10s with no sweat. Trading gas for fuel and switching from carbs to the Hilborn injectors that Chrysler officials authorized for drag racing duty in February 1965 allowed for equally easy bursts into the 9-second bracket. NHRA killjoys also banned the 1965 altered-wheelbase Mopars, leaving Landy to again head for AHRA tracks with his, posting a best pass of 9.52 seconds at 143.54 miles per hour. Mind altering, man!

Unaltered lightweight Dodge and Plymouth race Hemis also rolled over into 1965. Various tweaks came beneath those big scoops, most of them involving additional weight savings. The cast-iron heads used in 1964 were traded for aluminum units, a magnesium cross-ram intake replaced the aluminum piece used the year before, and aluminum housings appeared for the water pump, thermostat, and oil pump.

NHRA rules forbade the use of aluminum body parts on these so-called "A-990" Mopars, so they were fitted with various parts and panels stamped specially from lighter-gauge steel, including the scooped hood, front fender and bumper, doors, and radiator support. Lightweight Bostrum bucket seats went inside, while the back seat was yanked out, along with the window regulators, sun visors, heater,

This 1965 Plymouth Satellite convertible is one of only 65 built with the 426-S V-8. Of these, 44 were fitted with four-speed manual transmissions, 21 with automatic like this example.
Mike Mueller

dome lamp, armrests, carpet padding, and passenger-side windshield wiper. Side windows and the backlight consisted of thin Corning Chemcor tempered glass. Tan appointments appeared in place of the red interiors found inside all race Hemi cars in 1964.

As many as 500 pounds were deleted from the A-990 cars, which carried the VIN code "W051" in the Dodge Coronet's case, "R051" in the Plymouth Belvedere's. Translating that code, "W" was the Dodge designation, "R" was Plymouth's. The "0" meant "super stock," the "5" represented the 1965 model year, and the "1" signified the assembly plant (Lynch Road, Michigan).

Each division built 101 S/S Hemi cars in 1965. Of the 101 R051 Belvederes, 85 featured Torqueflites, 16 had four-speeds. The total for the W051 Dodges was 93 Torqueflites, 8 four-speeds. All 202 A-990 cars were built at the Lynch Road plant between November 1964 and May 1965.

No lightweight packages were offered for 1966, but the R0/W0 S/S deal did return the following year. All of these Hemi-powered Coronets and Belvederes were delivered in white and featured 10-inch drum brakes, 15×6 stamped-steel wheels, and trunk-mounted batteries. Carpet padding, undercoating, and body sealer were typically

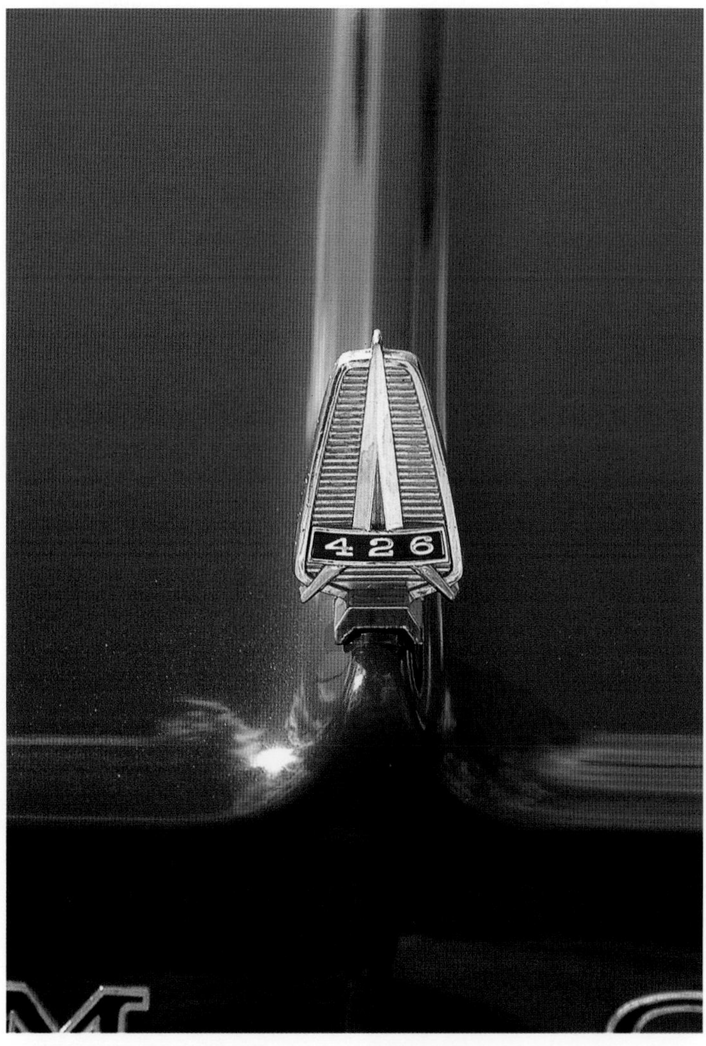

1966
Plymouth Satellite Hemi

Specifications

Model availability	two-door coupe, two-door convertible
Wheelbase	116 inches
Length	200.5 inches
Width	75.5 inches
Height	53.2 inches, hardtop
Weight	3,940 pounds
Price	$4,100, approximate
Track (front/rear, in inches)	59.5/58.5
Wheels	not available
Tires	not available
Construction	unitized body/frame with bolt-on front and rear subframes.
Suspension	long-arm/short-arm with longitudinal torsion bars in front; longitudinal leaf springs in back
Steering	recirculating ball
Brakes	four-wheel drums; 11.0×3.0 inches in front, 11.0×2.5 inches in back
Engine	425-horsepower, 426 "street Hemi" V-8
Bore and stroke	4.25×3.75 inches
Compression	10.25:1
Fuel delivery	two Carter four-barrel carburetors on inline intake
Transmission	four-speed manual or Torqueflite automatic
Axle ratio	3.23:1 with Sure-Grip differential, standard
Production	817 hardtops, 27 convertibles

The wedge-head 426 V-8 was soon lost in the shadow of the 426-cubic-inch street Hemi. But in 1965, this ornament signified Plymouth's hottest ticket as far as everyday operation was concerned. *Mike Mueller*

deleted, and a thin-gauge steel scoop was bolted onto the hood. An aluminum panel appeared beneath that scoop to help the Hemi's two carbs seal up to that opening using foam-rubber gaskets. Both this induction equipment and a set of tubular-steel Hooker headers were delivered from the factory in the trunk of a 1967 S/S Mopar.

A slightly re-ordered VIN, instituted in 1966, translated a little differently in the 1967 S/S Hemi's case. Plymouth's new tag was "R023," Dodge's was "W023." Those first two codes carried over, but the last two digits now signified the body style: two-door hardtop. As in 1965, all super-stock hardtops were built at Lynch Road in 1967. Production was 110: 55 Dodges, 55 Plymouths. Chrysler rolled out race Hemi super-stocks one last time, with help from Hurst, in 1968, this time using Plymouth's Barracuda and Dodge's Dart. For more on these, see chapters two and five, respectively.

Performance gains on the street during the early sixties included the 426S option introduced rather quietly for 1964. Plymouth promoters called this RB Wedge a "street version of our competition-designed 426 Hemi engine, which holds more records than our competitors care to count." Save for displacement, however, the 426S shared next to nothing with the race Hemi. It used civilized hydraulic lifters and a comparatively tame 10.3:1 compression, and its heads, rods, crank, and manifolds came right out of the 413's parts bins. Fed by a single Carter four-barrel, the 426S V-8 produced 365 horsepower.

Plymouth predictably called its version the "426 Commando V-8." A rarity in 1964, this Wedge turned a few more heads the next year when it was wrapped up in the new Satellite, Plymouth's latest flashy flagship. Both two-door hardtops and sexy convertibles were available in the Satellite lineup, as were standard bucket seats with a console.

Above:
Chrome dress-up was just the icing on the cake in the 426-S V-8's case in 1965. Advertised output was 365 horsepower. *Mike Mueller*

Left:
Plymouth continued using the Commando name for its high-performance V-8s throughout the sixties. The best of the best were the so-called Super Commandos. *Mike Mueller*

Opposite:
Hemi-powered Mopar convertibles were rare during any given year from 1966 to 1971. Only 10 Belvedere II convertibles were built with the street Hemi in 1966: 4 with four-speeds, 6 with automatics, as is the case here. *Mike Mueller*

Adding the 426S into the equation, at a cost of $500, also meant a beefed suspension and burly police brakes were installed too. Behind the 365-horse 426 was either a four-speed manual or Torqueflite automatic. Road tests claimed a 15.4-second quarter-mile for the 426S Plymouth.

Dodge also impressed customers a bit in 1965 with its 365-horse Coronet, then the gloves came off completely in 1966 after Chrysler's divisions unveiled their 426 street Hemi in order to go back racing on NASCAR tracks.

By homologating the latest Hemi for a return to stock-car competition, Mopar men also made lots of friends back on Main Street. It wasn't long before the 426 Hemi was being squeezed between the fenders of almost everything Dodge and Plymouth built, including a few four-door sedans. Belvedere, Satellite, Coronet, and Charger were the first to feel the joy in 1966. GTX, Coronet R/T, Super Bee, and Road Runner renditions quickly followed, as did perhaps the supreme Hemi variation, the lighter E-body 'Cudas and Challengers, in 1970. But while variety was present, proliferation wasn't. A high price tag limited Hemi sales, with roughly 2,700 delivered that first year. The total count for the breed, built from 1966 to 1971, was about 10,500.

Trading the "race" for "street" in the Hemi's makeup was no quick fix. As expected, a less radical cam (still bumping solid lifters)

01

Fed by two Carter four-barrel carburetors on an inline intake, the 426 street Hemi was rated rather conservatively at 425 horsepower. Compression was 10.25:1. *Mike Mueller*

This fender badge struck fear into the hearts of all challengers in 1966. "If you missed the San Francisco earthquake, reserve your seat here for a repeat performance," announced *Car and Driver* while introducing the street-going 426 Hemi. *Mike Mueller*

went inside, and those tube headers were dropped in favor of cast-iron manifolds. Compression was cut to 10.25:1 and the exotic cross-ram intake was replaced by a conventional inline manifold sporting two 650 cfm Carter four-barrels. Much of the race Hemi's super-tough foundation, however, carried over into 1966, as did that still-laughable 425-horse advertised output rating.

Familiar raves also returned. "If you missed the San Francisco earthquake, reserve your seat here for a repeat performance," began *Car and Driver*'s first review of the street Hemi, in this case a Plymouth. "Forget about your GTOs and your hot Fords—if you want to be boss on your block, rush down to your nearest Plymouth (or Dodge) dealer and place your order for a hemispherical combustion chamber 426 V-8. This automobile is the most powerful sedan ever, bar none."

Magazine road testers managed quarter-mile times as low as 13.25 seconds for a Hemi-powered B-body in 1966. Dodge advertisements that year called the Hemi-powered Charger "Boss Hoss," while Plymouth ads used the nickname "King Kong." In either case, the 425-horse Mopars were main attractions, but seeing that big show firsthand meant shelling out some serious coin. The Hemi alone cost more than $700, then came a long list of mandatory options, equipment required to keep the hot-tempered Hemi in line. On this list were items like an 11-inch clutch (with the A-833 four-speed; the A-727 Torqueflite automatic was also available), a Dana rear end with a Sure-Grip differential, 11-inch drum brakes, special tires, higher rate springs, and stiffer shocks.

In the Hemi's case, biggest bang for the buck was never the consideration. It was biggest bang, period.

In a *Car Life* test, a 1966 Hemi Satellite ran from rest to 60 miles per hour in 7.1 seconds. The quarter-mile clocking was 14.5 seconds. *Mike Mueller*

Both Dodge and Plymouth offered super-stock factory drag cars again in 1967. The option code for this package was "R023" for the Plymouth (shown here), "W023" for the Dodge. Production was 55 of each. *Mike Mueller*

Plymouth's R023 package included a street Hemi V-8, but the more exotic race Hemi has been substituted in this case. *Mike Mueller*

02

Plymouth Barracuda 1964–1974

Dangerous Waters

While we'll probably never, ever figure out which came first as far as chickens and eggs are concerned, none of us needs a veterinarian to help answer another, far more obscure, age-old question: which small animal followed the other, pony or predator fish? Back in April 1964, car-buyers simply couldn't get enough of the so-called new breed of compact that Ford called Mustang. An unprecedented automotive feeding frenzy ensued, and rival automakers quickly went to work creating copycats, with Chevrolet's 1967 Camaro ranking first and foremost, joined by the likes of Pontiac's Firebird, AMC's Javelin, and Mercury's Cougar. All these fun machines, they with their long hoods and short rear decks, were soon classed as "pony cars" for rather obvious reasons.

But hold on a sec. Lost under all the confetti spewed about 45 years back was the plain fact that Lee Iacocca's baby was beaten out of the box, by two weeks or so, by a comparable sporty compact, this one from Chrysler Corporation. Introduced to the public on April 1, 1964, Plymouth's cute little Barracuda was—if you want to get truly technical—Detroit's first pony car in that it, well, hit the streets first. So why, then, didn't it inspire the market segment name we all still use without question today?

For starters, let's talk sheer impact. Ford set all kinds of sales records with its early Mustangs while rolling more than a million off the line by February 1966. Plymouth let about 23,500 Barracudas loose in 1964, followed by 60,000 in 1965, and 36,000 in 1966. Not bad numbers, mind you, but a history-maker this Plymouth clearly wasn't. Nor did Dearborn earn milestone accolades by simply winning, by a humongous margin, a popularity contest.

- Plymouth introduced its A-body compact, Valiant, for 1960.
- The original Valiant-based Barracuda actually beat Ford's wildly popular Mustang out into the wild by two weeks in April 1964.
- All first-generation (1964–1966) Barracudas were fastback coupes.
- Ford's first fastback Mustang didn't appear until September 1964.
- An even sportier Barracuda, the Formula S, debuted for 1965.
- A redesigned second-generation Barracuda appeared for 1967.
- A "notchback" hardtop and convertible joined the lineup in 1967, as did optional big-block power.
- Promotional paperwork first used the "'Cuda" reference in 1967.
- Another redesign for 1970 featured a new foundation, Chrysler's compact E-body platform.
- Created to go racing on the Sports Car Club of America's Trans-Am circuit, the AAR 'Cuda was built for one year only, 1970.
- All V-8 Barracudas built from 1972 to 1974 featured small-blocks.

Opposite:
Plymouth's pony car rolled through three generations during its career. The first rendition ran from 1964 to 1966, the second from 1967 to 1969, and the third from 1970 to 1974. Up front is a 1966 Formula S; behind it is the last of the breed, a 360-equipped 1974 model. *Mike Mueller*

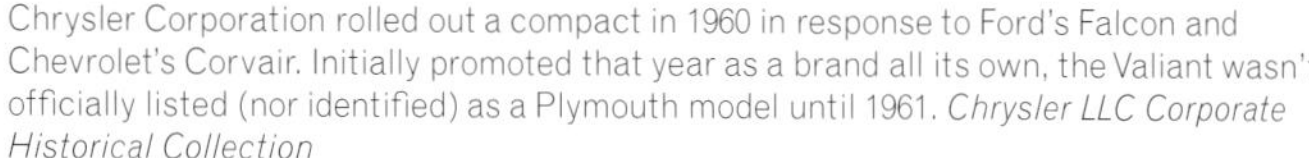

Chrysler Corporation rolled out a compact in 1960 in response to Ford's Falcon and Chevrolet's Corvair. Initially promoted that year as a brand all its own, the Valiant wasn't officially listed (nor identified) as a Plymouth model until 1961. *Chrysler LLC Corporate Historical Collection*

Plymouth designers created the original Barracuda, introduced in April 1964, by more or less grafting a glass fastback onto the division's existing Valiant Signet hardtop, shown here. *Chrysler LLC Corporate Historical Collection*

Ford people not only did much, much better concerning promotion and execution, they also deserve credit for original conception. Serious development work on the Mustang began not long after Iacocca was promoted to Ford Division general manager in November 1960, with final approval for a rush to market coming down from Henry Ford II's ivory tower in September 1962. Once Plymouth execs got wind of this plan, they hastily prepared a copy, speeding the Barracuda through short-order development in less than two years to hopefully upstage Iacocca at his own game.

Making this rapid response possible was the plain fact that Plymouth's design studio more or less took the division's existing two-door Valiant and melded on a sleek, sloping rear window. Designer Dave Cummins originally sketched this "Valiant Fastback" in the summer of 1962, inspired by a similar treatment first seen three years before on Plymouth's Super Sport, a sweet-looking midsized proposal that actually was considered for 1962 production. Transforming artwork into prototype sheet metal essentially was no sweat, with the final form all but agreed upon early in 1963.

From the cowl forward and beltline down, Plymouth's original Barracuda was essentially all garden-variety A-body, complete with a "Valiant" badge on its tail. But setting it miles apart from its plainly dull sibling was that huge rear window, then the largest expanse of glass ever installed on an American car. Missing this truly fresh profile was no easy task.

"To say that the Plymouth Valiant Barracuda is an attention-getter is an understatement," claimed a *Car Life* review. "A more accurate commentary is that it is a traffic-stopping, people-grabbing, where-do-I-sign-the-order-blank? sort of attention. The simple addition of a sweeping fastback roofline (from windshield header to a point just over the rear bumper) seems to transform the mundane Valiant into a thing of purpose and poise."

"Simple addition" qualified as a second understatement. Supplied by Pittsburgh Plate Glass, that 14.4-square-foot expanse of curved backlight didn't find a home atop the Valiant until various modifications were made. With the compact coupe's diagonal bracing and package shelf structure gone, the Barracuda's rear body section needed

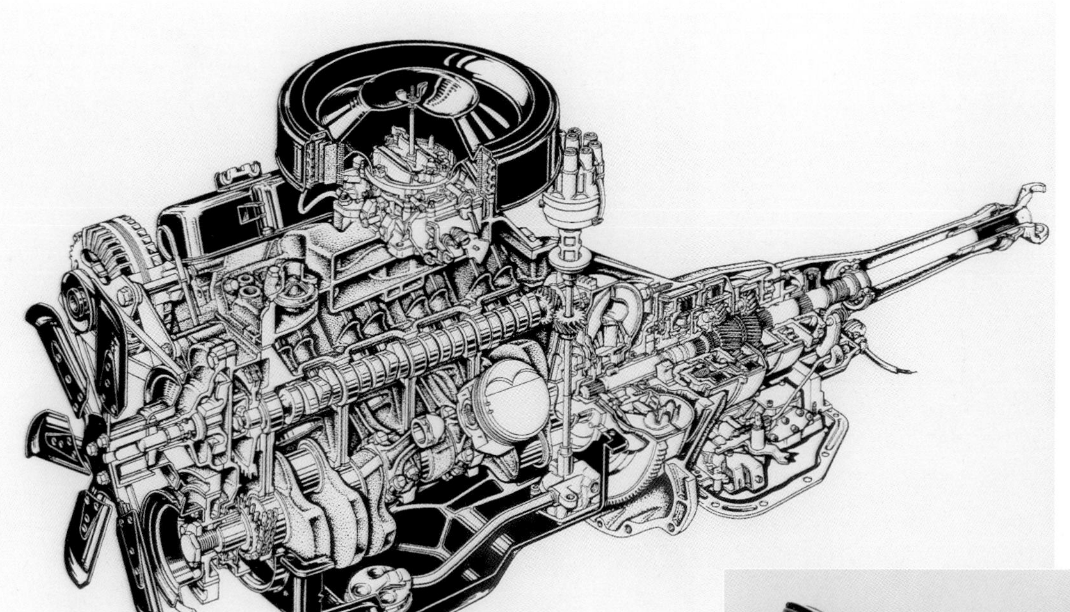

Left:
Chrysler Corporation's LA-series small-block was born in 1964 as an option for both Plymouth's Barracuda and Dodge's Dart. A 273-cubic-inch LA V-8 came first, joined by a 318 cid version in 1967. The hottest LA, the 275-horse 340, debuted the following year. Bore and stroke for the 273 V-8 (shown here) was 3.63 and 3.31 inches, respectively. *Chrysler LLC Corporate Historical Collection*

Below:
Hurst built the first of its famed "Hemi Under Glass" exhibition dragster Barracudas in 1965. Outrageous wheel stands were made possible by mounting this crowd-pleasing machine's Hemi V-8 behind the driver. *Chrysler LLC Corporate Historical Collection*

special reinforcement both to retain torsional rigidity and securely mount that heavy piece of safety glass. Tying the structure together and supporting the window at its leading edge was a box-section arch running up over the roof from wheelhouse to wheelhouse. A smaller boxed arch supported the glass at its trailing edge, and horizontal beams extended between these two trusses to add further confidence. Completing the transformation was special ventilation equipment designed to prevent interior air pressure build-up from unhinging that big transparent fastback.

Okay, so all that glass did tend to warm things up inside on seriously sunny days. But a warmly welcomed trade-off was expanded interior room, which could've been exploited further thanks to standard fold-down rear seats working in concert with a rear compartment panel that opened up into the trunk. Though that traditional storage compartment on its own was something to sneeze at, some seven feet of floor space was made available with the rear panel opened and back seats dropped down—all the better perhaps to allow you and your best girl to unroll a sleeping bag at the drive-in on a Saturday night.

Like its pony car rival from Ford, the 1964 Barracuda also came standard with bucket seats up front, just the ticket to tease the "young, sports-minded Americans who want to enjoy the fun of driving a car that also fills their general transportation needs," as Chrysler-Plymouth general manager P. N. Buckminster explained it. All other features were Valiant carryovers, including powertrain pieces. Front torsion bars and rear leaf springs suspended things, and four-wheel drums (measuring 9.0×2.5 inches in front, 9.0x2.0 inches in back) handled braking chores. Optional disc brakes weren't offered, at least not at first.

More and more performance potential appeared as the Barracuda splashed on into the sixties, beginning with the nimble Formula S, introduced for 1965. Available big-block power debuted along with a totally redesigned platform in 1967, and the legendary Hemi 'Cuda exploded onto the scene three years later, again in cahoots with a major redesign, this one based on Chrysler's all-new E-body foundation. Plymouth built its last Barracuda in 1974.

02

1964
Barracuda V-8

Specifications	
Model availability	two-door "fastback" coupe
Wheelbase	106 inches
Length	188.2 inches
Width	70.1 inches
Height	53.8 inches
Weight	3,150 pounds
Base Price	$2,496
Track (front/rear, in inches)	55.9/55.6
Wheels	13-inch stamped steel
Tires	7×13 inches
Construction	unitized body/frame
Suspension	independent wishbones with torsion bars, front; solid axle with longitudinal leaf springs, rear
Steering	recirculating ball
Brakes	four-wheel drums
Engine	180-horsepower, 273-cubic-inch V-8
Bore and stroke	3.63×3.31 inches
Compression	8.8:1
Fuel delivery	single two-barrel carburetor
Transmission	three-speed manual
Axle ratio	2.93:1
Production	23,433

All Barracudas built from 1964 to 1966 were sport coupes with fold-down rear seats. The rear compartment panel also opened up into the trunk, enhancing the car's cargo capacity even further. *Mike Mueller*

1964

The Barracuda's family ties were demonstrated rather painfully in base form. Standard beneath that hood was the Valiant's totally frugal 170-cubic-inch slant-six engine topped by a one-barrel carburetor. Output was a paltry 101 horsepower. First on the options list was a 145-horse, 225-cube bent-six, priced at $47.35. The closest thing to a performance mill was the 273-cubic-inch LA small-block fed by a two-barrel carb, a 180-horse engine included in the basic V-8 Barracuda deal, itself wearing a $2,496 bottom line. A Barracuda six started out at $2,365 that year.

A three-speed manual transmission was standard too, but it could've been replaced by a Hurst-shifted four-speed when one of the two optional engines was installed. Available, as well, was the Torqueflite automatic with its push-button controls set to the instrument panel's left side. Power assists for steering and brakes were typically available at extra cost, as was a Sure-Grip rear end, but that was it as far as mechanicals were concerned.

At 14.4 square feet, the first-generation Barracuda's rear window represented the largest piece of glass ever installed on an American car to that point. It was supplied by Pittsburgh Plate Glass. *Mike Mueller*

Without any real muscle available, Plymouth's first Barracuda wasn't quite ready to run with Ford's supreme Mustang, which could've been fitted with the optional 289 High Performance V-8, rated at 271 horsepower. Although sporty impressions clearly were present, true seat-of-the-pants responses were plainly lacking. According to *Car Life*, the 1964 Barracuda "needs some development if it is to match with performance the promise of its racy good looks. As it is right now, it's just a novel little hardtop that won't swim away from anything."

Fortunately lessons at the pool were in the works.

"The simple addition of a sweeping fastback roofline seems to transform the mundane Valiant into a thing of purpose and poise," claims a *Car Life* review of the 1964 Barracuda. Base price for the V-8 version that year was $2,486. *Mike Mueller*

Like Ford's new Mustang that year, Plymouth's original Barracuda also offered standard bucket seats in 1964. Both slant-six and V-8 models were offered, and a three-speed manual transmission was standard in both cases. *Mike Mueller*

The only V-8 available between Barracuda fenders in 1964 was a 273 LA small-block topped by a two-barrel carburetor. Output was 180 horsepower. *Mike Mueller*

Chrysler's quaint push-button automatic transmission controls appeared for one year only inside Plymouth's first Barracuda. *Mike Mueller*

02

1965
Barracuda Formula S

Specifications	
Model availability	two-door "fastback" coupe
Wheelbase	106 inches
Length	188.2 inches
Width	70.1 inches
Height	53.8 inches
Weight	3,170 pounds
Price	Formula S package added $258 to the V-8 Barracuda's $2,586 Base Price
Track (front/rear, in inches)	55.9/55.6
Wheels	14.0×5.5 inches
Tires	6.95×14.00 Goodyear Blue Streak
Construction	unitized body/frame
Suspension	independent wishbones with heavy-duty torsion bars and thickened stabilizer bar, front; solid axle with longitudinal heavy-duty leaf springs, rear; Firm Ride shock absorbers
Steering	recirculating ball
Brakes	four-wheel drums
Engine	235-horsepower, 273-cubic-inch V-8
Bore and stroke	3.63×3.31 inches
Compression	10.5:1
Fuel delivery	single four-barrel carburetor
Transmission	three-speed manual
Axle ratio	3.23:1
Production	not available

Above:
Plymouth people preferred to call their Barracuda "an action car," hence this action-packed image of a V-8-equipped 1965 model, base-priced that year at $2,586. *Chrysler LLC Corporate Historical Collection*

Below:
Plymouth officials opted to distance the Barracuda from its mundane roots in 1965 by deleting the Valiant badge seen on the car's tail the year before. The racing stripe seen here was a $31.25 option in 1965. The simulated chrome-wheel wheel covers were available in 13- and 14-inch sizes that year. *Chrysler LLC Corporate Historical Collection*

1965

After rolling out 23,443 Barracudas for 1964, Plymouth produced another 60,168 for 1965, and that latter total represented the all-time high for the line. Ford's zenith, on the other hand, amounted to some 607,000 Mustangs built for 1966.

Changes for 1965 were minimal, with perhaps the biggest news involving the removal of the "Valiant" badge in back as Plymouth people obviously decided to distance their sporty compact from its yeoman roots. An updated dashboard went inside, and a floor shifter replaced those quaint pushbuttons in Torqueflite applications. Base six-cylinder and V-8 renditions were again offered, priced at $2,502 and $2,586, respectively. The former relied only on the 225 slant-six, since officials opted, and rightly so, to drop the little 170 six from the Barracuda lineup.

New on the options list were the Performance Group and the Sports Group, the latter featuring a three-spoke simulated wood-

Above:
Scott Harvey's Barracuda finished fifth overall in the SCCA's inaugural Trans American Sedan Series season, which was kicked off at Sebring, Florida, on March 25, 1966. Trans-Am racing quickly became a proving ground of sorts for all of Detroit's pony cars. *Chrysler LLC Corporate Historical Collection*

Right:
An avid road racer himself, engineer Scott Harvey was responsible for both creating and testing the Formula S Barracuda, introduced for 1965. No, his wife and kids weren't along for the ride whenever he took his family car onto SCCA tracks. *Chrysler LLC Corporate Historical Collection*

grain steering wheel, whitewall tires, and wheel covers that mimicked bolt-on mags. This package was available with both six-cylinder and V-8 models. The Performance Group added the Rallye suspension and a four-barrel-fed small-block V-8, the "Commando 273." Also listed as a separate option, Rallye underpinnings consisted of predictably beefed-up torsion bars and leaf springs, as well as a stiffened 0.82-inch front stabilizer bar.

Plymouth's Commando 273-cubic-inch V-8 produced 235 horsepower, 55 more than the base small-block, thanks primarily to a more aggressive solid-lifter cam and a compression increase from 8.8:1 to 10.5:1. Bringing up the exhaust end was a single low-restriction system with a resonator and rectangular dress-up exhaust tip. Black-painted, finned valve covers and chrome dress-up for the air cleaner and oil filler cap completed the Commando deal.

Those 235 horses instantly transformed the 1965 Barracuda, as *Car and Driver* explained, "from a flabby boulevardier into a rugged middleweight." Zero-to-60 performance was 8 seconds flat, according to *Car Life*, which also published a so-so quarter-mile time slip of 16.1 seconds at 87 miles per hour. At least this was a start.

As it was, straight-line brute strength wasn't Plymouth's goal during the Barracuda's early years. Witness the efforts of engineer Scott Harvey, who spent his free time winning rally championships in SCCA racing. Harvey was the driving force behind a third new 1965 options group, the Formula S package. Though it did include the 235-horse 273, the Formula S deal's main focus was handling. Hence, the Rallye foundation, complemented with Firm Ride shock absorbers, was included, as were widened (5.5 inches) 14.0-inch wheels shod in specially prepared Goodyear Blue Streak 6.95x14.00 tires. Accenting this wheel/tire combo were those simulated bolt-on wheel covers.

Appropriate "Formula S" badges went on each front fender, and a 6,000 rpm tach was standard inside. A Walter Mitty type also could've enhanced the image further with an optional racing stripe that ran down the middle of the car from nose to tail. Available on its own without the Formula S option, this stripe was done in five colors, depending on exterior paint choice.

"If any single general observation can be made about the Formula S it might be that it really earned its stripes," wrote *Hot Rod* magazine's Eric Dahlquist in praise of the nimble 1965 Barracuda. "The first encounter with twisting roads revealed that corners could be safely negotiated at double or even triple posted limits."

"Just don't try this one at home, kids," he didn't say, but we'll forgive him.

02

1966
Barracuda Formula S

Specifications	
Model availability	two-door "fastback" coupe
Wheelbase	106 inches
Length	188.2 inches
Width	70.1 inches
Height	53.8 inches
Weight	3,170 pounds
Price	Formula S package added $257.75 to the V-8 Barracuda's $2,637 base price
Track (front/rear, in inches)	55.9/55.6
Wheels	14.0×5.5 inches
Tires	6.95×14.00 Goodyear Blue Streak
Construction	unitized body/frame
Suspension	independent wishbones with heavy-duty torsion bars and thickened stabilizer bar, front; solid axle with longitudinal heavy-duty leaf springs, rear; Firm Ride shock absorbers
Steering	recirculating ball
Brakes	four-wheel drums
Engine	235-horsepower, 273-cubic-inch V-8
Bore and stroke	3.63×3.31 inches
Compression	10.5:1
Fuel delivery	single four-barrel carburetor
Transmission	three-speed manual
Axle ratio	3.23:1
Production	not available

The Formula S package cost $257.75 in 1966. Humble fender badges were included in the deal from the beginning. *Mike Mueller*

1966

Updates for 1966 included a revised grille and taillights and new fender-mounted turn signal indicators. Another dash makeover happened inside as an actual oil pressure gauge replaced the old idiot light and a vacuum gauge was added when the optional tachometer took its place. The Barracuda's standard bucket seats also were changed to a sportier shell-type.

Making the biggest splash were new front disc brakes, 11.125-inch units supplied by Kelsey-Hayes and priced at $81.95. Available front discs had appeared in 1965 but only as a dealer-installed option. Plymouth customers in 1966 could order them direct, with or without optional power assist. In *Car and Driver*'s words, this new option was "indispensible."

All other mechanicals carried over unchanged from 1965. At the top again was the Formula S with its 235-horse small-block, and this handling machine once more took its sweet time completing a quarter-mile, finishing in 17.6 seconds according to *Car and Driver.* "No, the Formula S Barracuda, in its present form, won't capture the hearts of teen-age America," concluded the *C/D* crew. "It could, provided Plymouth stuffed in its 383 V-8 or even the Hemi, but this would utterly destroy the beautiful balance of the automobile. And in this case, we're four-square behind maintaining the status quo."

For now, that is.

Along with Plymouth's 273-cubic-inch four-barrel V-8, the 1965–1966 Formula S also came standard with the division's heavy-duty Rallye suspension. Output for the 273 Commando V-8 was 235 horsepower. Production of the 1966 Formula S (shown here) was 3,702. *Mike Mueller*

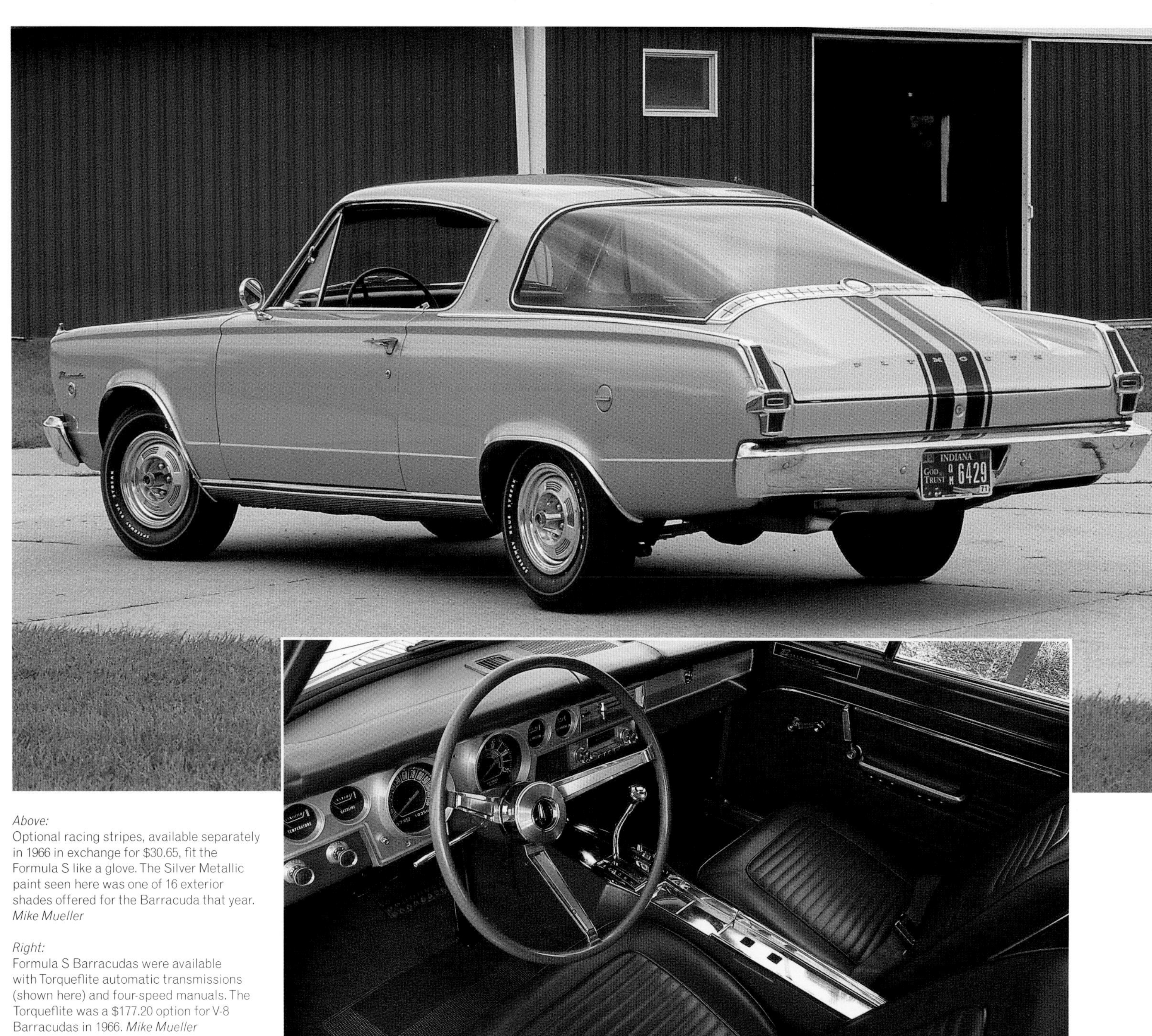

Above:
Optional racing stripes, available separately in 1966 in exchange for $30.65, fit the Formula S like a glove. The Silver Metallic paint seen here was one of 16 exterior shades offered for the Barracuda that year. *Mike Mueller*

Right:
Formula S Barracudas were available with Torqueflite automatic transmissions (shown here) and four-speed manuals. The Torqueflite was a $177.20 option for V-8 Barracudas in 1966. *Mike Mueller*

Above, left:
Firm Ride shock absorbers were included in the Formula S package, as were Goodyear Blue Streak 6.95×14.00 tires and those simulated bolt-on wheel covers. *Mike Mueller*

Above, right:
A four-speed stick was a $175.45 option for V-8 Barracudas in 1966. *Mike Mueller*

Left:
The four-barrel-fed 273 Commando small-block was available on its own, without the Formula S option, for the 1966 Barracuda at a cost of $97.30. *Mike Mueller*

02

1967
Barracuda Formula S

Specifications	
Model availability	two-door fastback, coupe and convertible
Wheelbase	108 inches
Length	192.8 inches
Width	71.6 inches
Height	53.5 inches (fastback)
Weight	3,310 pounds (273 V-8)
Price	Formula S package cost $177.50
Track (front/rear, in inches)	57.4/55.6
Wheels	14.0×5.5 inches
Tires	D70×14 Firestone Wide-Oval
Construction	unitized body/frame
Suspension	independent wishbones with heavy-duty torsion bars and thickened stabilizer bar, front; solid axle with longitudinal heavy-duty leaf springs, rear
Steering	recirculating ball
Brakes	four-wheel drums, standard; front discs, optional (mandatory with 383 V-8)
Engine	235-horsepower, 273-cubic-inch V-8 or 280-horsepower, 383-cubic-inch V-8
Bore and stroke	3.63×3.31 inches (273); 4.25×3.38 inches (383)
Compression	10.5:1 (273); 10.0:1 (383)
Fuel delivery	single four-barrel carburetor
Transmission	four-speed manual or Torqueflite automatic
Axle ratio	3.23:1
Production	5,352 with 273 small-block V-8; 1,841 with 383 big-block

Former Studebaker designer Milt Antonick garnered the bulk of the credit for the A-body Barracuda's 1967 makeover. According to *Car and Driver*, Plymouth's second-generation pony car featured the "tautness of line and integrity of design matched by few American cars of any vintage." *Mike Mueller*

1967

The pony car market blossomed full force in 1967 as General Motors unveiled its new Camaro and Firebird and Mercury introduced Cougar. All rolled right out of the blocks bragging about available big-block power, as did an equally new Mustang that was redesigned primarily to make that possible. Like Plymouth's first-generation Barracuda, Ford's early pony simply didn't have room between its flanks for the company's biggest horsepower churns. The choice in Dearborn had been simple once word got out about GM's pending introductions: enlarge the Mustang's engine bay or be content to eat the dust left behind by all those Camaro SS 396s and Firebird 400s.

Along with eyes, Plymouth people also had ears, and they, too, had heard about the new direction the pony car market would take in 1967. Thus they recognized the same need to put the spurs to their pony. Building a bigger, better Barracuda was the only thing to do, a certified no-brainer, but what about visual impact? Ford's 1967 Mustang still clearly looked like a Mustang; should Plymouth's redesign stick with those Valiant ties?

Hell no! Led by former Studebaker man Milt Antonick, the division's design team opted for a totally blank sheet of paper, and their bold efforts paid off with a sleek, sexy body that overnight changed the way critics looked at Plymouth's previously demure pony car. Sure, the second-generation Barracuda still shared its A-body foundation with Valiant and Dodge's Dart, but the connection was no longer visible, not even if you squinted. Nothing Chrysler offered looked like this baby, and many felt the same applied industry-wide.

"The new Barracuda is unquestionably the best-looking car out of Detroit in 1967," crowed a December 1966 *Car and Driver* review. "It

Above:
A new convertible model, base-priced at $2,779, debuted along with the restyled second-generation Barracuda fastback in 1967. Total topless production (exports included) that year was 4,228. Notice the sport stripe, a $30.65 option that year. *Chrysler LLC Corporate Historical Collection*

Right:
Total fastback Barracuda production for 1967 was 30,110. The Formula S option carried over basically unchanged from 1966, wearing a price tag of $177.50. *Mike Mueller*

The Barracuda's highly useful fold-down rear seat rolled over from 1966 into 1967 for the fastback body style. And again the passenger compartment's rear panel opened up into the trunk for maximum cargo capacity—or added stretch-out space. *Mike Mueller*

The 235-horsepower, 273-cubic-inch Commando V-8 also continued on unchanged into 1967. Total Barracuda installations that year numbered 10,242. *Mike Mueller*

A second new body style debuted in 1967, the "notchback" coupe, base-priced at $2,449. Introduced that year, too, was the Barracuda's first optional big-block, the 383-cubic-inch Commando V-8. *Mike Mueller*

has tautness of line and integrity of design matched by few American cars of any vintage. It's been several years since either division of the Chrysler Corporation has produced a notably handsome car; Plymouth's old Barracuda was hardly the exception."

Frontal impressions were downright dramatic thanks to a crisp, clean split grille treatment, while a Euro-style Kamm-back treatment brought up the rear. Antonick was a sucker for European sports cars, and this affliction showed up in other areas too, most prominently by way of the competition-style gas cap located in the driver-side quarter panel. Triumiles per hour's use of similar external fuel fillers inspired this addition, which got an enthusiastic two thumbs up from design chief Elwood Engle after Antonick popped one open in his presence.

All that eye-popping styling was enhanced further by the lower, longer, wider parameters made possible by Chrysler's redesigned A-body platform, which now rolled on a 108-inch wheelbase (up two clicks) in Plymouth applications. Overall length jumped nearly

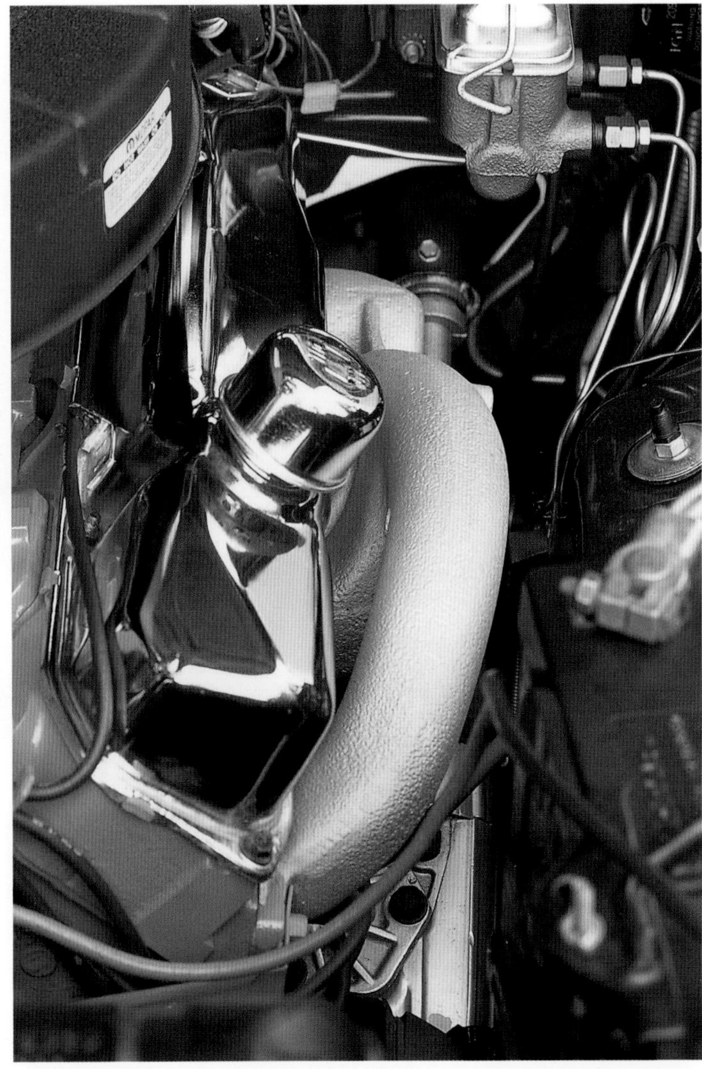

Above:
Concessions made to fit the 383 big-block into the A-body Barracuda included more restrictive exhausts, which translated into an output drop from 325 horsepower to 280 in this application. *Mike Mueller*

Right:
The fit was especially tight on the driver side of the A-body engine compartment, where the B-series big-block's exhaust manifold ruled out the installation of an optional power-steering pump. *Mike Mueller*

5 inches to 192.8, and width went from 70.0 inches to 71.6. Meanwhile, height dropped, about 1.5 inches to 53.0 inches, as did ground clearance, from 6.0 inches to 5.7.

Increasing, too, were 1967's body choices, since the familiar fastback was joined by a "notchback" hardtop and a care-free convertible, meaning Plymouth finally matched Ford, which had been marketing three Mustang bodies since September 1964. Only the topless Barracuda featured standard bucket seats; the other two models came standard with a typical front bench, and buckets were moved to the options list. The fastback, of course, retained the standard fold-down rear seat known far and wide to submarine racers everywhere since April 1964.

As expected, more interior room was a product of that extra width and length. But far more important was the extra space created beneath the hood. The available engines (the 225 six and two 273 V-8s) that carried over identically from 1966 looked lost in there. But not so concerning the Barracuda's first optional big-block, a hefty V-8 that had entered the developmental picture more or less at the last minute.

Reportedly, Plymouth engineers originally planned to incorporate an enlarged small-block into the Supreme Performance package for 1967. While designers were busy widening the Barracuda engine bay by two inches, the engine crew was preparing to modify Chrysler's existing 318-cubic-inch V-8 for this application. They hoped 35 more cubes would do the trick, but these hopes faded rapidly once they heard

The redesigned 1967 Barracuda rolled on a 108-inch wheelbase, compared to 106 inches for its predecessor. Overall length also increased 5 inches to 193. Width went from 70.0 inches to 71.6. *Mike Mueller*

The second-generation Barracuda's competition-style, pop-open gas cap, located on the driver-side rear quarter panel, demonstrated designer Milt Antonick's affection for European sports-racing machines. *Mike Mueller*

about the big big-blocks slated for Ford and GM's latest, greatest pony cars. Plan B, requiring the use of a shoehorn, then went into effect.

As *Car and Driver* told the tale, "Plymouth pushed aside the 318 and set about wedging their big, fat 383 into the 'Cuda. Tight fit, but—whew!—they made it." But not without losing the power-steering pump, which couldn't coexist with the driver-side exhaust manifold. Space constraints also ruled out the installation of optional air conditioning, leaving drivers no choice but to sweat their rumps off while muscling up to turn that wheel during parallel parking attempts.

That tight fit also contributed to a noticeable power outage. Dropping Chrysler's 325-horse B-series big-block, previously reserved for the larger B- and C-body models, into the smaller A-body platform required the use of a more restrictive exhaust system, and this installation, in turn, translated into a little less horsepower. A tamer cam in this case also helped cut advertised output down to 280 horses for the 1967 Barracuda's optional 383-cubic-inch Commando V-8.

According to a *Car and Driver* test, a 383-powered 1967 notchback could run from rest to 60 miles per hour in a tidy 6.6 seconds. Quarter-mile performance was 15.4 seconds at 92 miles per hour, and these figures came from a car equipped with the Torqueflite automatic and 3.23:1 "highway" gears. Greater potential clearly was present.

While the big-block option, at $52, surely looked affordable in 1967, the true price actually was a little higher thanks to two mandatory installations: the $177 Formula S suspension package

Production of 273-equipped Formula S Barracudas in 1967 was 5,352. The count for their big-block counterparts was 1,841. *Mike Mueller*

Front disc brakes were mandated whenever the 383 Commando V-8 was installed between Plymouth pony car flanks in 1967. Supplied by Kelsey-Hayes, these brakes incorporated 11.88-inch rotors. *Mike Mueller*

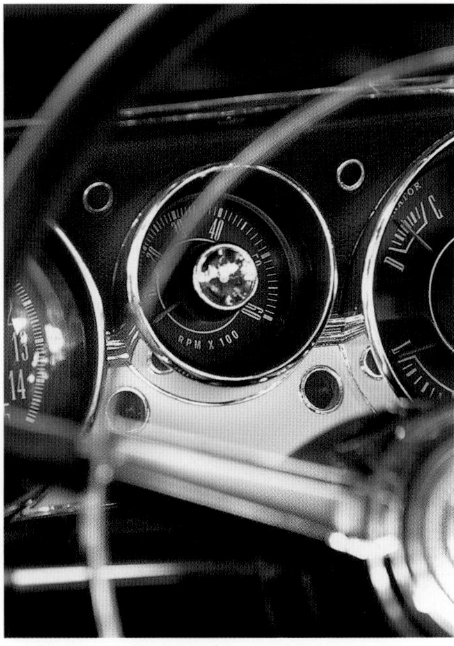

A 6,000 rpm tachometer was again included in the Formula S deal in 1967. *Mike Mueller*

$69 Kelsey-Hayes front disc brakes. Reining in those 280 horses was deemed every bit as important as whipping them on, and handling them safely and surely, too, obviously was made a priority.

Unfortunately, at least from a sports-car-minded guy's perspective, the 383's extra weight compromised the original Formula S ideal. In *Car and Driver*'s words, the 383 Formula S was "something of an oddball, more at home on a dragstrip or a turnpike than on a winding mountain road." Of course the same thing could've been said about the 390 Mustang GT, Camaro SS 396, and Firebird 400. All these nose-heavy muscle machines represented obvious compromises, yet they still stirred the souls of pony car buyers like never before. Apparently they shook 'em too.

Available with either the 383 big-block or 273 small-block, the Formula S package rolled over from 1966 with few changes. New were Firestone D70 Wide Oval redline tires, which in standard trim were complemented by small "poverty caps" covering each hub. New options for 1967 included the Decor Trim package, which consisted of a 150-miles-per-hour speedometer, bright pedal dress-up, simulated wood-grain panels for the dash and doors, and rear armrests with ashtrays. A rally-ready quick-steering ratio also appeared for manual operation only. Total Formula S production, for all three body styles, was 5,352 with the small-block, 1,841 with the big-block.

A center console was a $48.70 option for the 1967 Barracuda. It was not available with the base three speed manual transmission. *Mike Mueller*

1968
Barracuda Formula S

Specifications	
Model availability	two-door fastback, coupe, and convertible
Wheelbase	108 inches
Length	192.8 inches
Width	71.6 inches
Height	53.5 inches (fastback)
Weight	3,310 pounds (340 V-8)
Price	Formula S package cost $186.30 with 340 small-block V-8, $221.65 with 383 big-block
Track (front/rear, in inches)	57.4/55.6
Wheels	14.0×5.5 inches
Tires	E70×14 Red Streak
Construction	unitized body/frame
Suspension	independent wishbones with heavy-duty torsion bars and thickened stabilizer bar, front; solid axle with longitudinal heavy-duty leaf springs, rear
Steering	recirculating ball
Brakes	four-wheel drums, standard; front discs, optional
Engine	275-horsepower, 340-cubic-inch V-8 or 300-horsepower, 383-cubic-inch V-8
Bore and stroke	4.04×3.31 inches (273); 4.25×3.38 inches (383)
Compression	10.5:1 (340); 10.0:1 (383)
Fuel delivery	single four-barrel carburetor
Transmission	four-speed manual or Torqueflite automatic
Axle ratio	3.23:1
Production	3,917 with 340 small-block V-8; 1,279 with 383 big-block

The Formula S package was again available for all three Barracuda body styles in 1968. Two hot V-8s remained available beneath Formula S hoods that year, with the 383 big-block carrying over from 1967. The 273 Commando, however, was replaced in 1968 by the 340-cubic-inch LA-series V-8. *Mike Mueller*

1968

That hot bod, again done in three styles, returned for 1968 wearing a new grille and taillights, and nearly all basic features carried over from 1967. A few notable changes were made beneath the hood, with the first involving a new standard LA small-block as the 273 was traded for a 230-horsepower-rated 318. The optional 273 Commando was also dropped, but with nary a tear shed over its demise. In its place was the new 340-cubic-inch LA, conservatively (in many opinions) rated at 275 horsepower. Topping the options list off was the 383-cubic-inch big-block, which was pumped up to 300 horsepower thanks to the addition of better-breathing cylinder heads and an improved intake manifold.

The latest, greatest LA was created solely for performance applications and thus never appeared with anything less than a four-barrel on top. Its parts list included beefy rods, a bulletproof forged-steel crank, excellent-flowing cylinder heads, and a superb cam grind. Compression was 10.5:1, and that carb was a Carter AVS unit. Called a "giant killer from Hamtramck," the 340 quickly established itself as one of Detroit's hottest small-blocks and would remain so well into the seventies. According to a *Car Life* road test, a 1969 340 Formula S could smoke the quarter in 14.93 seconds at 96.63 miles per hour.

Thanks to its LA parameters, the 340 encountered no difficulties entering the Barracuda engine bay, and thus optional air conditioning also could've been installed. Its relative light weight, compared to its 383 big-block running mate, also meant there was no compromising the Formula S Barracuda's original intentions. This little fish could swim just as hard through the twisties as it could down the straight and narrow.

Three Barracuda body styles returned for 1968. Base prices (with V-8 power) were $2,711 for the notchback, $2,868 for the fastback, and $3,013 for the convertible. *Chrysler LLC Corporate Historical Collection*

As in 1967, the Formula S package was required when the hottest small-block and 383 big-block were specified. Both Formula S models featured bright hood plates that announced which engine was resting beneath. One minor change to the package involved standard rubber, which that year consisted of E70x14 Red Streaks. Front stabilizer bars used in the two Formula S applications measured 0.88 inch for the 340, 0.94 for the 383.

New on the 1968 options list was a set of red wheelhouse liners, as if the second-generation Barracuda needed any help standing out in a crowd. Returning go-fast goodies included quicker manual steering and the Rallye instrument cluster, which featured a 150-miles-per-hour speedometer and simulated wood-grain trim. A simulated wood-grain three-spoke steering wheel with padded hub also was available at extra cost.

Production breakdown for the 340 Formula S was 2,857 fastbacks, 867 notchbacks, and 193 convertibles. The numbers for the big-block Formula S read 963 fastbacks, 252 notchbacks, and 64 convertibles.

The year 1968 was also the year Tom Hoover's engineers rolled out the most extreme Barracuda yet by stuffing a few 426 Hemis between A-body fenders. Coordinated by Chrysler's Dick Maxwell, these super-stock conversions were created in conjunction with the Hurst shifter guys for serious drag racers. All 70 of these purpose-built machines were done in white primer, leaving the final paint scheme up to the owner. All also featured weight-saving fiberglass hoods and fenders, and door skins and bumpers were stamped from light-gauge steel to cut away even more unwanted pounds.

Fitting the Hemi into the Barracuda was made possible by moving the battery to the trunk (where it aided weight transfer anyway), reshaping the right shock tower, and relocating the master brake cylinder. Hurst added unique headers, its own excellent shift linkages for four-speed cars, and heavy-duty 9.75-inch Dana rear axles. Both manual transmissions and Torqueflites were installed. Quarter-mile blasts in the mid-10-second range were no problem for the S/S Hemi Barracuda.

02

Of the 867 small-block Formula S notchbacks built for 1968, 351 had four-speed manual transmissions (shown here), 516 had Torqueflite automatics. The deluxe steering wheel with simulated wood rim was a $25.95 option in 1968. *Mike Mueller*

New for 1968 was the 340-cubic-inch small-block, created by boring out the LA-series V-8 to 4.04 inches. Stroke remained at 3.31 inches. Meant only for high-performance applications, the 340 never settled for anything less than dual exhausts and a four-barrel carburetor. Output was 275 horsepower. *Mike Mueller*

Base price for a 1968 V-8 Barracuda convertible was $3,013. A 318-cubic-inch LA small-block was standard. The simulated bolt-on wheel covers seen on this topless 1968 Formula S added an extra $44.90 to the bottom line that year. *Mike Mueller*

Above, left:
Many Chrysler Corporation engines featured exhaust manifolds that were veritable works of art during the sixties and seventies, and the 340 LA small-block was no exception. *Mike Mueller*

Above, right:
When ordered with the 340 small-block, the Formula S package cost $186.30 in 1968. The price for the 383/Formula S combo was $221.54. *Mike Mueller*

Left:
The total count for 340-powered Formula S convertibles was 193 in 1968. Of these, 133 were fitted with Torqueflite automatics, and 60 had four-speed manuals. *Mike Mueller*

1969
Barracuda Formula S

Specifications	
Model availability	two-door fastback, coupe, and convertible
Wheelbase	108 inches
Length	192.8 inches
Width	71.6 inches
Height	52.7 inches (fastback)
Weight	3,470 pounds (340 V-8)
Price	Formula S package cost $186.30 with 340 small-block V-8, $221.65 with 383 big-block (convertible Prices varied $162.15 with 340, $197.55 with 383)
Track (front/rear, in inches)	57.4/55.6
Wheels	14.0×5.5 inches
Tires	E70×14 Red Streak
Construction	unitized body/frame
Suspension	independent wishbones with heavy-duty torsion bars and thickened stabilizer bar, front; solid axle with longitudinal heavy-duty leaf springs, rear
Steering	recirculating ball
Brakes	four-wheel drums, standard; front discs, optional
Engine	275-horsepower, 340-cubic-inch V-8 or 330-horsepower, 383-cubic-inch V-8
Bore and stroke	4.04×3.31 inches (273); 4.25×3.38 inches (383)
Compression	10.5:1 (340); 10.0:1 (383)
Fuel delivery	single four-barrel carburetor
Transmission	four-speed manual or Torqueflite automatic
Axle ratio	3.23:1
Production	1,839 with 340 small-block V-8; 718 with 383 big-block

Above:
Tom Hoover's engineers got to play with one final factory super-stock model in 1968, working in conjunction with Hurst to roll out 70 competition-ready Barracudas armed with race Hemi V-8s. The hoods and fenders on these machines were made of fiberglass. Hurst also teamed up with Dodge that year to create a similar run of Hemi-powered Dart super-stocks. *Chrysler LLC Corporate Historical Collection*

Below:
The 383 Commando big-block option was available in all three Barracuda bodies in 1969, and it also could've been installed in both base models and Formula S cars, as well as the new 'Cuda. *Chrysler LLC Corporate Historical Collection*

1969

The Formula S package was once more offered for all three bodies and again could've complemented the 340 small-block or 383 big-block. But product planners in 1969 opted to discriminate a bit more finely, promoting the Formula S as a "gentleman's hot rod," if you will. For the less refined, Plymouth introduced the bolder "'Cuda" models. Already accepted lexicon on the street, this abbreviated name was applied to no-nonsense street racers that also relied on small- or big-block power. The 'Cuda 340 package (code A56) was priced at $309.35, while its 'Cuda 383 counterpart (code A57) cost $344.75.

Included in either deal was a four-speed manual transmission, dual exhausts with chrome tips, the beefed-up Rallye suspension, Firm Ride shock absorbers, and redline tires on 14.0×5.5 heavy-duty wheels. Simulated hood scoops, a black grille, and black accents on the hood and lower body sides helped set these two apart from their more polite Formula cousins. More black tape on the fenders identified either model as a 'Cuda 340 or 'Cuda 383. Both were limited to notchback and fastback applications; no convertibles were offered.

Formula S production was 2,034 fastbacks (1,431 340s, 603 383s), 423 notchbacks (325 340s, 98 383s), and 100 convertibles (83 340s, 17 383s). The breakdown for the 'Cuda 340 was 568 fastbacks, 98 notchbacks; for the 'Cuda 383, 378 fastbacks, 83 notchbacks.

Left:
Psychedelic times begat psychedelic measures. Hip chicks were the target market in 1969 when Plymouth designers concocted the Mod Top option for that year's Barracuda notchback. "We've been designing cars with women in mind for years," began an advertisement for what Plymouth promotional people called "the car you wear." A similar floral-style vinyl roof (done in blue) also was offered that year for Plymouth's Satellite, and Dodge put Mod Tops on Darts, Coronets, and Super Bees in 1969. *Mike Mueller*

Below, left:
A groovy rear-quarter window decal also helped announce a Mod Top Barracuda's arrival in 1969. The option was available again in 1970 for Barracudas and 'Cudas. Reportedly 937 Mod Tops were fitted atop Barracuda coupes in 1969. *Mike Mueller*

Below:
Complementing interior appointments also were available for Mod Top Barracudas in 1969. The floral roof could've been ordered alone without this upholstery, and the reverse apparently was true too. *Mike Mueller*

02

Right:
Engineers bored out the LA V-8 in 1967 to 3.91 inches, resulting in a small-block that shared dimensions with Chrysler Corporation's aging 318-cubic-inch A-block engine. Plymouth's new 318 then became the V-8 Barracuda's base engine in 1968. Like the 1968 edition, the 1969 Barracuda's 318 (shown here) was rated at 230 horsepower. A two-barrel carburetor supplied fuel/air. *Mike Mueller*

Below:
The Formula S once again appeared as a coupe, fastback, or convertible in 1969. Total production of the topless variety was a mere 100. Of these, 83 featured the 340 small-block (shown here), and 17 were fitted with the 383 big-block. *Mike Mueller*

Below, right:
The Formula S option cost $162.15 when ordered along with the 340 small-block for a Barracuda convertible in 1969. The package (again with the 340) was priced at $186.30 for that year's coupe and fastback.
Mike Mueller

Left:
Total Barracuda convertible production for 1969 was only 1,442. Base price that year for a V-8 Barracuda drop-top was $3,082. Notice the rare aluminum wheels on this 340 Formula S. *Mike Mueller*

Below, left:
This optional aluminum wheel (code W23) was introduced for 1969 in 14- and 15-inch sizes for both Dodge and Plymouth models. But problems with lug nuts staying tight forced Chrysler officials to recall them soon after their release. The few that escaped into the wild remain valued collector items today. *Mike Mueller*

Below:
The Torqueflite automatic transmission was a $216.20 option behind the 340 small-block in 1969. Also notice the optional sport steering wheel. *Mike Mueller*

1969
440 'Cuda

Specifications	
Model availability	two-door fastback
Wheelbase	108 inches
Length	192.8 inches
Width	71.6 inches
Height	53 inches
Weight	3,405 pounds
Price	A13 440 Engine Conversion Package cost $344.75
Track (front/rear, in inches)	58/56
Wheels	14.0×5.5 inches
Tires	E70×14 Red Streak
Construction	unitized body/frame
Suspension	independent wishbones with heavy-duty torsion bars and thickened stabilizer bar, front; solid axle with longitudinal heavy-duty leaf springs, rear
Steering	recirculating ball
Brakes	four-wheel drums
Engine	375-horsepower, 440-cubic-inch V-8
Bore and stroke	4.32×3.75 inches
Compression	10.1:1
Fuel delivery	single Carter four-barrel carburetor
Transmission	Torqueflite automatic
Axle ratio	3.55:1 or 3.91:1 gears in Sure-Grip differential
Production	not available

As was the case in 1967 when engineers stuffed the Barracuda's first big-block between A-body flanks, the 440 installation in 1969 created a tight fit, to say the least, on the driver side where the exhaust manifold met the steering gear. *Mike Mueller*

1969 440 'Cuda

More than one bystander, innocent or otherwise, had noticed in 1967 that Plymouth's first big-block Barracuda represented only the beginning. "Is the 383 enough?" queried *Car and Driver* in its April 1967 Formula S road test. "The drag racing fraternity is already asking, 'why not the 440?' Indeed, the 440 ci block is essentially the same as the 383, so it would be a natural. For now, Plymouth is saying that a Barracuda 440 would be too much, but competition might change their minds."

Chrysler introduced its 440-cubic-inch RB-series V-8 in 1966 by boring out the 426 "street wedge," resulting in the "440 TNT" big-block, rated at 350 horsepower. This torque monster was then morphed into the 375-horse "Super Commando 440" in 1967 for Plymouth's first GTX, and in 1968 it began appearing in aftermarket A-body installations performed at Mr. Norm's Grand-Spaulding Dodge in Chicago. Only 48 of Mr. Norm's awesome 440-powered "GSS" Dart conversions were sold.

Well aware of Grand-Spaulding's shenanigans, Chrysler officials opted to pick up were Norm Kraus' people left off. New for 1969 was the 440 Engine Conversion Package, available for both Dodge's Dart and Plymouth's Barracuda. The option code in either case was A13, and the price was $363.65 for Dart GTS customers, $344.75 for their pony car counterparts. Plymouth introduced its 440 'Cuda in April 1969, purposefully flopping the term to emiles per hourasize the big engine over the little car. On the cars themselves, the displacement figure tape was moved to the top on each front fender; it was on the bottom in the case of the 'Cuda 340 and 'Cuda 383.

The meanest, nastiest Barracuda for 1969 was created by checking off option code A13, which specified the installation of a 440-cubic-inch RB-series V-8. The price for this package was $344.75. *Mike Mueller*

Plymouth introduced its new 'Cuda models for 1969 with either small- or big-block power. The former was the 'Cuda 340, the latter was the 'Cuda 383. But when the division's biggest big-block was dropped between A-body fenders, Plymouth promotional people chose to place the emiles per hourasis on the engine over the car. The name in this case was "440 'Cuda." *Mike Mueller*

The A13 conversion option was offered for both Plymouth's Barracuda and Dodge's Dart GTS in 1969. Included in this deal was the 440 Super Commando V-8, rated at 375 horsepower. *Mike Mueller*

The A13 option was available for Barracuda coupes and fastbacks in 1969. Total production for both body styles was 340, all with Torqueflite automatic transmissions. *Mike Mueller*

Playing with the name was one thing; actually putting the 440 into a Barracuda was by no means such a simple task. The 440-cubic-inch RB was slightly larger than the 383 B-series big-block, which in 1969 was upgraded to 330 horsepower. Squeezing the RB into the A-body platform required a unique driver-side exhaust manifold, and the swap also not only barred the installation of power steering, power brakes were also out of the question. And with the brake booster not possible, front discs became taboo as well. Optional air conditioning? Are you kiddin'?

Also missing was an available four-speed stick because engineers didn't trust the car's driveline to handle all those hefty torque jolts, as many as 480 of 'em. The Torqueflite was the only transmission offered. Additional standard equipment included a Sure-Grip Dana rear end containing 3.55:1 or 3.91:1 gears, a heavy-duty suspension, the equally heavy-duty 14.0x5.5 rims, and those ever-present Red Streak tires.

The arguably insane sum of these parts equaled swift 0–60 bursts in 5.6 seconds, according to *Car Life*. A *Super Stock and Drag Illustrated* road test produced a 13.89-second, 103.2-miles-per-hour time slip for the quarter-mile.

Impressive, yes, but scary too. Calling it in some ways, "a disturbing automobile," *Car Life*'s critics were quick to point out "obvious discrepancies between the superb way the 440 'Cuda goes, and the way it does other things . . . like, for example, stop. Possibly the 1970 Barracuda will have suitable brakes and steering with the 440, but until they do the car will suffer."

As it was, those very considerations had become top priorities immediately after Cliff Voss' Advanced Styling Studio began work on the latest next-generation Barracuda in February 1967. And wouldn't you know it? When the redesigned E-body 'Cuda appeared three years later, customers instantly noticed how easily it served as a home for the 440 RB without any compromises. Preferred comforts and conveniences—power steering and brakes, air conditioning, etc.—weren't sacrificed. That, however, was then.

In 1969 any card-carrying musclehead knew that real men didn't need such girlie stuff. And, plainly put, Plymouth's 440 'Cuda clearly was a machine meant for real men.

The facade on this E-body design proposal looks familiar, but fortunately stylists put a little more thought into the Shaker hood idea before putting it into production. *Chrysler LLC Corporate Historical Collection*

1970
Hemi 'Cuda

Specifications	
Model availability	two-door hardtop or convertible
Wheelbase	108 inches
Length	186.7 inches
Width	74.9 inches
Height	50.9 inches
Weight	3,880 pounds
Price	Hemi engine alone cost $871.45
Track (front/rear, in inches)	59.7/60.7
Wheels	15×7 inches
Tires	F60×15
Construction	unitized body/frame
Suspension	independent wishbones with heavy-duty torsion bars and thickened stabilizer bar, front; solid axle with longitudinal heavy-duty leaf springs, rear
Steering	recirculating ball
Brakes	four-wheel, 11-inch, heavy-duty drums (front discs, optional)
Engine	425-horsepower, 426-cubic-inch Hemi V-8
Bore and stroke	4.25×3.75 inches
Compression	10.25:1
Fuel delivery	two Carter four-barrel carburetors
Transmission	four-speed manual or Torqueflite automatic
Axle ratio	3.23:1 ratio (standard) in Dana rear end with 9.75-inch ring gear
Production	652 hardtops, 14 convertibles

1970

The goal at Voss' studio in 1967 was to develop a truly fresh face for the Barracuda that, at the same time, made even more room beneath the skin for as much motor as possible. To that end, the all-new E-body pony car was some 5 inches wider than its A-body forerunner. The wheelbase remained at 108 inches, but all that extra girth translated into just the expansion engineers needed to install any of Plymouth's monster mills with more or less no muss or fuss. Power steering and brakes also were no problem.

Every optional V-8 right on up to the vaunted Hemi slipped right in between Plymouth pony car fenders in 1970. Designers managed seemingly to stuff 10 pounds of stuff into a 5-pound bag by basing the E-body foundation on the bigger B-body's cowl structure, hence an explanation for all that extra overall width.

On top went some groovy, rakish sheet metal—credited primarily to stylist John Herlitz—that was shaped into only two body styles when the Barracuda's original flowing form was dropped in favor of the notchback coupe and convertible. But that wasn't necessarily a bad thing. "The svelte fastback styling has had its day," claimed a November 1969 *Motorcade* review. "The restyled [Barracuda] is mean and lean this year, with bulges where they ought to be."

New, as well, for 1970 was a revised model lineup. First came the base Barracuda, available in six-cylinder and V-8 forms. A bit more prestigious was the Gran Coupe, with its leather bucket seats and overhead console. Gran Coupes were also broken up into six and V-8 lines, with the 318 small-block serving as the base engine in this case and in the Barracuda's. Both models could've been equipped optionally with two 383 big-blocks, one with a two-barrel carb, the other a four-barrel.

Most important, at least from a performance buyer's perspective, was the reborn 'Cuda, one of five members (Road Runner, Fury GT,

Plymouth's redesigned E-body pony car was offered in three distinct lines in 1970: the base Barracuda, upscale Gran Coupe (shown here), and performance-conscious 'Cuda. Available in both six-cylinder and V-8 forms, the Gran Coupe came standard with leather bucket seats and an overhead console. *Chrysler LLC Corporate Historical Collection*

GTX, and Duster 340 were the other four) of Plymouth's new Rapid Transit System, introduced late in 1969. Among 'Cuda accoutrements for 1970 were front foglamps, hood pins, simulated hood scoops, a blacked-out rear panel, and "hockey stick" body-side stripes that incorporated engine displacement identification out back. Engine choices included the 275-horse 340 small-block, the 335-horse 383 big-block, the 375-horse 440 RB, and the 390-horse 440 Six Barrel—for more on this latter engine, see chapter seven detailing the Road Runner story.

The 'Cuda's hockey stripes simply read "Hemi" when this model's top power source was installed in 1970. Still fed by twin four-barrels, the 425-horse 426 had experienced a change or two since 1966, beginning with the addition of a windage tray, hotter cam, and revised valvetrain in 1968. Yet another revised cam appeared in 1970 along with hydraulic lifters in place of the previously used solid tappets, improvements made with an eye toward civilizing, albeit subtly, this big ape.

In 1970, the Hemi was only available for the hot-to-trot 'Cuda, which then took on the expected name "Hemi 'Cuda" even though it wasn't officially listed as an individual model. The new Shaker hood scoop was standard, as was a 9.75-inch Dana rear end and fat F60 tires on 15x7 Rallye wheels. Buyers typically chose between a four-speed or tough Torqueflite. A heavy-duty radiator also was mandated for the Hemi 'Cuda, along with large 11-inch drum brakes all around. Power front discs were optional.

The Shaker simply stuck right through the hood to allow cooler, denser outside air an easy path into those two Carters and was optional atop other 'Cuda V-8s, both big and small. Shakers on Rallye Red cars were painted red, while others were black. By year's end, buyers could've also chosen a blue Shaker for Blue Fire Metallic cars, and argent became available too.

As for function, when that baby really started shakin', look out. Hemi 'Cudas produced some of the hottest quarter-mile numbers ever seen on magazine pages 40 years back. Most tests showed elapsed

Above:
Plymouth's 335-horsepower, 383-cubic-inch big-block was the 'Cuda's base engine in 1970. The 275-horsepower, 340-cubic-inch small-block shown here was a no-cost option. *Mike Mueller*

Above, right:
Chrysler's new E-body platform, introduced for 1970, incorporated some of the midsized B-body's cowl structure to make for a wider engine compartment, which in turn, of course, supplied ample room for optional big-block installation. A twin-scooped hood was standard for the 'Cuda in 1970. Total 'Cuda convertible production that year was 635, including 548 domestic deliveries. *Mike Mueller*

Right:
An optional sport steering wheel enhanced the already sexy 'Cuda interior even further in 1970. *Mike Mueller*

times running well down into the 13-second bracket, with *Car Craft*'s lead-foots managing a sizzling 13.1 run after some typical tinkering.

As impressive as Hemi 'Cudas were, they also were majorly expensive and terribly tough to live with in everyday applications. No wonder they were rarely seen on Main Street U.S.A. back in the day. Hemis went into only 652 hardtops and 14 convertibles in 1970, and 1971's count was only 107 hardtops, 7 convertibles. Considerably more plentiful were the new-for-1970 400+6 'Cudas, mean machines that offered nearly as much brute force for much less money. Like the Hemi, the triple-carb 440 appeared on the 'Cuda options list one more time before getting the axe in 1971.

Right:
Three Holley two-barrel carburetors on a cast-iron intake shot the juice to the 440+6 V-8 in 1970. Available for the 'Cuda only that year, the 440+6 option cost $249.55.
Mike Mueller

Below:
Three optional big-blocks were available for the 1970 'Cuda: the 375-horse 440 four-barrel, 390-horse 440+6 triple-carb RB (demonstrated here), and legendary 426 Hemi. The 1970 production tally for 440+6 'Cuda hardtops was 1,755. Another 29 triple-carb convertibles also were built that year.
Mike Mueller

Optional Rallye road wheels debuted in 1970 in 14- and 15-inch diameters. The bigger rims were shod in wide 60-series rubber. *Mike Mueller*

The unforgettable Shaker hood scoop was a $97.30 option atop the 440+6 RB big-block in 1970. *Mike Mueller*

Production of Hemi 'Cuda hardtops was 652 in 1970. The count for Hemi convertibles that year was a mere 14. *Mike Mueller*

Humble "hockey stick" tape stripes announced the arrival of a Hemi 'Cuda in 1970. *Mike Mueller*

Above:
The 'Cuda's Hemi engine option carried a hefty $871.45 price tag in 1970. Fifteen-inch wheels and tires were mandated when the 425-horsepower Hemi was installed. *Mike Mueller*

Right:
The transmission breakdown for 1970 Hemi 'Cuda hardtops read 368 automatics, 284 four-speeds. Notice this automatic model's column-mounted shifter and the red knob beneath the dash—the latter item opened the cable-operated Shaker scoop to let the good air in. *Mike Mueller*

1970
AAR 'Cuda

Specifications	
Model availability	two-door hardtop
Wheelbase	108 inches
Length	186.7 inches
Width	74.9 inches
Height	51.9 inches
Weight	3,585 pounds
Price	$3,966
Track (front/rear, in inches)	59.7/60.7
Wheels	15×7 inches
Tires	Goodyear, E60×15 in front, G60×15 in back
Construction	unitized body/frame
Suspension	independent wishbones with heavy-duty torsion bars and thickened stabilizer bar, front; solid axle with longitudinal heavy-duty leaf springs, rear
Steering	recirculating ball
Brakes	power front discs, rear drums
Engine	290-horsepower, 340-cubic-inch V-8
Bore and stroke	4.04×3.31 inches
Compression	10.5:1
Fuel delivery	three Holley two-barrel carburetors
Transmission	A-833 four-speed manual (with Hurst shifter) or 727 Torqueflite automatic
Axle ratio	3.55:1 ratio in 8.75-inch Sure-Grip differential
Production	2,724

Three Holley two-barrel carburetors helped the AAR 'Cuda's (and Challenger T/A's) exclusive 340-cubic-inch small-block engine make 290 horsepower. Both four-speed manuals and Torqueflite automatics were bolted up behind. *Mike Mueller*

1970 AAR 'Cuda

Another tri-carb engine, this one a small-block, also appeared in 1970 beneath 'Cuda hoods, as well as those belonging to the Dodge's new E-body, Challenger. Both divisions opted that year to go racing on the Sports Car Club of America's Trans-Am circuit, which had opened for business in 1966. The following year Chevrolet had put together its Camaro Z/28 to allow race-ready versions to legally run with the SCCA crowd, and Ford then followed suit with its Boss Mustang in 1969. Chrysler officials just couldn't resist jumping onto the bandwagon.

The result was Dodge's Challenger T/A and Plymouth's AAR 'Cuda, the latter named for Dan Gurney's All American Racers team. Both were equipped in similar fashion, with racing versions relying on a four-barrel-fed, destroked, 305-cubic-inch version of Chrysler's LA small-block. Street-going models featured a hopped-up 340 topped by three Holley two-barrel carburetors on an Edelbrock aluminum

Above:
Both Dodge and Plymouth introduced Trans-Am pony cars in 1970: the former's Challenger T/A Six Pack, the latter's AAR 'Cuda. Plymouth's acronym referred to Dan Gurney's All American Racers team. Base price for an AAR 'Cuda was $3,966. *Mike Mueller*

Right:
Fully functional fresh-air hoods made of fiberglass were standard for both Dodge's Challenger T/A and Plymouth's AAR 'Cuda in 1970, but the scoop designs differed in a big way. *Mike Mueller*

The commonly quoted estimation for AAR 'Cuda production is 2,724. Side-exiting exhausts were standard for the AAR 'Cuda and Challenger T/A in 1970. *Mike Mueller*

intake manifold. Called a "340 Six Pack" by Dodge, the AAR 'Cuda's standard V-8 was known as a "340 Six Barrel" in Plymouth parlance.

Engineers already had themselves a hot little small-block when they went to work on the 340 Six Barrel. To enhance things even further, they recast the block to add extra main bearing web reinforcement and reworked the cylinder heads to make room for larger ports. Hydraulic lifters, pushrods, rocker arms, and rocker shafts were all special heavy-duty items intended for high-rpm operation. Compression was a healthy 10.5:1. Advertised output was 290 horsepower, yet again considered conservative by those in the know.

Additional standard features included a fiberglass hood crowned by a large, gaping scoop that opened up directly to the air cleaner below. The exhaust system was equally exotic: spent gases were sent through a low-restriction system that exited race-car-style directly in front of each rear wheel. Along the way, those gases entered special mufflers in typical fashion, made a U-turn inside, came back out the same end, and finally cut a sharp arc back rearward through bent pipes, dumping finally through chrome "megaphones." Yowza!

Hood pins, blackout treatment for the grille and hood, a competition-type fuel filler, and a rear ducktail spoiler were all part of the deal too. Beauty beneath the skin included either a 727 Torqueflite automatic or an A-833 close-ratio four-speed with Hurst shifter, an 8.75-inch Sure-Grip differential with 3.55:1 cogs, power front disc brakes, and the Rallye suspension package. Standard tires were E60×15 Goodyears in front, G60×15 in back, a combination that created a pronounced forward rake. Though quite common today, the AAR's big-tire/small-tire combo was a Detroit first in 1970.

SCCA homologation rules in 1970 mandated a minimum production run of 2,500 units to make a particular model legal for Trans-Am racing. No problem, at least for Plymouth, which managed to roll out an estimated 2,724 AAR 'Cudas for 1970. Plymouth built about 2,400 T/A Challengers that year, but apparently nobody was counting. Both cars were one-hit wonders.

02

1971
'Cuda

Specifications	
Model availability	two-door hardtop or convertible
Wheelbase	108 inches
Length	186.7 inches
Width	74.9 inches
Height	51.9 inches
Weight	3,585 pounds
Price	$3,144, hardtop; $3,391, convertible
Track (front/rear, in inches)	59.7/60.7
Wheels	14×6 inches
Tires	F70×14
Construction	unitized body/frame
Suspension	independent wishbones with torsion bars; solid axle with longitudinal leaf springs, rear
Steering	recirculating ball
Brakes	four-wheel, 11-inch, heavy-duty drums
Engine	300-horsepower, 383-cubic-inch V-8, standard (275-horsepower, 340-cubic-inch V-8, no-cost option); 426 Hemi and 440 six-barrel V-8s, optional
Bore and stroke	4.25×3.38 inches (383 V-8)
Compression	8.5:1
Fuel delivery	single Carter four-barrel carburetor
Transmission	three-speed manual
Axle ratio	3.23:1 in 8.75-inch rear end
Production (including exports)	6,228 hardtops, 374 convertibles

1971

Plymouth's 1971 E-body was quickly identified by its four headlights, two more than the 1970 models carried. New, too, was a restyled "cheese grater" grille and slightly revised taillights. 'Cuda models were adorned with four small simulated louvers on each front fender, and the grille was painted to match the body whenever the optional color-keyed elastomeric bumper group was ordered.

Three body styles were offered for 1971: a bargain-basement coupe with a 198 cid slant-six, a Barracuda hardtop with a 225 six, and a sexy convertible in its last year. The three-tiered model line rolled over, with the base Barracuda (coupe or hardtop) followed by the classy Gran Coupe and the performance-packed 'Cuda, fitted with its twin-scooped hood. Available engines carried over, save for the 440 four-barrel, which was dropped from the E-body options list after 1970. Compression cuts led to power drops for the 383 and 440+6 (down 5 ponies to 385 horsepower), but the Hemi retained its long-established 425-horse tag.

As much as the Barracuda line had to offer, 1971 sales fell off in a big way, a clear clue that attitudes were changing.

Above:
Quad headlights appeared for Plymouth's E-body for 1971 only. Base price for the 'Cuda convertible that year was $3,391. *Mike Mueller*

Below:
Plymouth offered a convertible E-body in 1970 and 1971 only. As in 1970, the 383 B-series big-block was standard for the 'Cuda in 1971. Options that year included the 340 small-block, 440+6 big-block, and 426 Hemi. *Mike Mueller*

Above:
So-called "billboard" tape stripes appeared for 1971 to help show off which engine a 'Cuda customer had chosen. This was the last year for big-block options in E-body ranks. *Mike Mueller*

Far right:
A six-way manually adjustable bucket seat (for the driver only) was a $32.20 option in 1971. The rear seat speakers seen here are non-stock customizations. *Mike Mueller*

Right:
Plymouth's four-barrel-fed 383 Super Commando V-8 was rated at 300 horsepower in 1971. Compression was 8.5:1. A 383 two-barrel V-8 also was available that year for base Barracudas and Gran Coupes.
Mike Mueller

Right:
Foglamps were E-body 'Cuda standard features from the get-go. *Mike Mueller*

Below, right:
Of the 7 Hemi 'Cuda convertibles built for 1971, 5 featured Torqueflite automatics, the other 2, of course, used four-speed manuals. The breakdown for Hemi hardtops that year was 48 automatics, 59 four-speeds. *Mike Mueller*

Below, left:
While most V-8s were experiencing compression cuts across the board in Detroit in 1971, the vaunted Hemi didn't give an inch. Its squeeze remained at 10.25:1 that year. Two Carter four-barrels stuck around too, as did those 425 rip-snortin' ponies. *Mike Mueller*

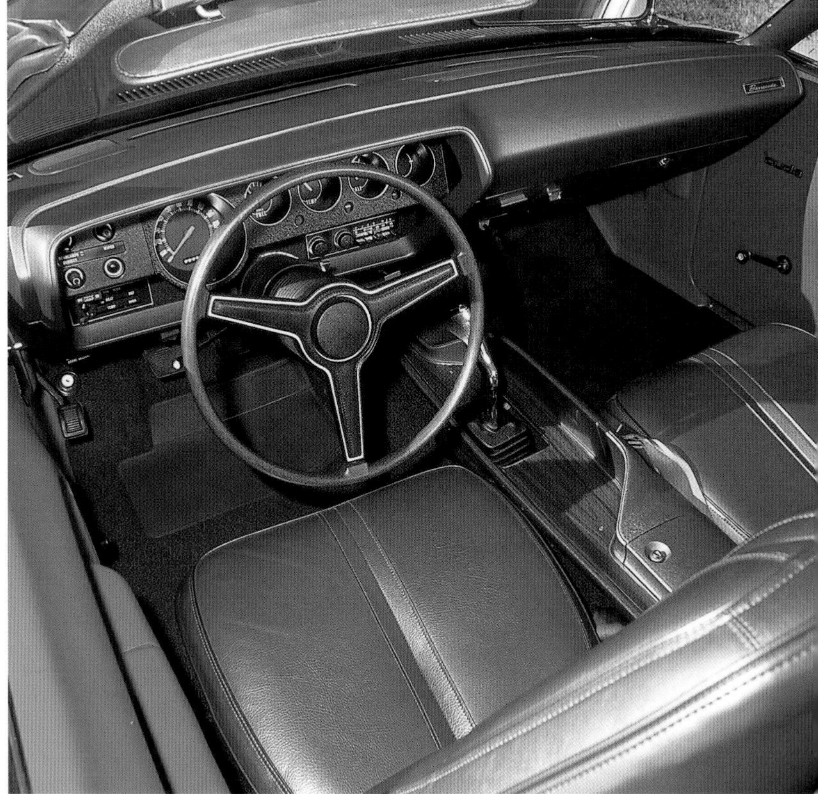

Above:
Revised taillights with separate backup lamps (they had been integral units in 1970) appeared for the 1971 Barracuda. A blacked-out rear cove panel was a 'Cuda feature again in 1971. *Mike Mueller*

Left:
The optional 426 Hemi, priced at $883.90 in E-body ranks, made one final appearance in 1971. Only 107 'Cuda hardtops and 7 convertibles were released with Hemi power that year. *Mike Mueller*

Below:
These fender-mounted "gills" represented another way to pick out a new 'Cuda at a glance in 1971. *Mike Mueller*

02

1972
'Cuda

Specifications	
Model availability	two-door hardtop
Wheelbase	108 inches
Length	186.6 inches
Width	74.9 inches
Height	50.9 inches
Weight	3,520 pounds
Price	$3,105
Track (front/rear, in inches)	59.7/60.7
Wheels	14×5.5 inches
Tires	F70×14 Goodyear
Construction	unitized body/frame
Suspension	independent wishbones with torsion bars; solid axle with longitudinal leaf springs, rear; sway bars, front and rear
Steering	recirculating ball
Brakes	four-wheel drums
Engine	240-horsepower, 340-cubic-inch V-8
Bore and stroke	4.04×3.31 inches
Compression	8.5:1
Fuel delivery	single Carter four-barrel carburetor
Transmission	three-speed manual
Axle ratio	3.23:1
Production (including exports)	7,828

1972

Single headlights returned for 1972, and two pairs of large, round taillights appeared in back. A two-door hardtop remained the only body choice after 1971's low-budget coupe was axed along with the short-lived E-body convertible. Like the topless body, the luxury-minded Gran Coupe model also failed to roll over from 1971, leaving only the base Barracuda and sporty 'Cuda to carry on. Still standard for the former was the 225 slant-six, while the latter relied on the 318 small-block in base form. The 340 was the only optional power choice for 'Cuda buyers, while both the 340 and 318 were options for the base Barracuda. Manual front disc brakes became standard equipment for each 1972 model. Front and rear sway bars came standard beneath the 'Cuda.

All three engines could've been backed by the optional Torqueflite in 1972, but the available four-speed manual was saved for the still-hot 340 small-block. Like the Hemi and 440+6 big-blocks, that way-cool Shaker hood, the various spoilers, and the big 15-inch wheels all failed to return in 1972's options collection. The only rear end option remaining was the Performance Axle package, which included a heavy-duty 3.55:1 Sure-Grip differential, a fan shroud, and a 26-inch high-performance radiator. This extra-cost group also included a power-steering oil cooler when optional steering assist was added. The Performance Axle package was only offered with 340-equipped models.

Single headlights returned for the 1972 Barracuda. Only the base Barracuda and sporty 'Cuda were offered that year when the Gran Coupe failed to carry over from 1971. The convertible body style didn't return, either. *Chrysler LLC Corporate Historical Collection*

1973

Basically everything carried over into 1973 save for new, highly noticeable front and rear bumper guards designed to withstand 5-miles-per-hour impacts. Two model lines again were home to one body style, the hardtop, but the base six was gone, leaving the 318 and 340 small-block V-8s to keep the power coming. Though sales actually went up this year, only one more performance remained for Plymouth's long-running pony car.

1973
'Cuda

Specifications	
Model availability	two-door hardtop
Wheelbase	108 inches
Length	193 inches
Width	75.6 inches
Height	50.9 inches
Weight	3,230 pounds
Price	$3,105
Track (front/rear, in inches)	60.2/60.7
Wheels	14.0×5.5 inches
Tires	F70×14 Goodyear
Construction	unitized body/frame
Suspension	independent wishbones with torsion bars; solid axle with longitudinal leaf springs, rear; sway bars, front and rear
Steering	recirculating ball
Brakes	four-wheel drums
Engine	240-horsepower, 340-cubic-inch V-8
Bore and stroke	4.04×3.31 inches
Compression	8.5:1
Fuel delivery	single Carter four-barrel carburetor
Transmission	three-speed manual
Axle ratio	3.23:1
Production (including exports)	10,626

Safety-conscious bumper guards appeared at both ends of the 1973 Barracuda, available only in hardtop form with V-8 power that year. Base price for the still-cool 'Cuda was $3,033. *Chrysler LLC Corporate Historical Collection*

1974
'Cuda

Specifications	
Model availability	two-door hardtop
Wheelbase	108 inches
Length	195.6 inches
Width	75.6 inches
Height	50.9 inches
Weight	3,230 pounds
Price	$3,252
Track (front/rear, in inches)	60.2/60.7
Wheels	14.0×5.5 inches
Tires	F70×14 Goodyear
Construction	unitized body/frame
Suspension	independent wishbones with torsion bars; solid axle with longitudinal leaf springs, rear; sway bars, front and rear
Steering	recirculating ball
Brakes	four-wheel drums
Engine	245 net-horsepower, 360-cubic-inch V-8
Bore and stroke	4.00×3.58 inches
Compression	8.4:1
Fuel delivery	single Carter four-barrel carburetor
Transmission	three-speed manual
Axle ratio	3.23:1
Production (including exports)	4,989

Above:
Introduced for 1971, Plymouth's 360-cubic-inch small-block was the only LA V-8 that didn't use a 3.31-inch stroke. Bore and stroke measurements for this enlarged LA were 4.00 and 3.58 inches, respectively. As a new option for the Barracuda in 1974, the 360-cubic-inch four-barrel was net-rated at 245 horsepower. *Mike Mueller*

Below:
Bigger didn't mean better when Plymouth's 360-cubic-inch V-8 superseded the popular 340 as a 'Cuda option in 1974. With the 340 finally retired, the days of real Mopar muscle were truly over. *Mike Mueller*

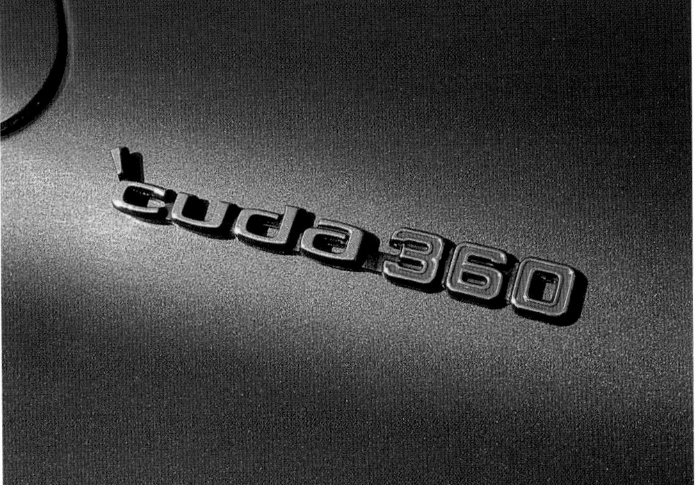

1974

No longer wanted by America's no-longer-so-young car buyers, Plymouth's sporty Barracuda rolled off into history at year's end. No major changes came in 1974, save for a lone exception under the hood as the 340 was replaced by the 360-cubic-inch V-8. Bigger didn't mean better in this case: witness the 360's 170 net-rated horses.

Lee Iacocca downsized his Mustang in 1974 to allow it to survive into a new era. Chrysler wasn't about to subject its veteran pony cars to a similar fate, and so came a fitting end for both Plymouth's Barracuda and Dodge's Challenger.

The 360-cubic-inch LA V-8 replaced the 340 as an option for both the base Barracuda and top-shelf 'Cuda in 1974. Priced at $188.50, the 360 small-block made its way into 1,194 'Cudas that year. *Mike Mueller*

Four round taillights first graced the Barracuda's tail in 1972. They remained in place until the end of the line came for the breed in 1974. *Mike Mueller*

03

Dodge Charger 1966–1971

Leader of the Pack

Chrysler engineers certainly were no strangers to making horsepower during the early sixties; witness the 413/426 super-stock V-8s and the awesome 426 race Hemi. Maybe so, but the Dodge Boys still couldn't quite capture the attention of the then-burgeoning muscle car market, not like Pontiac people did with their ground-breaking GTO in 1964. As it still is today, image was everything around Detroit 40-something years ago, and the wildly popular "Goat" had it all over anything Chrysler had to offer up through 1965 as far as certified sex appeal was concerned. Sure, the new-for-1966 street Hemi easily inspired lust wherever it went. More than one critic, however, was more than willing to point out that all that throbbing performance came off a little limp when wrapped up in a garden-variety Coronet, which was the only midsized B-body offering available from Dodge when the 1966 model year began.

Fortunately a major dose of image enhancement came along shortly afterward when sleek new Chargers started showing up in showrooms in January 1966. Called the "Leader of the Dodge Rebellion" by ad guys, the head-turning Charger was created to compete in Detroit's newborn specialty car field, a wide-open lot if there ever was one. At the lower end of this lineup was Chevrolet's compact Corvair Monza, Ford's budget-conscious Mustang, and Plymouth's pony car rival, the Barracuda. At the top were the pricey Thunderbird, Studebaker's Euro-style Avanti, and Buick's regal Riviera. Clearly a major gap yawned in between, a reality not lost on Dodge general manager Byron Nichols. "Give us a car halfway between the Barracuda and T-bird and we'll have a big chunk of market to ourselves," he said.

Base-priced at about $3,100, the 1966 Charger dropped right into that gap and was immediately paired up in the automotive press with American Motors' year-old Marlin, another fastback specialty

- Dodge's first Charger dream machine, based on a Polara convertible, debuted on the auto show circuit in November 1962.
- The prescient Charger II show car toured the auto show circuit with great success in 1965.
- The new Charger, the "Leader of the Dodge Rebellion," was introduced to television watchers during college football's Rose Bowl game in Pasadena, California, on January 1, 1966.
- The 1966 Charger's hideaway headlights were Chrysler Corporation's first since the 1942 De Soto's.
- Looking much like a Corvette, Dodge's sensational Charger III dream car made the auto show rounds in 1968.
- Dodge's R/T package became a Charger option in 1968.
- Midsized B-body Chargers were built from 1966 to 1974.
- A full-sized Charger, based on the Chrysler Cordoba, was built from 1975 to 1978.
- The Charger nameplate reappeared in February 2005 as a 2006 model.

Opposite:
Advertisements called the new Charger the "Leader of the Dodge Rebellion" in 1966. Dodge's flashy fastback easily represented one of Detroit's most exciting releases that year. *Mike Mueller*

03

Above:
Based on a 1964 Polara convertible, the two-seat Charger roadster debuted on the auto show circuit in November 1962. A 365-horsepower, 426-cubic-inch wedge powered this topless baby. *Chrysler LLC Corporate Historical Collection*

Below:
Dream car designers teased Dodge fans in 1965 with their Charger II concept car, created specifically to promote the regular-production Charger to come the following year. *Chrysler LLC Corporate Historical Collection*

machine that came in at around $2,850 in basic trim. Some wags called the Charger a "good-looking Marlin," a backhanded compliment of sorts that couldn't have sat well with the men behind the machine. According to a much more enthusiastic Byron Nichols, his latest, greatest baby was "a fresh new concept in styling and engineering excellence from bumper to bumper."

"Every style line in metal and glass has been smoothly blended to provide the Charger with a forward-thrusting look and a low silhouette," added design director William Brownlie. "From the swept-back roofline and full-width taillights to the tapering forward-side sculpturing and scoop effect of the frontal area, the Charger is the ultimate in sporty car design."

Dodge designers had held out on their specialty field entry for nearly three years trying to get this look right, unlike their Plymouth counterparts, who had hastily introduced the Barracuda in April 1964 by more or less tacking a sloping rear window onto a Valiant body. Burt Bouwkamp, then Dodge's product planning manager, explained the situation during a presentation in 2004:

"Lynn Townsend was at odds with Dodge dealers and wanted to do something to please them. So he asked me to come to his office. He noted that one of the Dodge Dealer Council requests was for a Barracuda-type vehicle. The overall dealer product recommendation theme was the same—we wanted what Plymouth had. [Townsend] directed me to give them a specialty car but he said 'for God's sake,

Though longer and with a more dramatic tail, the Charger II clearly showed off the fastback lines that would make its regular-production successor the talk of Detroit in 1966. *Chrysler LLC Corporate Historical Collection*

don't make it a derivative of the Barracuda.' So the 1966 Charger was born."

Of course, anyone with eyes surely noticed that the first Charger was little more than a Coronet with a trendy fastback roof spliced in place. The two did share the same unitized B-body platform, with its 117-inch wheelbase, so the resemblance was plainly present. But not so fast. Based on the rather daring Charger II dream machine, the 1966 Charger represented an exceptional job of face-lifting a rather mundane model into an exciting and fun machine. Overall, the look was truly fresh.

You'd have to go back to the Cadillac's 1953 Eldorado convertible to find a better example of an American automaker putting one of its show cars onto the street. This was the first time one of Chrysler's many dream cars went from turntable to driveway, though those ever-present eyeballed witnesses might have also noted that the Charger II was campaigned with the specific intent of previewing an upcoming regular-production counterpart, as opposed to previous corporate show cars, which appeared for no reason other than to prove just how truly crazy the guys in corporate design studios were.

The Charger was reborn in 1975, this time based on Chrysler's full-sized Cordoba. The SE model was the only Charger offered that year. Cordoba-based Chargers were built up through 1978. *Chrysler LLC Corporate Historical Collection*

The Charger badge was revived again in 1982 for Dodge's tiny Omni. An 84-horsepower, 2.2-liter four-cylinder powered this little imposter. The Omni-based Charger stuck around through 1987. *Chrysler LLC Corporate Historical Collection*

Dodge's latest, greatest Charger debuted in February 2005 as a 2006 model. Both R/T and Daytona R/T (left) models appeared that year, the latter with a standard 350-horsepower, 5.7-liter Hemi. A Ram truck Daytona (right) also was introduced for 2005. *Mike Mueller*

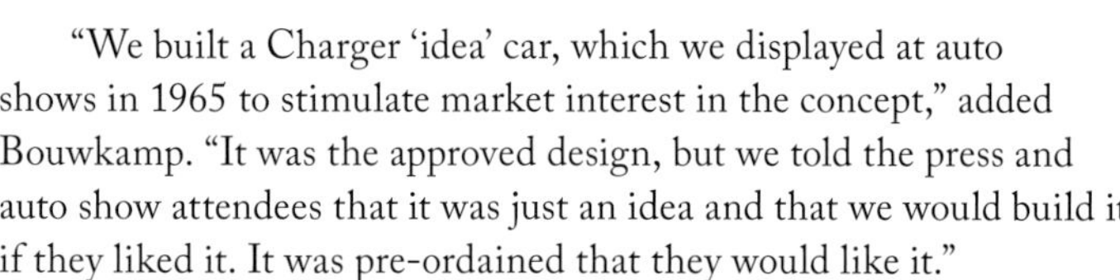

"We built a Charger 'idea' car, which we displayed at auto shows in 1965 to stimulate market interest in the concept," added Bouwkamp. "It was the approved design, but we told the press and auto show attendees that it was just an idea and that we would build it if they liked it. It was pre-ordained that they would like it."

In the Dodge studio, William Brownlie's team was busy sculpting the 1966 Charger even as the crowd-pleasing Charger II was touring the auto show circuit. Except for its tubular grille and rectangular headlights, the Charger II more or less predicted the shape of things to come two years later. A sweeping fastback created the focal point in both cases, while the Charger II's full-width taillight ideal carried over in similar fashion into regular production. Up front, a thoroughly modern grille with hideaway headlights both announced the 1966 Charger's impending arrival in rival machines' rearview mirrors and helped disguise the fact that the grille surround was the same style used by that year's Coronet. When those headlights were exposed, the new Charger's B-body bloodlines were made plainly obvious.

A few features may have been familiar on the outside, but a Charger buyer in 1966 discovered an interior treatment unlike anything out of Detroit then or now. Bucket seats and a console were standard. While the base three-speed manual transmission (which few Charger customers stood still for) came with a column shift, all optional tranny choices used a sporty floor shifter. Standard equipment also included a 6,000 rpm tachometer, mounted on the dash in easy eyeshot where it belonged.

An optional clock could've been added at the head of a unique console that ran the length of the passenger compartment, splitting the rear seat into twin buckets. At first glance, marketing a car with so much interior room as a four-seater appeared awfully frivolous, especially in the Charger's price range. But once scoffers saw those rear buckets fold down and the back panel open up into the trunk, disapproving scowls turned into impressed smiles. In this respect the Charger was truly special; at the same time it featured a sexy, sporty flair while also offering ample utilitarian purposefulness.

And with its relatively slippery styling, the Charger was a natural for NASCAR superspeedways. Though Richard Petty got all the headlines at the wheel of a Hemi-powered Plymouth in 1966, Dodge's Hemi Chargers definitely were a force to be reckoned with that year, especially after racers worked out an early high-speed handling problem by adding a small rear-deck spoiler.

Hemi-equipped Chargers back on Main Street U.S.A. offered all the bite to match their bark, but it was suggested to not ask how much these doggies were in the window, at least not before a buyer had taken a seat. Throw in a collection of mandatory options, and a 1966 Hemi Charger went from $3,100 to about $4,600 in a hurry. At that price level, Dodge's new Charger didn't exactly fit into the plan Byron Nichols spoke of during the car's early planning stages. But then how could the Dodge Boys expect to stage a rebellion without any rebels?

1966

While the 1966 Charger's standard powertrain—a 230-horsepower, 318-cubic-inch two-barrel V-8 mated to a three-speed manual transmission—served to keep the bottom line down, a few tasty options were present to help prove the beauty of this beast went more than skin deep. Engine choices included a 265-horse, 361-cubic-inch V-8 sporting another two-barrel carburetor and a single exhaust—not bad, but that was still ma-and-pa stuff. Things really started getting hot once the 383 four-barrel big-block fell into place. Regular fuel wouldn't do for this baby, not with its 10:1 compression.

Certainly sport bucket seats and a console were standard inside the 1966 Charger. A 150-miles-per-hour speedometer and 6,000-rpm tachometer also were included in the base interior package. *Mike Mueller*

1966 Charger

Specifications

Model availability	two-door fastback
Wheelbase	117 inches
Length	203.6 inches
Width	75.3 inches
Height	53 inches
Weight	3,499 pounds
Base Price	$3,122
Track (front/rear, in inches)	59.5/58.5
Wheels	14.0×5.5
Tires	7.75×14.00
Construction	unitized body/frame
Suspension	independent A-arms with torsion bars, front; solid axle with longitudinal leaf springs, rear
Steering	recirculating ball
Brakes	four-wheel drums
Engine	230-horsepower, 318-cubic-inch V-8
Bore and stroke	3.91×3.31 inches
Compression	9:1
Fuel delivery	two-barrel carburetor
Transmission	three-speed manual
Axle ratio	3.23:1
Production (including exports)	37,344 (31,209, domestic)

Adding that sweeping roofline helped most witnesses forget all about the Charger's Coronet roots, as did a full-width taillight treatment featuring six lamps. *Mike Mueller*

Base price for the second-edition Charger in 1967 was $3,263. Hideaway headlights were again standard that year. *Mike Mueller*

Beneath that sloped rear window was about 86 inches of possible floor space with the 1967 Charger's rear seats folded down. *Mike Mueller*

Fed by Premium only, the 383-cube B-series V-8 came standard with a Carter four-barrel. Specs for its hydraulic cam were 256 degrees duration on intake, 260 on exhaust, with 32 degrees of overlap. Valve sizes were 2.08-inch intakes, 1.60 exhausts. A free-breathing dual exhaust system, with 2.25-inch main tubes and 1.88-inch tailpipes, also was included. Output was 325 horsepower. According to *Car Life*, a 383-powered Charger could run from 0–60 in 7.2 seconds and do the quarter in 15.6 seconds.

At the top of the top was the vaunted 426 Hemi, which became available for the new Charger as an option in February 1966. Adding all that Hemi power instantly boosted a 1966 Charger's bottom line by about $800. A long list of mandatory options also upped the ante, equipment like an 11-inch clutch (with the A-833 four-speed; the A-727 Torqueflite automatic was also available), heavy-duty springs and shocks, 11-inch "Cop" brakes, oversized tires, and a Sure-Grip differential in a 9.75-inch Dana rear end. This package's high price helped explain why only 468 Hemi Chargers were built in 1966.

As expected, a four-speed manual and the Torqueflite automatic were available behind all the Charger V-8s in 1966. Ratios for the fully synchronized New Process Gear Division four-gear were 2.66:1 first, 1.91:1 second, 1.39:1 third, and 1.00:1 high. The standard three-speed featured synchronizers in the top two gears and carried ratios of 3.02:1 first, 1.76:1 second, and 1.00:1 third.

The Torqueflite was the overwhelming favorite among 1966 Charger buyers, and understandably so in most opinions. "Part of the [Charger's] performance credit is due to Chrysler's three-speed automatic transmission," claimed a *Car Life* road test. "Since its first appearance in 1957, this transmission has become the standard, in terms of performance, for others to see. So far, no one has come close to it for responsiveness. The Chrysler unit's controllability factor is also high: It can be held in first and second for low-speed or town traffic work, or it can be left in high and, with a light touch on the throttle, provide smooth, fuss-less through-all-three acceleration."

Total 1966 Charger production, with all available engines and trannies, was 31,209.

A 230-horsepower, 318-cubic-inch V-8 was standard in both 1966 and 1967. New for 1967 was Dodge's 440 Magnum big-block, a 375-horse option that offered much of the Hemi's muscle at a fraction of the cost. The count that year for 440-equipped models was 660. The Hemi Charger shown here was one of only 117 built for 1967. *Mike Mueller*

The Charger's Coronet heritage was most evident in 1966 and 1967, when the hideaway headlights were exposed. *Mike Mueller*

A NASCAR-inspired rear deck spoiler appeared for Hemi-powered Chargers in 1967. *Mike Mueller*

1967 Charger

Specifications	
Model availability	two-door fastback
Wheelbase	117 inches
Length	203.6 inches
Width	75.3 inches
Height	53 inches
Weight	3,480 pounds
Base Price	$3,128
Track (front/rear, in inches)	59.5/58.5
Wheels	14.0×5.5
Tires	7.75×14.00
Construction	unitized body/frame
Suspension	independent A-arms with torsion bars, front; solid axle with longitudinal leaf springs, rear
Steering	recirculating ball
Brakes	four-wheel drums
Engine	230-horsepower, 318-cubic-inch V-8
Bore and stroke	3.91×3.31 inches
Compression	9:1
Fuel delivery	two-barrel carburetor
Transmission	three-speed manual
Axle ratio	3.23:1
Production (including exports)	15,788 (14,666, domestic)

The Magnum road wheel was a Charger option in 1967. Simulated mag-style wheel covers also were available at extra cost. *Mike Mueller*

1967

Only minor changes appeared for the second-edition Charger. A few trim adjustments and the addition of new fender-mounted turn signal indicators set the 1967 Charger apart from its 1966 forerunner on the outside. Inside, the center console became an option and was shortened considerably to allow rear seat passengers to move freely from side to side. A new option for 1967 was a fold-down center armrest that replaced the console up front to allow seating for three instead of two. A column shift was again standard for three-speed models, as well as Torqueflite cars not equipped with optional consoles. Adding the console moved the automatic shifter to the floor.

While the standard 230-horse 318 rolled over from 1966, new for 1967 was a two-barrel 383, rated at 270 horsepower, in place of the 361-cubic-inch V-8 option. The 325-horsepower, 383-cubic-inch four-barrel returned, as did the mean and nasty 426 Hemi. New also to the 1967 options list was the exciting 375-horsepower 440 Magnum V-8, a musclebound big-block that offered a major portion of the Hemi's might at a relative fraction of the price. To read all about the 440 Magnum, see the GTX tale in chapter four.

Both the 440 Magnum and 426 Hemi, as expected, were supported by a heavy-duty suspension, which featured stiffer 0.92-inch torsion barsand a thicker 0.94-inch sway bar up front. Six-leaf springs went underneath in back. Hemi-powered Chargers in 1967 were also fitted with the rare rear-deck spoiler option.

Total domestic production fell to 14,666 for the 1967 Charger, with only 117 of those featuring the 426 Hemi. Production of the new 440 Magnum Charger was 660. According to *Car Life*, the top-dog Hemi could run from 0–60 miles per hour in 6.40 seconds. Quarter-mile performance was 14.16 seconds at 96.15 miles per hour.

Above:
No way anyone could've missed the Charger's optional 426 Hemi in 1967. As in 1966, this beastly big-block was token-rated at 425 horsepower. Compression was 10.25:1 *Mike Mueller*

Left:
Rear bucket seats also were part of the interior attraction in 1966 and 1967. Folding them down opened up loads of space back there for almost anything a Charger owner might have in mind. *Mike Mueller*

1968
Charger R/T

Specifications	
Model availability	two-door hardtop
Wheelbase	117 inches
Length	203.6 inches
Width	75.3 inches
Height	53 inches
Weight	3,650 pounds
Base Price	$3,480
Track (front/rear, in inches)	59.5/58.5
Wheels	14.0×5.5
Tires	F70×14 Red Streak Wide Tread
Construction	unitized body/frame
Suspension	independent A-arms with heavy-duty torsion bars, front; solid axle with longitudinal heavy-duty leaf springs, rear
Steering	recirculating ball
Brakes	four-wheel, heavy-duty, 11-inch drums
Engine	375-horsepower, 440-cubic-inch Magnum V-8, standard (426 Hemi, optional)
Bore and stroke	4.32×3.75 inches
Compression	10.1:1
Fuel delivery	Carter four-barrel carburetor
Transmission	four-speed manual or Torqueflite automatic
Axle ratio	3.23:1
Production	17,584

Charger production soared by more than 600 percent for 1968. Base price that year for the garden-variety sports hardtop was $3,104. Hideaway headlights remained a Charger trademark. *Mike Mueller*

1968

As exciting as Dodge's first-generation Charger looked, buyers still stayed away in droves. Sales for 1966 were lukewarm, to say the least; they were downright chilly the following year. But fortunately the story began turning around after a stunning new Charger began bringing customers running into Dodge dealerships in 1968. William Brownlie's team had this beautiful body well in the works almost before the clay had dried on the 1966 model—just in time, in other words. Many still feel the 1968 Charger ranks as the best-looking of the breed.

Both sales numbers (about 96,000 units) and praises soared off the scale that year. *Car and Driver* gave the Charger top styling honors for the year going away, with only Chevrolet's new 1968 Corvette coming close, a somewhat ironic ranking, since the pair shared more than one cue. With its Coke-bottle body, tunneled rear window, and dual round taillights, the 1968 Charger sure looked a lot like the restyled third-generation 'Vette. Or did Bill Mitchell's "Shark" look like Dodge's gorgeous second-generation Charger?

Enhancing the appeal further in 1968 was the new R/T package, announced boldly by a set of soon-to-be familiar stripes added out back. This tail treatment honored the Charger R/T's membership in Dodge's equally new Scat Pack, made up of, in promotional people's words, "the cars with the bumblebee stripes." Adding this distinctive striping around the trailing end of any Dodge muscle car, from Charger down to Dart, was a choice left up to each driver joining the Scat Pack. Most did, instantly turning heads in the process.

"Dodge's stripes scooped the industry," claimed *Car Life* about the Scat Pack touch. "Others had stripes down the center, down the driver's side, across the hood and down the front fenders. But only Dodge has 'bustle stripes.' As one observer put it, 'Those cars must really be fast—they almost got past the striper.'"

Charger stripes differed slightly in style compared to those used on Dodge's Super Bee, also introduced for 1968, and appeared in three colors: black, white, and red. They also could've been deleted on request, but why cut such a cool fashion statement?

Above:
The Charger III showed up on the auto show circuit in 1968 looking very much like a Corvette. It was only 42 inches tall and featured a periscope for rearward vision because there was no back window. *Chrysler LLC Corporate Historical Collection*

Left:
Designers typically toyed with various taillight styles before settling on the idea at left for the 1968 Charger. Notice that this mockup does not have the door scallops seen on the second-generation Charger. *Chrysler LLC Corporate Historical Collection*

Critics writing for *Car and Driver* claimed the restyled second-generation Charger was the hottest-looking thing out of Detroit in 1968, and that was saying a lot considering Chevrolet also rolled out its "Shark-bodied" Corvette that year. *Mike Mueller*

Most witnesses with eyes couldn't miss the similarities shared out back by the Charger and Chevrolet's radically restyled third-generation Corvette in 1968. *Mike Mueller*

A cool competition-style fuel filler was standard on the driver-side rear quarter panel on the 1968 Charger. *Mike Mueller*

Fourteen-inch wheels wearing small hubcaps were standard for the 1968 Charger. Options included three full wheel cover styles (including this code 584 unit) and the five-spoke Magnum 500 road wheel. *Mike Mueller*

Above:
Two 383 big-blocks were optional for the 1968 Charger, a 290-horsepower two-barrel version and the four-barrel-fed Magnum, rated at 330 horsepower. The 383 Magnum was topped by a dual-snorkel air cleaner, while its two-barrel counterpart got a single-snout unit. *Mike Mueller*

Left:
A 150-miles per hour speedometer was again included in the Charger's standard instrumentation in 1968. *Mike Mueller*

The 375-horse 440 Magnum V-8 came as standard R/T equipment. So, too, did heavy-duty drum brakes, special handling equipment, and F70 Red Streak tires. The excellent Torqueflite automatic transmission was standard with the R/T, while the four-speed manual was a no-cost option. Optional, of course, was the ever-present 426 Hemi with its mandatory heavy-duty suspension and 15-inch wheels. According to *Car and Driver*, quarter-mile performance for the Hemi Charger R/T in 1968 was 13.5 seconds at 105 miles per hour. The 0–60 clocking read only 4.8 clicks.

Another new option, the High Performance Axle Package, also appeared in 1968, but only for Chargers ordered with the 383-cubic-inch four-barrel V-8. This deal added a 3.55:1 Sure-Grip axle, a high-capacity radiator, and a seven-blade "Slip Drive" (viscous) fan with shroud. Curiously, Dodge also rolled out a 225 cid slant-six engine for the base Charger, but only 904 were built.

New for 1968 was the Charger R/T, one of the three founding members of Dodge's Scat Pack clan. Completing this trio were the Coronet R/T and Dart GTS. *Mike Mueller*

Like its Scat Pack running mates, the Charger R/T came standard with trademark bumblebee stripes wrapped around its tail. These stripes were available in three colors: black, white, and red. *Mike Mueller*

Base price for the Charger R/T in 1968 was $3,480. This R/T features specially customized Magnum 500 wheels (widened to 10 inches) in back. *Mike Mueller*

R/T badges appeared at both ends of the 1968 Charger. Heavy-duty drum brakes, a beefed suspension, and F70 Red Streak tires were included in the R/T deal. *Mike Mueller*

Above, left:
Bucket seats were standard for both the base Charger and R/T in 1968, as was a certainly sporty dash with full instrumentation. This Rallye instrumentation was also standard inside Dodge's Super Bee, introduced midyear in 1968. It was optional for that year's Coronet R/T. *Mike Mueller*

Above:
The combination clock/tachometer, the so-called "tick-tock-tach," was a $48.70 option in 1968. *Mike Mueller*

Left:
Only two engines were available for the 1968 Charger R/T: the standard 375-horsepower 440 Magnum (shown here) and optional 426 Hemi. Production of Magnum-powered models that year was 17,109. *Mike Mueller*

03

1969
Charger R/T

Specifications	
Model availability	two-door hardtop
Wheelbase	117 inches
Length	203.6 inches
Width	75.3 inches
Height	53 inches
Weight	3,646 pounds
Base Price	$3,592
Track (front/rear, in inches)	59.5/58.5
Wheels	14.0×5.5
Tires	F70×14 Red Streak Wide Tread
Construction	unitized body/frame
Suspension	independent A-arms with heavy-duty torsion bars, front; solid axle with longitudinal heavy-duty leaf springs, rear
Steering	recirculating ball
Brakes	four-wheel, heavy-duty, 11-inch drums
Engine	375-horsepower, 440-cubic-inch Magnum V-8, standard (426 Hemi, optional)
Bore and stroke	4.32×3.75 inches
Compression	10.1:1
Fuel delivery	Carter four-barrel carburetor
Transmission	four-speed manual or Torqueflite automatic
Axle ratio	3.23:1
Production (including exports)	20,057 (18,776, domestic)

A revised split grille was new for the 1969 Charger. Total production of base models (non-R/T), exports included, was 69,142. *Mike Mueller*

1969

A new split grille and long, horizontal taillights constituted the most notable exterior upgrades for 1969. Mechanicals carried over essentially unchanged, with the R/T deal again coming standard with the 440 Magnum. The Hemi also returned as an R/T option.

New for 1969 was the upscale Special Edition package, which dressed up the refreshed Charger with even more prestige. An SE Charger featured leather and vinyl bucket seats, a sport steering wheel, bright pedal trim, the light package, and a simulated wood-grain instrument pane inside. Hood-mounted turn signals, deep-dish wheel covers, and appropriate "SE" badges on the C-pillars went in place outside. Price for this option, coded A47, was $161.85.

Various rear axle options also debuted in 1969. First came the Performance Axle Package, offered with 383, 440, and Hemi V-8s backed by either automatic transmissions or four-speeds. Included in this deal, coded A36, was a 3.55:1 Sure-Grip axle, the heavy-duty Hemi suspension, a seven-blade torque-drive fan with shroud, and a 26-inch high-capacity radiator. Available only for the 383 four-barrel V-8 (with Torqueflite or four-speed), the High Performance Package (code A31) featured a 3.91:1 Sure-Grip rear, Hemi suspension, and the same extra cooling gear. The Super Performance Axle Package (A32) was available for the 440 and 426 Hemi with Torqueflite and included the big radiator and fan, power front disc brakes, and a 4.10:1 Sure-Grip differential in a heavy-duty 9.75-inch Dana axle. Air conditioning and A32 were not compatible options.

The Track Pack (A33) appeared for manual-transmission 440 and Hemi Chargers, and it, too, could not be ordered with air conditioning. The four-speed used in this case was a special heavy-duty box featuring a reverse warning light and a Hurst shifter wearing a wood-grain knob. Remaining A33 hardware included a 3.54:1 Sure-

Above:
New taillights complemented the Charger's restyled grille in 1969. Base price for the V-8 Charger hardtop that year was $3,109. As in 1968, a six-cylinder Charger also was available in 1969. *Mike Mueller*

Left:
An unsilenced air cleaner appeared late in 1968 for the four-barrel, 383-cubic-inch Magnum V-8, still rated at 330 horsepower in 1969. This B-series big-block was a $137.55 option that year. *Mike Mueller*

Optional turn signal indicators were available in the 1968–1970 Charger hood's simulated air vents. This little trick (option code L31) cost a tidy $10.80 in 1969. *Mike Mueller*

Above:
The Charger's attractive dash featured this full instrumentation layout for (left to right) fuel level, coolant temperature, oil pressure, and alternator from 1968 to 1970. *Mike Mueller*

Right:
A sport steering wheel, with simulated wood rim, was a $26.75 option for the 1969 Charger. The Torqueflite automatic transmission cost $227.05 behind the 383 Magnum V-8. *Mike Mueller*

Grip differential in a 9.75-inch Dana axle, a dual-breaker distributor (standard with the Hemi), and the familiar extra-capacity cooling pieces. Topping things off was the Super Track Pack (A34), which was nearly identical to the Track Pack save for the addition of power front disc brakes and 4.10:1 gears in place of the 3.54:1 ratio.

Above:
As was the case with all Scat Pack models, deleting those bumblebee stripes was a customer option in the Charger's case too. This stripe-delete 1969 R/T also features the Special Edition package introduced that year. *Mike Mueller*

Left:
Charger R/T production, including exports, was 20,057 for 1969. The domestic count was 18,776. The tally for R/T SE combinations that year was 4,243. *Mike Mueller*

1969
Charger 500

Specifications	
Model availability	two-door hardtop with flush-mounted grille and rear window
Wheelbase	117 inches
Length	206.6 inches
Width	76.7 inches
Height	54.2 inches
Weight	3,305 pounds
Base Price	$3,843
Track (front/rear, in inches)	59.5/58.5
Wheels	14.0×5.5 (15-inch rims with Hemi option)
Tires	F70×14 Red Streak Wide Tread (white-sidewall F70 Wide Tread, available as no-cost option; F70×15 with Hemi option)
Construction	unitized body/frame
Suspension	independent A-arms with heavy-duty torsion bars, front; solid axle with longitudinal heavy-duty leaf springs, rear
Steering	recirculating ball
Brakes	four-wheel, heavy-duty, 11-inch drums
Engine	375-horsepower, 440-cubic-inch Magnum V-8, standard (426 Hemi, optional)
Bore and stroke	4.32×3.75 inches
Compression	10.1:1
Fuel delivery	Carter four-barrel carburetor
Transmission	four-speed manual or Torqueflite automatic
Axle ratio	3.23:1
Production	392 estimated (U.S. shipments)

The aerodynamically enhanced Charger 500 appeared for 1969 with a flush-mounted grille borrowed from Dodge's Coronet. This modification, in turn, meant fixed headlights were standard. *Mike Mueller*

1969 Charger 500

Yet another new variation, the Charger 500, debuted in the fall of 1968 to hopefully help make Dodge's bodacious B-body more competitive in NASCAR competition. The "500" name came from NASCAR's new rule mandating that a manufacturer build at least that many regular-production versions of a particular machine to make it legal for stock-car racing.

While the second-generation Charger looked sleek enough to scream around a superspeedway at supersonic speeds, those looks were deceiving. In truth that recessed grille and tunneled rear window induced loads of unwanted drag at high speeds, especially so beyond 170 miles per hour. NASCAR drivers by 1967 had discovered a "wall" apparently existed at about 175 miles per hour, and even the awesome Hemi couldn't bust through. Ford Motor Company was the first to go over this barrier in 1968 with its restyled Fairlane and Cyclone fastbacks, cars that cut through the wind far easier than the 1968 Charger.

Dodge's response was the Charger 500, built outside the company's realm at Creative Industries in Detroit. There the Charger's air-trapping recessed front cavity was transformed into a flush nose (complete with fixed headlights) using the grille from a 1968 Coronet. Meanwhile, a steel plug filled the rear window tunnel to help the Charger's top end increase by 5 miles per hour, just the edge it needed to stay ahead of FoMoCo's newly restyled Fairlane and Cyclone fastbacks.

Above:
The typical Charger's recessed rear window also was traded for flush-mounted glass in the Charger 500's case. These modifications were performed by Creative Industries in Detroit. *Mike Mueller*

Left:
Dodge rushed the Charger 500 into production to make it legal for the 1969 NASCAR season. But rivals got wind of the plan quickly, resulting in Ford's introduction of its long-nosed Talladega, which proved aerodynamically superior to the special Charger. Dodge then went back to the drawing board, trading the Charger 500 (shown here) early in the year for the high-flying Charger Daytona. *Chrysler LLC Corporate Historical Collection*

03

Plain hubcaps on conventional stamped-steel wheels were standard for the Charger 500 in 1969. Five-spoke road wheels were typically optional. *Mike Mueller*

In 1969 this badge was reserved for a Charger created specifically to go racing on NASCAR speedways. A second Charger 500 model appeared the following year, but this one only featured an extra dash of pizzazz, no extra performance. *Mike Mueller*

Unfortunately, Dodge announced the Charger 500 before the 1968 NASCAR season's close, leaving Ford to quickly retaliate with its long-nose Talladega, the first factory "showroom racer" (*Hot Rod* magazine's words) to top 190 miles per hour at the track. Talladega teams won 26 NASCAR races in 1969, compared to 18 Charger 500 victories.

Apparently that name was a bit of a misnomer. Estimates today commonly list only 392 Charger 500s built for 1969, although it's possible as many as 450 might've rolled out of the Creative Industries facility that year. Either way, someone obviously looked the other way while Dodge's first aero-racer was slipping onto NACAR tracks.

Street-going Charger 500s were equipped with either the Hemi or the 375-horsepower, 440-cubic-inch wedge, either one backed by a Hurst-shifted four-speed or the durable A727 Torqueflite automatic. Just so you know, the latter's chrome shift knob was a leftover from the 1968 Charger's parts bin. Other automatic-trans 1969 Chargers used a wood-grain knob. Additional unique items included filler pieces for the headlight bezels and a Coronet headlight switch. While those headlights were fixed, a vacuum tank remained in place beneath a Charger 500's hood because the hoses that would have activated the standard model's hideaway lamps were simply cut. Since all Charger 500s began life as R/T models, all came standard with the R/T's special handling package, which included 11-inch drum brakes, F70x14 tires, extra-heavy-duty shocks and springs, and larger-diameter torsion bars up front. The front anti-sway bar was also thickened. A special "bumblebee" stripe appeared at the tail with appropriate "500" identification used in place of the typical "R/T" label. A small "500" badge appeared as well, below the right taillight. Heavy-duty steel rims with dog-dish hubcaps were standard, with optional deluxe wheel covers or sporty road wheels available at extra cost.

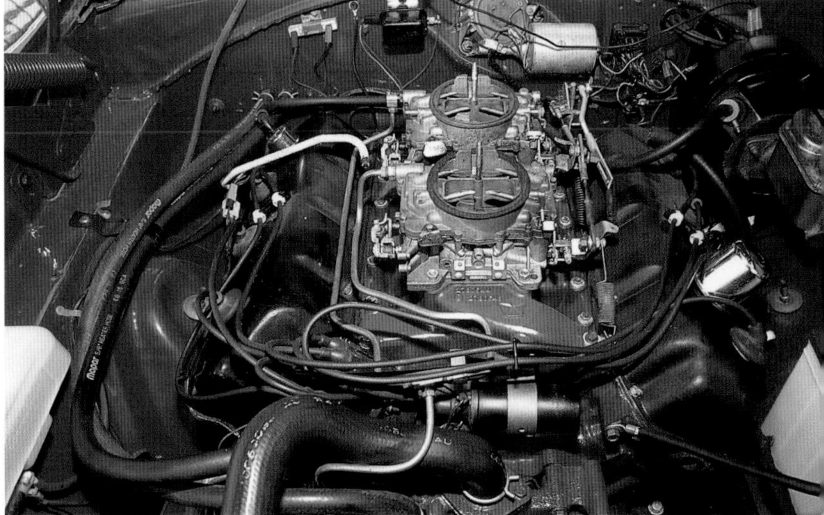

Charger 500s were powered by either the 375-horsepower 440 Magnum or 426 Hemi with its trademark twin Carter four-barrels. Either big-block could've been backed by the Torqueflite automatic or four-speed manual transmission in 1969. *Mike Mueller*

Though lost in Ford's shadow at the track, the Charger 500 was a big winner on the street, especially so when equipped with Hemi power. A 425-horse Charger 500 fitted with a four-speed ranked as *Car Life*'s quickest test car for 1969, clocking a 13.68-second quarter-mile.

Above, left:
Combining the racing-inspired Charger 500 with the luxury-conscious SE option in 1969 made for one rare animal. Only 13 of these odd combos are known. *Mike Mueller*

Above:
The SE treatment, code A47, was a $161.85 option in 1969. It was available for all models; the basic hardtop, hot R/T, and limited-edition 500. *Mike Mueller*

Left:
Along with polite badges on each rear roof pillar, the Special Edition option also added spruced-up leather/vinyl trim inside and hood-mounted turn signals outside. Included as well were the sport steering wheel (rimmed with fake wood), bright pedal trim, and more simulated wood grain for the instrument panel. *Mike Mueller*

1969
Charger Daytona

Specifications	
Model availability	two-door hardtop with aerodynamic nose and tall rear wing
Wheelbase	117 inches
Length	208.5 inches
Width	76.6 inches
Height	53 inches
Weight	not available
Base Price	$3,993
Track (front/rear, in inches)	59.7/58.2
Wheels	14.0×5.5 (15-inch rims with Hemi option)
Tires	F70×14 whitewall (F70×15 with Hemi option)
Construction	unitized body/frame
Suspension	independent A-arms with heavy-duty torsion bars, front; solid axle with longitudinal heavy-duty leaf springs, rear
Steering	recirculating ball
Brakes	four-wheel, heavy-duty, 11-inch drums
Engine	375-horsepower, 440-cubic-inch Magnum V-8, standard (426 Hemi, optional)
Bore and stroke	4.32×3.75 inches
Compression	10.1:1
Fuel delivery	Carter four-barrel carburetor
Transmission	four-speed manual or Torqueflite automatic
Axle ratio	3.23:1
Production	503

Above:
Dodge followed up the Charger 500 in 1969 with the truly exotic Daytona, introduced for the street in April that year. Up front the Daytona featured an extended steel nose to help make it easily the slipperiest factory racing machine yet. *Mike Mueller*

Below:
Charger Daytona production was 503. Base price was $3,993. *Mike Mueller*

1969 Charger Daytona

While no slouch, the Charger 500 did represent old news even before it had a chance to make news. But Dodge still managed to inspire some serious headlines in 1969 by one-upping Ford with an even more aerodynamic Charger, the Daytona. With its pointed steel beak and soaring "towel-rack" spoiler in back, this radical wind-cheater was the first machine to break the 200-miles-per-hour barrier on NASCAR tracks. Plymouth's similar Superbird followed in 1970 to tack an exclamation point onto perhaps the most outlandish factory racing effort ever seen around Detroit. However, like the Charger 500 and Daytona, Plymouth's Superbird was a one-hit wonder. Apparently 200 miles per hour was fast enough as far as NASCAR mogul Bill France was concerned. New rules changes ruled out all of Detroit's showroom racers almost before they got comfortable parked in NASCAR winner's circles.

A Charger Daytona was the first to run 200 miles per hour on a NASCAR superspeedway. The Daytona's NASCAR competition debut came in September 1969 at the Alabama International Motor Speedway near Talladega, Alabama. *Chrysler LLC Corporate Historical Collection*

Introduced in April 1969, Dodge's original Charger Daytona clearly was the product of some serious wind-tunnel testing, and it was again left to the guys at Creative Industries to handle the modifications. Included were the aforementioned steel nose with a chin spoiler (a fully functional modification that stretched the car by about a foot and a half) and that cast-aluminum high wing in back.

Both the Charger 500 and Daytona used the same exclusive A-pillar moldings and sloping rear window with its sheet metal plug. Adding that flush-mounted glass required a radically shortened rear-deck lid, which *Hot Rod*'s Steve Kelly described as being "about as big as a glovebox door." "As much grain as you'd care to pour into the trunk can be carried, but suitcase size is restricted to ultra-slim designs," Kelly explained. "With a little jockeying, though, you can fit a lot in there, but nonetheless it's not an easy job. Okay, it may be a gripe, but [NASCAR drivers] Buddy Baker, Charlie Glotzbach, or Bobby Isaac will probably never care about it. They travel light, and always on the same road."

Dodge's winged warrior was also equipped with either 440 or 426 Hemi power in street guise. Production this time was completely legit: 503 were built during a three-month run.

Above:
The noses of the 1969 Charger Daytona (right) and 1970 Plymouth Superbird (left) appeared quite similar at a glance. But differences included a continuation of the hood's center crease in the Superbird's case. *Mike Mueller*

Right:
The Superbird's wing (orange) was taller and wider at its base compared to the Daytona unit. *Mike Mueller*

Above:
Like the Charger 500, the 1969 Daytona was powered by either the 440 Magnum (shown here) or 426 Hemi. *Mike Mueller*

Left:
Daytona wings were adorned with tape striping in 1969 while Superbird spoilers weren't in 1970. *Mike Mueller*

Far left:
The Charger Daytona's hood-mounted air extractors actually were functional. The differently shaped scoops on the 1970 Superbird were for looks only. *Mike Mueller*

1970
Charger R/T

Specifications	
Model availability	two-door hardtop
Wheelbase	117 inches
Length	208.5 inches
Width	76.6 inches
Height	53 inches
Weight	3,638 pounds
Base Price	$3,711
Track (front/rear, in inches)	59.7/58.2
Wheels	14×6
Tires	F70×14 whitewall Goodyear Polyglas
Construction	unitized body/frame
Suspension	independent A-arms with heavy-duty torsion bars, front; solid axle with longitudinal heavy-duty leaf springs, rear
Steering	recirculating ball
Brakes	four-wheel, heavy-duty, 11-inch drums
Engine	375-horsepower, 440-cubic-inch Magnum V-8, standard (426 Hemi and 440 Six Pack V-8s, optional)
Bore and stroke	4.32×3.75 inches
Compression	10.1:1
Fuel delivery	Carter four-barrel carburetor
Transmission	four-speed manual or Torqueflite automatic
Axle ratio	3.23:1
Production (including exports)	10,337 (9,370 domestic)

Simulated vents appeared on Charger R/T doors in 1970, and these additions served as suitable mounting points for prominent model identification. Notice the optional engine callout tape treatment (code V24) on this Hemi Charger's hood. *Mike Mueller*

1970

Yet another revised grille appeared for 1970, this one completely surrounded by a chromed loop bumper. Mechanical news included an easier-to-live-with hydraulic cam for the optional Hemi. Among new options added midyear were a rear spoiler, dual color-keyed mirrors, and a performance hood treatment that spelled out "440" or "Hemi" in silver reflective tape.

Discounting the mundane slant-six, yeoman 318, and meek 383 two-barrel, the 1970 Charger's engine lineup featured four great choices. First on the list was the 335-horsepower, 383-cubic-inch four-barrel V-8, followed by the 375-horsepower 440 four-barrel, the new 390-horsepower 440 Six Pack with its three two-barrel carburetors, and the still-tough Hemi. For more on the Six Pack big-block, see chapter seven, home to Plymouth's Road Runner.

Also new for 1970 was a totally different Charger 500. No special aerodynamic modifications were included this time; instead, a 1970 Charger 500 owner received a nice bit of pizzazz in the form of vinyl-covered bucket seats, an electric clock, wheel lip moldings, and appropriate external identification. Equally tidy was the extra cost: only about $150.

Another $161.85 could've added the prestigious Special Edition package, coded A47. Included again in the A47 group were genuine leather seat inserts, simulated wood-grain touches for the steering wheel and instrument panel, bright pedal dress-up, deep-dish wheel covers, hood-mounted turn signal indicators, and a courtesy light group. According to factory paperwork, no way could the Hemi and SE options be combined. Apparently it was kinda like asking dogs and cats to live together. Yet 13 such combos were built—9 with automatic transmissions, 4 with four-speeds.

Another restyled grille adorned the Charger in 1970, as did a new loop bumper that totally surrounded the grille. Base price for the R/T that year was $3,711. *Mike Mueller*

Total Charger R/T production for 1970 was 10,337, of which 9,370 were delivered domestically. The count for the R/T SE combination (shown here) was 1,452. *Mike Mueller*

Optional Rallye wheels, available in 14- and 15-inch sizes, debuted for the Charger in 1970. The price in either case was $43.10. *Mike Mueller*

The 1970 R/T's bumblebee stripes were available in five colors: white, black, red, blue, and green. *Mike Mueller*

Above:
Dodge designers repackaged their B-body line on a shorter 115-inch wheelbase for 1971. The bottom line for a Charger R/T that year began at $3,223. Front and rear spoilers were optional, as were a vinyl roof and power sunroof. *Mike Mueller*

Above, right:
The 425-horsepower, 426-cubic-inch Hemi was a $648.25 option for the Charger R/T in 1970. Production was 112: 56 four-speeds, 56 automatics. *Mike Mueller*

Right:
The Charger's optional four-speed manual transmission was fitted with Hurst's unforgettable Pistol Grip shifter in 1970. *Mike Mueller*

As in 1969, the SE option was available along with the R/T package, which again featured heavy-duty drum brakes, a beefed Rallye suspension, and some aggressive image enhancements. New-for-1970 R/T touches included dummy scoops on the doors and a choice of longitudinal tape stripes or Dodge's trademark bumblebee-striped tail. Standard Charger R/T power came from the 440 four-barrel, with the Six-Pack V-8 and Hemi available at an additional cost.

1971

American muscle was on its last legs when Dodge designers radically reshaped their B-body models for 1971. The bulk of the Chargers sold that year existed on their looks alone as available performance fell off noticeably. Rolling this time around on a shortened 115-inch wheelbase, the 1971 Charger's attractive Coke-bottle body helped make it look real fast even if it wasn't, and the basic coupe clearly wasn't. Standard power came from either a 225 cid slant-six or the ever-present 318 cid V-8. Priced at $2,707—$300 less than the lowest Charger sticker in 1970—this bargain-basement Dodge kept costs down by incorporating fixed rear quarter windows (instead of the roll-up units used by the more expensive hardtops) and fully fixed headlights.

The same two engines also were standard for the base Charger hardtop, which featured color-keyed carpeting and various pieces of simulated wood-grain interior trim. Base price for the slant-six hardtop was $2,975.

1971
Charger R/T

Specifications	
Model availability	two-door hardtop
Wheelbase	115 inches
Length	205.3 inches
Width	75.9 inches
Height	52.2 inches
Weight	3,685 pounds
Base Price	$3,777
Track (front/rear, in inches)	59.7/60.1
Wheels	14×6
Tires	G70×14
Construction	unitized body/frame
Suspension	independent A-arms with heavy-duty torsion bars, front; solid axle with longitudinal heavy-duty leaf springs, rear
Steering	recirculating ball
Brakes	four-wheel, heavy-duty, 11-inch drums
Engine	370-horsepower, 440-cubic-inch Magnum V-8, standard (426 Hemi and 440 Six Pack V-8s, optional)
Bore and stroke	4.32×3.75 inches
Compression	9.7:1
Fuel delivery	Carter four-barrel carburetor
Transmission	four-speed manual or Torqueflite automatic
Axle ratio	3.23:1
Production (including exports)	3,118 (2,743 domestic)

Black-out tape also appeared on the Charger R/T's domed hood in 1971. Total R/T production that year was 3,118, including 2,743 delivered in the United States. *Mike Mueller*

Exclusive door treatments were again an R/T feature in 1971. Longitudinal body-side tape replaced the traditional bumblebee stripes issued as standard equipment from 1968 to 1970. *Mike Mueller*

The central intake flap first used by Plymouth's Air Grabber system in 1970 became part of Dodge's Ramcharger hood option in 1971. *Mike Mueller*

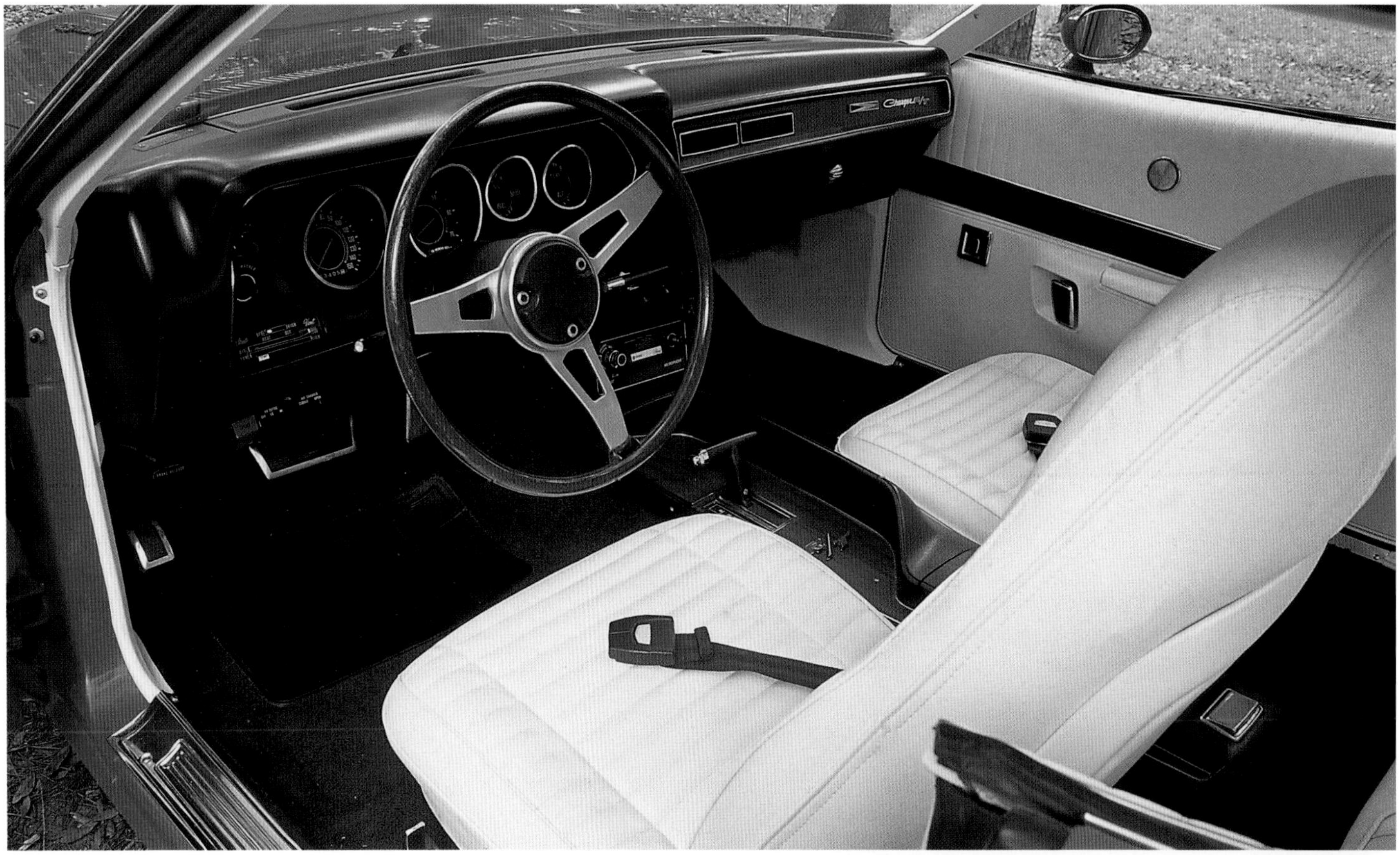

Above:
Options on this heavily loaded 1971 R/T SE include power steering and windows, rim-blow sport steering (with simulated wood rim), rear window defogger, six-way driver seat, console, tachometer, AM/FM stereo with rear seat speakers, and variable-speed wipers. *Mike Mueller*

Right:
Dodge also offered an intriguing cassette recorder with microphone in 1971. *Mike Mueller*

The Charger 500 came only with V-8 power, beginning with the 230-horsepower 318. Various upgrades for the 500 included standard bucket seats with integral head restraints. Next up was the upscale Charger SE, which featured all the 500's standard items plus, among other things, hideaway headlights and a vinyl landau roof. A bench seat was standard inside the SE, with leather buckets optional. The 440 Magnum V-8 was the top power option in the 1971 SE; the triple-carb 440 and Hemi weren't available.

In its final year (like the Hemi and Six Pack), the Charger R/T was still a prominent player in 1971. Now rated at 370 horsepower, the 440 Magnum was still standard, as was the floor-shifted Torqueflite automatic. Again a four-speed stick was a no-cost option.

Dodge rolled out one last Super Bee in 1971, this one based on the Charger because the Coronet was retired after 1970. *Mike Mueller*

The optional Hemi and 440 Six Pack were history after 1971, as was the racy R/T. But at least the Rallye package was still around in 1972 to help keep Charger buyers running in what was left of Detroit's fast lane. *Chrysler LLC Corporate Historical Collection*

Exterior identification included "Charger R/T" badges on the fenders and deck lid, a louvered, domed hood with a flat-black center section, and unique doors incorporating "gills" indented in their forward sections. Body-side stripes, done in black only, were standard and once more could've been deleted.

The same heavy-duty suspension was standard one more time beneath the last Charger R/T, as were heavy-duty drum brakes and G70x14 tires on stamped-steel wheels. Power front discs were a popular option, and buyers also could've chosen between two extra-cost wheel styles: the ever-present 14-inch chrome road wheel and the familiar Rallye wheel, which came in either 14×6 or 15×7 sizes. Choosing the 15-inch Rallye rims meant also bringing home G60×15 rubber.

Still a fun machine, the Charger R/T was given *Cars* magazine's "Top Performance Car of the Year" award in 1971, a suitable send-off for the last of Dodge's great midsized muscle cars. The Charger remained an attractive offering up through 1974, but the days of true high performance disappeared along with the Hemi at year's end.

04

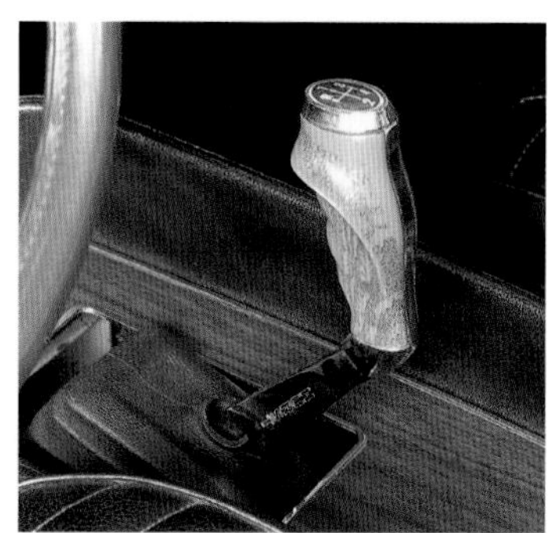

Plymouth GTX 1967–1971

Face in the Race

- Plymouth's midsized B-body lineup for 1967 consisted of the base Belvedere, Belvedere I, Belvedere II, and upscale Satellite.
- Though described as a "Belvedere GTX" in Plymouth promotional paperwork in 1967, the original GTX technically was based on the supreme Belvedere variation, the Satellite—both shared much of the same top-shelf trim, various standard features, and the division's "CR2-P" model series code.
- The 440-cubic-inch wedge and 426 Hemi V-8 were the only Engines used by the GTX during its five-year run.
- A convertible GTX was offered from 1967 to 1969.
- Plymouth's triple-carb, 440-cubic-inch V-8, rated at 390 horsepower, became a GTX option in 1970.
- The triple-carb 440 V-8's name was changed to 440+6 in 1971.
- The GTX name stuck around after 1971 for Plymouth's hottest Road Runner, which used an optional 440 big-block up until 1974.

Like their counterparts at Dodge, Plymouth people also encountered an identity crisis during the mid-sixties. From an engineering perspective in 1966, they were known as the builders of perhaps the most exciting road rocket available to mere mortals. Anyone that year who dared ask a Plymouth B-body driver "that thing got a Hemi in it?" sure found out in a hurry. But therein lay the rub. Dropping an utterly awesome 425-horsepower, 426-cubic-inch V-8 into a Belvedere or Satellite instantly jacked up the price by a thousand bucks or so, and for all that excess green a Hemi owner still would find himself lost in a crowd, at least while standing still. As thrilling as Plymouth's best midsized performers were mechanically in 1966, they remained damned dull visually.

Car and Driver's critics couldn't have agreed more, 40-odd years back. "When we tested the 1966 Plymouth, equipped with a street Hemi and four-speed transmission, we were rather upset that [it] didn't look like anything special. A Plain-Jane car sometimes fits well into life's order, but when a buyer forks over extra money for a fast car at the top of the line, he wants it to have a distinctive identification."

General Motors had four definitely distinctive musclebound intermediates up and rolling by 1966: Pontiac's ground-breaking GTO, Oldsmobile's 4-4-2, Buick's Gran Sport, and Chevrolet's Chevelle SS 396, all powered by suitably strong big-block V-8s. Plymouth, on the other hand, had the king of Detroit's big-blocks but nothing in the way of a snazzy supporting cast, not one wit of special packaging that screamed "no need to ask, you know I'm bad to the bone!" To be so strong under the hood yet so weak in the eyes of the casual observer—a classic conundrum, no?

Fortunately one puzzled person at Plymouth decided it was high time to rejoin this split personality. Jack Smith, the division's chief product planning manager, simply couldn't believe his company didn't have anything to stand up to the GTO crowd as far as eye-appeal was concerned. He also had watched rather enviously as Dodge began reaping the rewards of an exciting image makeover after rolling out its head-turning Charger for 1966. What was working for one corporate cousin would surely do the same for the other, right?

Opposite:
The 1967 GTX, offered in both hardtop and convertible forms, was Plymouth's first complete muscle car package. Base price for the hardtop rendition was $3,178. *Mike Mueller*

Above:
The 1967 GTX was technically based on Plymouth's B-body Belvedere, but it also came standard with some of the same features (bucket seats most notably) included on the Belvedere line's flagship, the Satellite. Basic Satellites wore "Aluma-plate" lower body-side trim; the 1967 GTX did not. *Chrysler LLC Corporate Historical Collection*

Opposite:
The Dodge truck guys dusted off the GTX name in 2004, sticking it onto a special run of high-profile pickups painted in Hemi Orange, Sublime Green, Plum Crazy Purple, or Banana Yellow. *Mike Mueller*

Smith's first move to hopefully put Plymouth's face into the muscle car race involved a few doodles on a legal pad. After noting that more than one factory hot rod of the day relied on a zinger of a name made up of three numerals or letters, he began a quest for a suitably groovy tag for an entirely new Plymouth supercar.

Being a card-carrying Detroit man, Smith had no qualms whatsoever about reusing another's idea and claiming it as his own. His label-making experiments began with the classic "GT," but how to make this a triplet? Adding an "O" was, of course, completely out of the question, Ford would have "GTA" in use (for automatic-transmission Mustang and Fairlane GTs) once its 1967 models arrived, and "GTS" would show up in Dodge lexicon that year. Smith then scrolled down through the alphabet until he arrived at "X," a letter that always has exuded its own particular coolness. "GTX," yeah that was the ticket.

Once he named his baby, Smith caught the ear of design studio head Richard McAdams, who proposed that they go right to the head of the Belvedere class and use the trimmed-out, top-shelf Satellite as a base for the GTX. Along with a full load of exterior flair, the Satellite featured standard bucket seats and was offered only in sporty hardtop and sexy convertible forms. Maximum impact and exclusivity, coupled with as much midsized luxury as Plymouth offered, were among Smith's goals from the get-go.

Maxing out the 1967 GTX's image was simply a matter of blacking out both ends, bolting two dummy scoops onto the hood, attaching a pair of chromed exhaust trumpets out back, and offering twin racing stripes as an option. Milt Antonick then supplied an exclamation point by adding an exposed competition-style gas cap to the driver-side rear quarter panel, a neat little trick he'd also applied to that year's redesigned Barracuda.

A 150-miles-per-hour speedometer went inside, and the Satellite's bucket seats naturally carried over with their saddle-grain vinyl upholstery that featured a "tooled leather" effect. A console was available in between, and the rear seats were designed to look a little like buckets too. A split bench with center armrest was available optionally for those who perhaps preferred to get a little closer to their passengers, either while on the move or at rest.

Making a heavy-duty chassis standard was a no-brainer. As for motivation, a standard big-block was a slam dunk, but which one? Going right for the throat with the street Hemi would've been the best choice for nuking the competition at all costs. But, even though Smith's ideal never did necessarily involve keeping costs down, there was a limit to his madness, and limiting the GTX only to the fattest of wallets was never his goal. Though the sky-high-priced Hemi obviously would be an option, a better candidate would have to surface for standard status if Plymouth officials expected to sell more than a hundred or so GTXs a year.

Presto, enter the "440 Super Commando," based on Chrysler's "440 TNT" RB big-block, itself introduced just the year before at 350 horsepower. Best suited for turning pulleys on power-steering pumps and air conditioning compressors between luxury car fenders, this torque churn was transformed into a real beast by adding better-breathing open-chamber heads, freer-flowing exhaust manifolds, a big Carter four-barrel carburetor, and a more aggressive hydraulic cam. The resulting Super Commando (and its 440 Magnum counterpart at Dodge) debuted for 1967 with 375 healthy horses at the ready.

Dual bright exhaust tips were part of the original GTX package, as was a competition-style gas cap on the driver-side rear quarter panel. Racing stripes on the hood and deck lid were optional. *Mike Mueller*

While some higher-placed GTX buyers did choose the optional Hemi, the majority stuck with the standard Super Commando, losing little in the deal, face or otherwise. What the 375-horse 440 lacked in advertised output, it made up for in overall ease of use compared to its cantankerous solid-lifter cousin. As *Hot Rod* magazine's Dick Scritchfield explained, the heart and soul of the 1967 GTX was "a street engine with racing ability without the problems of the finely tuned racing mill." Either a Torqueflite automatic or four-speed manual could've been installed behind each available V-8.

With either engine, this bodacious B-body stood taller than tall among Detroit's burgeoning supercar set in 1967, clearly raising the bar in the process as far as its parent company was concerned. "[GTX is] a model that has taken Plymouth out of the domestic snapshot album and put it right in the middle of the performance picture, and with a very sharp image I might add," continued Scritchfield's high praise. "It's exciting to look at and it's exciting to drive."

"GTO owners had better look to their defenses," went a *Car and Driver* conclusion. "Plymouth has given the GTX strong good looks and one of the best-handling sedan chassis we have ever driven." Sure sounds like Jack Smith hit his target right on the nose.

1967
GTX

Specifications	
Model availability	two-door hardtop and convertible
Wheelbase	116 inches
Length	200.5 inches
Width	76.4 inches
Height	54 inches, hardtop
Weight	3,869 pounds
Base Price	$3,178, hardtop; $3,418, convertible
Track (front/rear, in inches)	59.6/58.5
Wheels	14.0×5.5 inches
Tires	7.75×14.00
Construction	unitized body/frame
Suspension	independent A-arms with torsion bars, front; solid axle with longitudinal leaf springs, rear
Steering	recirculating ball
Brakes	four-wheel drums, standard; power front discs, optional
Engine	375-horsepower, 440-cubic-inch Super Commando V-8, standard; 426 Hemi, optional
Bore and stroke	4.32×3.75 inches
Compression	10.1:1
Fuel delivery	single Carter four-barrel carburetor
Transmission	Torqueflite automatic, standard; four-speed manual, optional at no extra cost
Axle ratio	3.23:1 with Torqueflite; 3.54:1 in Dana rear end with four-speed
Production	11,330 hardtops, 680 convertibles

Only two engines were available beneath a GTX hood in 1967: the standard 440 Super Commando or optional 426 Hemi. "Banzai-i-i-i" was all ads could say about the latter combination. *Mike Mueller*

1967

According to *Car and Driver*'s November 1966 test, a base GTX, with an automatic transmission, could roast the quarter-mile in 14.4 seconds at 98 miles per hour. Just as heart-warming were the numbers that appeared at the car's bottom line. A 1967 GTX hardtop started at $3,178, its convertible running mate at $3,418. Total production that first year was 11,330 coupes, 680 ragtops. Breakdown by engine was 11,277 Super Commando V-8s, 733 Hemis. Of the Hemi installations, 312 featured four-speeds, 408 automatics. Transmission choices for the standard 440 numbered 8,791 automatics, 2,486 four-speeds.

While compression, at 10.1:1, was the same for the 440 Super Commando and its TNT cousin, the 375-horse RB was topped off with its own low-restriction, dual-snorkel air cleaner to help the Carter carb below suck like nobody's business. Additional

The console, tachometer, and simulated wood-grain steering wheel seen here were all optional in 1967. Bucket seats were standard, as was the Torqueflite automatic. A four-speed manual transmission was a no-cost option. *Mike Mueller*

Red Streak tires were standard in 1967, but the attractive five-spoke road wheels required a customer to shell out an extra $97.30 that year. *Mike Mueller*

modifications included a revised valvetrain better suited to handle the lumpier cam's reciprocating demands. High-load valve springs (105 pounds at 1.86 inches of height, intake; 246 pounds at 1.36 inches, exhaust) helped resist valve float, and those springs incorporated surge dampers to limit unwanted harmonics. At 2.08 inches, intake valve size carried over from the TNT, but exhaust diameter was enlarged from 1.60 inches to 1.74.

Super Commando heads were massaged for better flow on both intake and exhaust, the intake manifold was revised to deliver the fuel/air mixture more efficiently, and exhaust manifolds incorporated large 2.38-inch outlets that dumped into 2.50-inch headpipes and 2.25-inch tailpipes. No resonators were used, making for an exhaust note that, in *Car Life*'s words, was "distinctly audible, though well within legal requirement."

The GTX's excellent standard chassis featured heavy-duty ball joints, thickened torsion bars (0.92 inches, compared to 0.88), and a strengthened 0.94-inch anti-sway bar up front. Those thicker torsion bars translated into a front spring rate of 118 lbs/in, compared to 102 lbs/in for the standard B-body bars. Beefier springs in back used six leaves instead of five and boosted the rear rate from 115 lbs/in to 159. Stiffer shock absorbers were predictably added all around, as were

Chrysler's 350-horsepower 440 TNT V-8 was converted into Plymouth's 375-horse Super Commando by adding better-breathing heads, a more aggressive cam, a big Carter four-barrel carb, and less-restrictive exhausts. *Mike Mueller*

wider (14.0x5.5K) station wagon rims wrapped in 7.75-inch red-stripe tires. Attractive five-spoke Magnum 500 road wheels were optional.

Standard brakes were 11-inch drums (with 3-inch-wide shoes in front, 2-inchers in back) that left more than one driver in 1967 wondering how they'd possibly counteract all those horses. Optional power front discs (with four-piston calipers) were offered, but they, too, didn't quite measure up, a situation not uncommon in sixties supercars.

Trading the 1967 GTX's standard Torqueflite automatic for the four-speed, a no-cost option, mandated the installation of a few other extra cost items, including a dual-point distributor, a viscous-drive fan, and a windage tray in the oil pan to prevent horsepower loss as the crankshaft whipped up the lubricant supply. Four-speed GTX models were also fitted with a heavy-duty Dana rear axle containing 3.54:1 gears in a Sure-Grip differential. The Dana unit's ring gear measured 9.75 inches, compared to the standard axle's 8.75-inch gear.

The sum of these parts equaled what Plymouth ads called "a machine of many talents . . . the most well-rounded Supercar to come out of Detroit (or anywhere, for that matter) in a long time."

1968
GTX

Specifications	
Model availability	two-door hardtop and convertible
Wheelbase	116 inches
Length	202.7 inches
Width	76.4 inches
Height	54.7 inches
Weight	3,870 pounds (hardtop)
Base Price	$3,355, hardtop; $3,590, convertible
Track (front/rear, in inches)	59.5/59.2
Wheels	14.0×5.5 inches
Tires	F70×14 Red Streak
Construction	unitized body/frame
Suspension	independent A-arms with torsion bars, front; solid axle with longitudinal leaf springs, rear
Steering	recirculating ball
Brakes	four-wheel drums, standard; power front discs, optional
Engine	375-horsepower, 440-cubic-inch Super Commando V-8, standard; 426 Hemi, optional
Bore and stroke	4.32×3.75 inches
Compression	10.1:1
Fuel delivery	single Carter four-barrel carburetor
Transmission	Torqueflite automatic, four-speed manual, optional at no extra cost
Axle ratio	3.23:1 with Torqueflite; 3.54:1 in Dana rear end with four-speed
Production (including exports)	17,914 hardtops, 1,026 convertibles

Plymouth people picked up the promotional pace in 1968, adding major "GTX" identification just ahead of each rear wheel. *Mike Mueller*

1968

A nicely restyled B-body platform served as a base for Plymouth's second-edition GTX. In place of all the body-side sculpturing seen in 1967 were an expanse of mild contouring and a slight "Coke-bottle" bulge behind the doors. "GTX" identification was added to the grille, rear cove panel, and lower rear quarters just ahead of the wheels. Completing the image were parallel hood bulges that proved to be the perfect place to mount engine displacement badges, a job handled in 1967 by a dated hood ornament. Dual lower body accent stripes could've been added in a choice of five colors: white, black, red, blue, or green. Bucket seats and a 150-miles-per-hour speedometer were again standard inside, and all mechanicals carried over unchanged beneath that restyled skin.

As it did in 1967, a small "GTX" badge appeared near the passenger-side taillight in 1968. *Mike Mueller*

A new B-body shell and official recognition in the grille appeared for the second-edition GTX in 1968. Again, both hardtop and convertible models were offered that year. *Mike Mueller*

The 1968 GTX's body-side stripes were supplied by 3M and done in five colors: red, black, white, green, and blue. These stripes could've been deleted on customer request. *Mike Mueller*

Bucket seats were again standard in 1968 and could've been topped by optional headrests. No bench was available; no way, no how. The console seen here was a $52.85 option. *Mike Mueller*

Power again came from either the standard 440 Super Commando or optional Hemi. According to *Car Life* magazine's test crew, they'd "never tested a standard passenger car with the accelerative performance of the Hemi GTX. This is the winner. The most powerful standard car built in America. And the 440 is not far behind."

"As a performance car, the GTX has few equals," continued *Car Life*'s February 1968 report. "With the Hemi engine, it is the fastest quarter-miler among current domestic Supercars. With the 440 engine, it offers as much performance-per-dollar as anything on the market, and more than most. The standard 440 GTX should appeal to the man who wants a very fast passenger car with sporty styling and reasonable smoothness and economy. The Hemi GTX will appeal to the acceleration enthusiast who wants the ultimate."

The numbers for the Hemi GTX (a convertible, by the way, with an automatic transmission, stock F70x15 Goodyear Wide Tread tires, and standard 3.23:1 gears) read 13.97 seconds for the quarter-mile at 103.50 miles per hour. Its 440 running mate, a similarly equipped

An optional tachometer, priced at $48.70, moved to the instrument panel's far right in 1968 and superseded the installation of a clock, itself a $16.05 option that year. *Mike Mueller*

F70x14 Red Streak tires, mounted on conventional 14.0x5.5 stamped-steel wheels, were standard in 1968, as were mundane "dog-dish" hubcaps. *Mike Mueller*

GTX hardtop, posted a 14.34/97.93 time slip. A little tweaking (trading the standard-issue gears for dealer-offered 4.56:1 cogs and bolting up a pair of 14-inch slicks) resulted in a best run of 13.44 clicks at 104.89 miles per hour for the Hemi. Adding the same size slicks and 4.30:1 gears to the 440 hardtop produced a 13.97/99.77 run.

"That, friends, is really outstanding performance for a car with no on-track tuning (we never even checked the spark plugs though the test period), with standard reverse-flow mufflers, and carrying a heavy convertible body—with power windows, yet," concluded the *Car Life* gang about their Hemi test car. No kidding.

Production of the second-edition GTX was 17,083 hardtops, 917 convertibles. Base prices were $3,355 for the GTX hardtop, $3,590 for the convertible.

04

1969
GTX

Specifications	
Model availability	two-door hardtop and convertible
Wheelbase	116 inches
Length	202.7 inches
Width	76.4 inches
Height	54.7 inches
Weight	3,465 pounds (hardtop); 3,590 pounds (convertible)
Base Price	$3,416, hardtop; $3,635, convertible
Track (front/rear, in inches)	59.5/59.2
Wheels	14.0×5.5 inches
Tires	F70×14 Red Streak
Construction	unitized body/frame
Suspension	independent A-arms with torsion bars, front; solid axle with longitudinal leaf springs, rear
Steering	recirculating ball
Brakes	four-wheel drums, standard; power front discs, optional
Engine	375-horsepower, 440-cubic-inch Super Commando V-8, standard; 426 Hemi, optional
Bore and stroke	4.32×3.75 inches
Compression	10.1:1
Fuel delivery	single Carter four-barrel carburetor
Transmission	Torqueflite automatic, four-speed manual, optional at no extra cost
Axle ratio	3.23:1 with Torqueflite; 3.54:1 in Dana rear end with four-speed
Production (including exports)	14,902 hardtops, 700 convertibles

Above:
A GTX convertible appeared for the final time in 1969. Total production (exports included) that year was 700. The domestic count was 551. *Chrysler LLC Corporate Historical Collection*

Opposite, top:
The bright rocker moldings seen in 1968 were replaced by black lower body paint the following year, and this change mandated a revised standard stripe treatment. Again supplied by 3M, this new thin stripe was done in either white or red. *Mike Mueller*

Opposite, below:
Total GTX production for 1969 (both body styles, exports included) was 15,602. Base price that year for the hardtop rendition was $3,416. *Mike Mueller*

1969

That Plymouth's totally fresh B-body carried over into 1969 nearly unchanged wasn't necessarily a bad thing, at least as far as *Motor Trend*'s Bill Sanders was concerned. In his humble opinion, "watching a '69 GTX in the rearview mirror, it looks like a mean, hungry animal, and we could imagine how it would feel to be slip-streamed by Richard Petty at Daytona or Charlotte."

Minor updates were made to the car's grille and taillights, and a wide flat-black paint band appeared in place of the bright rocker moldings seen in 1968. Trimming out that band was a thin bright strip that was accented with a pinstripe done in red (on cars equipped with redline tires) or white (on cars with optional whitewalls). New for all B-body Plymouths in 1969 were rectangular side marker lights. Round units had appeared the year before. All other standard features, inside and out, remained familiar.

Notable new options for 1969 included Plymouth's "Air Grabber" induction, which made those twin hood bulges functional by opening their vents. Like Dodge's Ramcharger hood, Plymouth's Air Grabber lid featured ductwork underneath that directed cooler, denser outside air through those vents into an oval air cleaner below. Activated mechanically by an under-dash knob, Air Grabber plumbing was automatically installed when the Hemi was chosen over the still-standard 375-horsepower 440 Super Commando.

GTX

PLYMOUTH
GTX
Plymouth
EAGLE ST
GOODYEAR

PLYMOUTH
24251
GTX
EAGLE ST
GOODYEAR

Right:
Engine identification was added to each hood vent in 1968 and 1969. These vents faced outward in 1968, upward in 1969. *Mike Mueller*

Below:
"GTX" identification grew in prominence and was relocated to the center of the model's tail in 1968. *Mike Mueller*

Also new was an optional paint treatment made up of parallel black bands that ran over the hood and fender tops from the grille to the windshield. Now facing upward instead of outward, 1969's twin hood vents incorporated red-colored inserts for contrast whenever these black bands were applied. A tasty collection of rear axle ratios debuted for 1969 too, each wrapped up in specific packages meant to maximize performance. First came the GTX's Performance Axle Package, which featured 3.55:1 gears in a Sure-Grip differential and extra cooling gear made up of a seven-blade viscous-drive fan and wider (26-inch) radiator. This option was limited to automatic-equipped GTX models. Next was the Super Performance Axle Package, made up of the Hemi suspension, power front disc brakes, 4.10:1 Sure-Grip gears in a 9.75-inch Dana 60 rear end, and the same cooling equipment mentioned above. Again this package was available only with an automatic transmission.

For GTX buyers who preferred to row their own, there were two more packages, the Track Pack and Super Track Pack, both of which included a Hurst shifter. The Track Pack was the same as the

The tried-and-true 440 Super Commando V-8 remained standard in 1969. Helping those 375 horses breathe easier that year was the new Air Grabber option (code N96), which allowed cooler, denser outside air a direct path into the 440's Carter carb through those now-functional parallel hood vents. *Mike Mueller*

A sport steering wheel, wrapped in simulated wood, cost $26.75 in 1969. The option code in this case was S81. *Mike Mueller*

Super Performance option save for the substitution of 3.54:1 gears and the deletion of front disc brakes. The Super Track Pack kept the discs and the 4.10:1 cogs. None of these axle options, except for the Performance Axle Package, could've been ordered along with air conditioning, as was the case with the Hemi V-8 and Air Grabber hood.

Hardtop and convertible renditions were once more offered for 1969. Domestic delivery totals were 14,048 for the former, 551 for the latter. The total Hemi hardtop count was 197: 98 four-speeds, 98 automatics. Another 11 Hemi GTX hardtops were sent to Canada. Hemi convertibles were rare birds indeed in 1969, with only 16 known: 5 four-speeds, 6 automatics, and 5 to Canada.

An under-dash knob opened the cable-operated Air Grabber plumbing for business. The N96 option cost $55.30 and also mandated the installation of the optional J25 three-speed windshield wipers. *Mike Mueller*

04

1970
GTX

Specifications	
Model availability	two-door hardtop
Wheelbase	116 inches
Length	204 inches
Width	76.4 inches
Height	not available
Weight	3,515 pounds
Base Price	$3,535
Track (front/rear, in inches)	59.7/59.2
Wheels	14×6 inches
Tires	F70×14 Red Streak
Construction	unitized body/frame
Suspension	independent A-arms with torsion bars, front; solid axle with longitudinal leaf springs, rear
Steering	recirculating ball
Brakes	four-wheel drums, standard; power front discs, optional
Engine	375-horsepower, 440-cubic-inch Super Commando V-8, standard; 426 Hemi and 440 Six Barrel V-8s, optional
Bore and stroke	4.32×3.75 inches
Compression	10.1:1
Fuel delivery	single Carter four-barrel carburetor
Transmission	Torqueflite automatic, four-speed manual, optional at no extra cost
Axle ratio	3.23:1 with Torqueflite; 3.54:1 in Dana rear end with four-speed
Production (including exports)	7,748

Only a hardtop GTX was offered for 1970, since the far less popular convertible rendition failed to carry over from 1969. Yet another B-body restyle helped the third-edition GTX, in many opinions, look its best yet. Note the new Air Grabber hood flap with its gnarly graphics. *Mike Mueller*

1970

Topless GTX models never did turn a lot of heads, and so it was understandable when Plymouth officials shelved the convertible rendition after 1969. But general popularity also continued to fall, undoubtedly thanks to the bite the Road Runner had been taking out of the division's performance pie since its 1968 introduction. The domestic count for the GTX hardtop in 1970 was a mere 7,141: 6,398 with the standard 375-horse 440 V-8, which this year experienced a slight compression drop to 9.7:1. Now fitted with civilized hydraulic lifters in place of the previously used solid tappets, the ever-present 425-horse Hemi was ordered only 71 times that year. New for 1970 was a third engine choice, Plymouth's 440 Six Barrel V-8, which had first appeared the previous year beneath the lift-off hoods of special Road Runner and Super Bee models. Six Barrel GTX production totaled 678.

Fed by three Holley two-barrel carburetors on a cast-iron intake, the 440-cubic-inch Six Barrel relied on 10.5:1 compression to make 390 horsepower. Inside was the same hydraulic cam used by the 375-horse 440. Cam specs were 276 degrees duration on intake, 292 on exhaust, and 54 degrees of overlap. Valves were the familiar 2.08-inch intakes, 1.74-inch exhausts. While the standard 440 used a single-breaker ignition, the triple-carb version shared the Hemi's dual-breaker distributor.

Base price for the 1970 GTX was $3,535. Production (exports included) was 7,748. Two optional engines were available: the ever-present Hemi and the 390-horse triple-carb 440. *Mike Mueller*

The Torqueflite automatic was again standard behind all three GTX engines, and a heavy-duty four-speed was once more a no-cost option. Like its 1969 forerunner, the 1970 GTX came standard with the battleship-tough Hemi suspension regardless of engine choice. This package included extra-heavy-duty everything: shocks, torsion bars, front stabilizer bar, and rear leaf springs. Those springs consisted of six leaves on the left side, five leaves plus two half-leaves on the right. The rear spring rate was 148 lbs/in, while the front rate was 124 lbs/in thanks to the addition of those thick 0.92-inch torsion bars. The stabilizer bar measured 0.94 inch in diameter.

Also behind all three engines were a 3.25-inch driveshaft (with heavy-duty U-joints) and a 9.75-inch Dana 60 heavy-duty rear end. The familiar 3.23:1 axle ratio remained standard in Torqueflite applications. A 3.54:1 Sure-Grip differential was included when a four-speed was bolted up. All the same optional axle packages offered for 1969 rolled over into 1970. The standard heavy-duty 11-inch drum brakes carried over too, as did optional power front discs.

While Plymouth's basic B-body shape continued into its third year for 1970, its sides were freshened up markedly with all sharp edges smoothed away and a simulated quarter-panel scoop added behind each door. More aggressive grille and taillight treatments appeared, while "GTX" badges showed up in all the familiar places.

The 1970 GTX hood reminded its driver what he was working with. The 375-horsepower 440 remained standard that year. *Mike Mueller*

Left:
A revised air cleaner appeared for the GTX's Air Grabber option in 1970. The 440 Super Commando V-8 experienced a slight compression drop (to 9.7:1) that year.
Mike Mueller

Below, left:
Air Grabber under-hood plumbing was noticeably simplified in 1970 thanks to the switch from two "scoops" to one central opening. And vacuum control replaced mechanical activation that year.
Mike Mueller

Below:
Chrysler Corporation's popular Rallye wheel debuted as a GTX option in 1970. Priced at $43.10, these rims were available in either 14- or 15-inch diameters. *Mike Mueller*

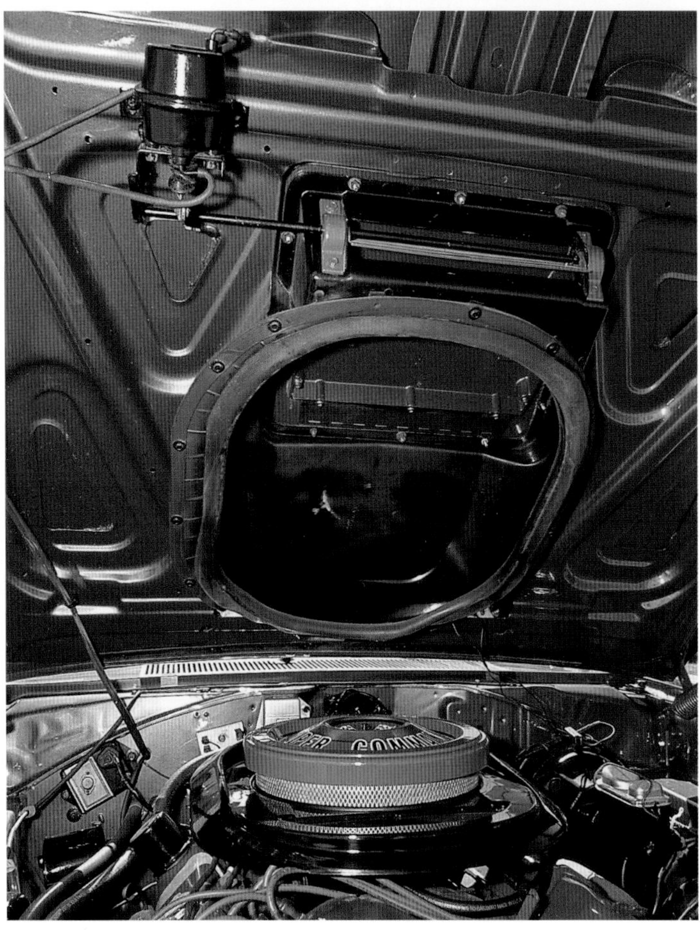

This 1970 GTX is one of only 71 fitted with the optional 426 Hemi. Another 678 featured the 440 Six Barrel V-8 that year. *Mike Mueller*

The N96 hood was included in the Hemi GTX deal in 1970; it was a $65.55 option atop the standard 440 that year. The 425-horsepower 426 was a $710.60 option for the 1970 GTX. *Mike Mueller*

Accenting the GTX image further was a body-side tape stripe that ran from the nose back into that simulated rear quarter scoop. These stripes were available in three colors: white, black, and gold. New, too, was a macho power-bulge hood that could've been optionally adorned in a revised blackout paint treatment, which this time consisted of a wide central stripe flanked by a pair of thin pinstripes, all running from grille to windshield.

The Air Grabber option was also revised. A witness barely noticed its presence until ambient atmosphere needed grabbing. By hitting a switch below the dash, a GTX driver forced open an unobtrusive panel cut into the hood's center bulge, opening the way for all those cooler, denser breezes to rush directly into the exposed air cleaner below. The Air Grabber scoop in 1970 also was adorned on each side with cartoonish artwork featuring a menacing, toothy mouth. The Air Grabber hood again was standard with the Hemi, optional for the two 440s.

Attractive Rallye wheels joined the GTX options list in 1970 and were offered in two sizes, 14.0×5.5 and 15.0×7.0. Big, fat F60 tires were available on those 15.0-inch Rallye rims.

Right:
The transmission count for Hemi GTX models in 1970 was 43 four-speeds (shown here), 29 automatics. *Mike Mueller*

Below, right:
The so-called "tick-tock-tach," a combination clock/tachometer, was a $68.45 GTX option in 1970. *Mike Mueller*

Below:
New for the 1970 GTX was the Rallye instrumentation layout that had been standard inside Dodge's Charger and Super Bee since 1968. The simulated wood-grain panel also was part of the Rallye deal. *Mike Mueller*

A large decal (in place of the previously used emblems) announced a 1971 GTX's presence from an aft perspective in 1971. *Mike Mueller*

1971
GTX

Specifications

Model availability	two-door hardtop
Wheelbase	115 inches
Length	203.2 inches
Width	79.1 inches
Height	53 inches
Weight	4,022 pounds
Base Price	$3,707
Track (front/rear, in inches)	60.1/62.0
Wheels	14×6 inches
Tires	G70×14
Construction	unitized body/frame
Suspension	independent A-arms with torsion bars, front; solid axle with longitudinal leaf springs, rear
Steering	recirculating ball
Brakes	four-wheel drums, standard; power front discs, optional
Engine	370-horsepower, 440-cubic-inch Super Commando V-8, standard; 426 Hemi and 440 Six Barrel V-8s, optional
Bore and stroke	4.32×3.75 inches
Compression	9.7:1
Fuel delivery	single Carter four-barrel carburetor
Transmission	Torqueflite automatic or four-speed manual
Axle ratio	3.23:1
Production (including exports)	2,942

1971

In Plymouth's own words, its radically restyled "fuselage" shell for its 1971 midsized models represented "the slickest new body shape this side of Modena." Taking the aircraft analogy further was a front bumper that wrapped completely around the grille, looking much like a jet engine nacelle in the process. This bumper was fully chromed in standard form but could've been optionally color-keyed to a particular exterior finish for a definitely dramatic effect.

Wilder than wild color choices—including the likes of Green Go, Lemon Twist, Tor-Red, Plum Crazy, and Citron Yella—added to the 1971 GTX's attraction, as did sporty options like a rear wing spoiler, backlight louvers, and high-profile striping that ran across the hood and down the fenders. And let's not forget that zany Air Grabber scoop with its gnarly grin.

The 1971 GTX's standard hood one once again used parallel vents that contained engine identification. Enlarged "GTX" badges returned in their same locations, and bucket seats reappeared as part of the basic deal, as did a beefed-up chassis and the good ol' choice between the Torqueflite and no-cost four-speed manual. Plymouth's Rallye instrument cluster was standard inside for 1971.

The engine trio offered for 1970 carried over with a few minor adjustments. The standard 440-cubic-inch V-8 was rated at 370 horsepower in 1971, while the renamed "440+6" dropped 5 horses to 385. No one dared touch the venerable Hemi's 425-horse advertised tag. GTX production for 1971 was only 2,703, with 30 of those featuring Hemi V-8s, 135 using triple-carb 440s. Both these gasoline-gulping legends were cancelled at year's end, signaling the end of an era as far as Plymouth's truly super supercars were concerned.

A radically restyled B-body shape appeared for 1971, as did a new platform rolling on a 115-inch wheelbase, down one click from 1970. Base price for the GTX hardtop that year was $3,707. *Mike Mueller*

The GTX legacy did manage to survive up through 1974, but it was basically in name alone. Road Runners built after 1971 with Plymouth's surviving 440 four-barrel V-8 were all dressed up with GTX identification. Production counts for this combo read 672 for 1972, 749 for 1973, and 386 for 1974.

Left:
The familiar 440 V-8 remained standard fare for 1971. *Mike Mueller*

Below:
The GTX's standard 440 Super Commando V-8 was detuned slightly to 370 horsepower in 1971. Domestic production of base 440 models that year was 2,538: 2,211 with Torqueflite automatics, 327 with four-speed manuals. *Mike Mueller*

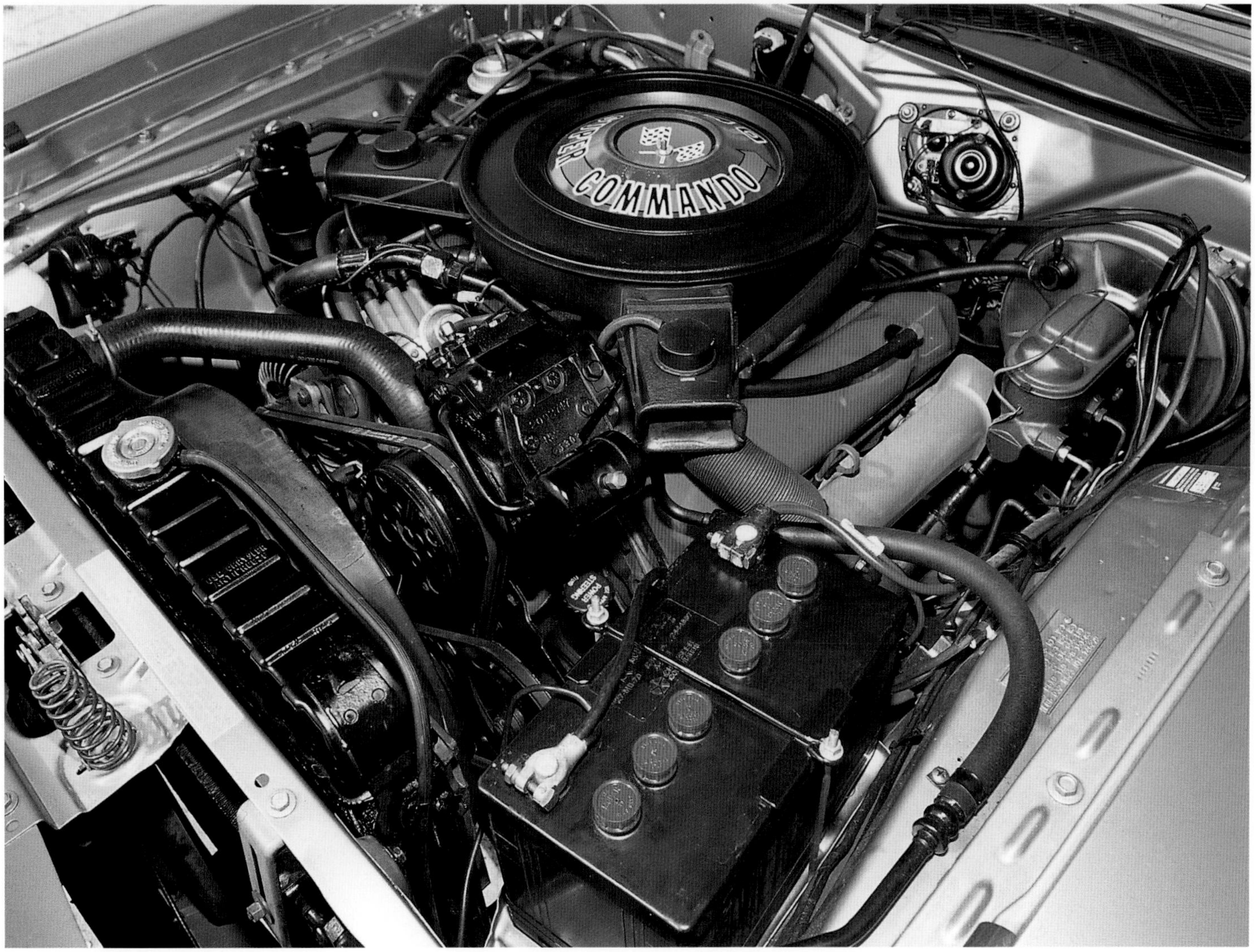

A radically restyled B-body shape appeared for 1971, as did a new platform rolling on a 115-inch wheelbase, down one click from 1970. Base price for the GTX hardtop that year was $3,707. *Mike Mueller*

Total GTX production, including exports, for 1971 was only 2,942. The domestic count was 2,703. *Mike Mueller*

Above, left:
The 1971 GTX's Air Grabber system employed the same eye-catching graphics used in 1970. *Mike Mueller*

Above:
The official name for the GTX's triple-carb RB big-block became "440+6" in 1971. Domestic production was 135: 73 with Torqueflites, 62 with four-speeds. *Mike Mueller*

Left:
The 440+6 also was downrated (to 385 horsepower) for 1971. Compression was 10.3:1. *Mike Mueller*

Left:
Air Grabber equipment rolled over basically unchanged from 1970. The price for the N96 package in 1971 was $68.90. *Mike Mueller*

Opposite, top:
Power steering was required whenever the diminutive Tuff steering wheel was installed in a 1971 GTX. The prices were $96.55 for the former, $20.10 for the latter. *Mike Mueller*

Opposite, below right:
Hurst's distinctive Pistol Grip shifter was included in all B-body four-speed installations beginning in 1970. The 1971 Pistol Grip, shown here, differed slightly in design compared to its forerunner. *Mike Mueller*

Opposite, below left:
Rallye instrumentation was again standard inside the GTX in 1971 and once more could've included the optional N85 clock/tachometer combination. *Mike Mueller*

40
50
60
70
TO REMOVE KEY

05

Dodge Dart & Demon 1967–1971

The A-Team

Okay, so maybe Chrysler's divisions didn't really have a direct response to Pontiac's popular GTO until 1967. But once Dodge's Coronet R/T and Plymouth's GTX arrived that year, things really got cooking. Within two years, another midsized performance Plymouth, Road Runner, was actually outselling GTO, and the success story didn't end there. By decade's end, Mopar muscle cars were seemingly everywhere in all sizes, colors, and flavors. Charger R/Ts, Super Bees and Birds, Barracudas in various forms and fashions, big-block Magnums and Super Commandos, small-block 340s—the choices were wide, to say the least.

Commonly lost in the shadows of all those bodacious B-bodies was Dodge's "A-team," yet another variation on the Mopar muscle theme. Offered in compact form from 1963 to 1976, the division's reasonably popular Dart shared Chrysler's A-body foundation with Plymouth's first- and second-generation Barracuda, and thus offered similar potential as far as performance enhancements were concerned. Bringing the Dart up to speed also may have been a somewhat slow process during the sixties, but once again the wait was more than worth it. In the end, Dodge buyers found themselves faced with one more group of factory hot rods to pick from. So many choices, so little garage space.

Dodge first used the name Dart, rather appropriately, for a futuristic show car unveiled in 1956. As its name implied, this long, low, four-wheeled spaceship pierced the air with ease, thanks to some pioneering wind tunnel work done in Europe. Reportedly, the four-passenger Dart encountered about a third of the aerodynamic drag produced by other supposedly sleek cars of the day. Other innovations included a large, heavily sloped windshield that wrapped around at the corners and at the top into a roof panel that could slide backward to allow open-air travel. Far out.

- Chrysler's A-body platform, born in 1960, served as a home for both Dodge's Dart and Plymouth's original Barracuda.
- The Dart name was first used for a show car in 1956.
- A B-body Dart was offered from 1960 to 1962.
- Dodge's new compact A-body Dart debuted for 1963.
- The sporty Dart GT stood as an individual model line, offered in hardtop and convertible forms with both six-cylinders and V-8s, from 1963 to 1969.
- All GTS models, offered in hardtop and convertible forms from midyear 1967 to 1969, were fitted with V-8s.
- The Dart's first optional big-block appeared midyear in 1967.
- Dodge teamed up with Hurst in 1968 to build a run of dragstrip-ready Hemi Darts.
- A 440-powered GTS was produced in 1969 only—all were hardtops.
- Dart Swinger 340s were offered domestically for 1969 and 1970 only.
- The Demon 340, built in 1971 and 1972, was basically repackaged as the Dart Sport 340 for 1973.

Opposite:
Dodge officials got things cooking in their A-body ranks midyear in 1967 by squeezing a big-block V-8 between Dart fenders for the first time. The resulting 383-horsepowered GTS was offered in hardtop and convertible forms. *Mike Mueller*

Chrysler Corporation first used the Dart name in 1956 for an innovative, wind-cheating show car. Pioneering wind tunnel testing helped produce the original Dart, at the time arguably the world's most aerodynamic passenger car. *Chrysler LLC Corporate Historical Collection*

The Dart badge came back down to earth in 1960, crowning Dodge's new downsized B-body platform, the division's first to feature thoroughly modern unitized body/frame construction. Two other new nameplates, Matador and Polara, also showed up that year on the company's full-sized line, which continued rolling on the same 122-inch wheelbase seen in 1959. Dart, meanwhile, used a 118-inch foundation and was segregated into three sub lines: Seneca, Pioneer, and Phoenix. More downsizing came in 1962 (wheelbase dropped to 116 inches), and the trio was renamed Dart, Dart 330, and Dart 440. More standard comfort and convenience features and extra trim were included as the base Dart evolved into the midlevel 330 then the top-shelf 440.

Less was the name of the game again in 1963 when an even smaller Dart appeared to supersede Dodge's first compact, Lancer, introduced for 1961. While the Lancer had relied on a definitely diminutive 106.5-inch wheelbase, the redesigned 1963 Dart's foundation measured 111.0 inches from hub to hub. Officials considered keeping the Lancer name for this slightly larger compact but in the end opted to bring the Dart moniker down to an all-new low. Relative affordability remained the main selling point for the Lancer's replacement, with base prices beginning at $1,983 for a two-door sedan.

All 1963 Darts, even the top-shelf GT, were powered by frugal six-cylinders; a plainly meek 101-horsepower, 170-cubic-inch slant-six in a standard model's case. The original GT package, available in two-door hardtop and convertible forms, also was all flash, no fire. Included were bucket seats, a padded dash, and fancy wheel covers. No meaty mechanicals were part of the deal.

Fortunately, optional V-8 power did appear for the Dart GT in 1964, though the only choice was a 273-cubic-inch LA small-block (topped by a two-barrel carburetor) rated rather tamely at 180 horsepower. Though it was a distant relative of the antiquated 318-cubic-inch A-engine, the 273 did represent real progress. New thin-wall casting techniques allowed the LA-series V-8 to do away with considerable unwanted weight, and this small-block family also quickly demonstrated a willingness to accept performance boosts—witness its evolution into the sizzling 340 in 1968.

Engineers, in the meantime, continued tinkering with the original LA V-8. Big news for 1965 involved the addition of a four-barrel carburetor and a compression boost from 8.8:1 to 10.5:1, upgrades that helped increase advertised output to 235 horsepower. Those ponies represented enough force to drive a 1965 Dart GT through the quarter in 16.4 seconds, not too bad for a former budget buggy that to this point had proved about as exciting as a visit from your mother-in-law.

This newfound performance, in turn, convinced product planners to pump up the GT image in 1966. Outward imagery was enhanced notably, and restyled buckets inside were complemented by an optional full-length console. A small die-cast floor plate (with a four-speed) and a mini-console of sorts (with an automatic) were the choices the year before. Max power for the 1966 GT still came from the four-barrel 273, again not a bad thing at all.

The Dart badge made it into regular production in 1960 on Dodge's new short-wheelbase B-body platform. Separated into three models (Seneca, Pioneer, and Phoenix), the first Dart featured a 118-inch stretch between front and rear hubs. Dodge's bigger B-bodies (Matador and Polara) rolled on a 112-inch wheelbase that year. *Chrysler LLC Corporate Historical Collection*

Dodge's truly compact A-body Dart debuted for 1963. Wheelbase in this case was 111 inches. The Dart flagship was the GT, which came standard with bucket seats. Dart GTs were offered as hardtops and convertibles. *Chrysler LLC Corporate Historical Collection*

Above:
Available V-8 power appeared for the Dart GT in 1964 in the form of the 180-horsepower, 273-cubic-inch LA-series small-block. *Chrysler LLC Corporate Historical Collection*

Below:
A crisp, clean restyle announced the Dart's arrival for 1967. The GT hardtop and convertible remained the hottest Darts available that year. Total GT domestic production (for both body styles) was 32,660. *Chrysler LLC Corporate Historical Collection*

Above:
Based, believe it or not, on the Dart, Dodge's Daroo I show car made the rotating stage rounds in 1968. Some resemblances appeared inside. *Chrysler LLC Corporate Historical Collection*

Left:
Dodge's Daroo II show car was powered by a 340-cubic-inch LA small-block. *Chrysler LLC Corporate Historical Collection*

1967
Dart GTS

Specifications	
Model availability	two-door hardtop and convertible
Wheelbase	111 inches
Length	195.4 inches
Width	69.7 inches
Height	52.9 inches
Weight	not available
Price	not available
Track (front/rear, in inches)	57.4/55.6
Wheels	14.0×5.5
Tires	F70×14 Red Streak Wide Tread
Construction	unitized body/frame
Suspension	independent A-arms with heavy-duty torsion bars, front; solid axle with longitudinal heavy-duty leaf springs, rear
Steering	recirculating ball
Brakes	front discs, rear drums
Engine	280-horsepower, 383-cubic-inch Magnum V-8
Bore and stroke	4.25×3.38 inches
Compression	10:1
Fuel delivery	single Carter four-barrel carburetor
Transmission	four-speed manual or Torqueflite automatic
Axle ratio	3.23:1
Production	457

Left:
Many sources still claim the first Dart GTS appeared in 1968. But that debut actually arrived, along with the model's first big-block power source, midyear in 1967. *Mike Mueller*

Below:
Mag-style wheel covers were seemingly all the rage around Detroit by 1967. Chevrolet had released a set for its first Chevelle SS 396 in 1965, and Dodge followed suit with a similar option for its A-, B-, and full-sized C-bodies two years later. *Mike Mueller*

1967

Dodge designers dressed up their A-body in neat new clothes for 1967 that helped make the latest Dart look a little larger, even though it was essentially the same size as its 1963–1966 forerunner. Notably freshened lines were crisp, clean, and uncluttered, and the GT hardtop and convertible were given higher profiles with more prominent identification. Next to no one could miss those major "GT" badges on the front fenders and in the grille this time around, nor could image-conscious customers resist Dodge's new mag-style wheel covers, an option that clearly copied a similar cap introduced by Chevrolet in 1965.

The 1967 Dart's restyled dash reminded many critics of the sporty layout found in that year's Charger. Bucket seats were standard inside the GT hardtop, optional in its convertible counterpart. Available for both at extra cost was a console that also could've included an optional tachometer. Still standard beneath the hood was that timid 170 slant-six, but few stuck with this meek mill. More than half of the 32,660 GTs built for 1967 were fitted with V-8s.

Only 457 big-block GTS Darts were built in hardtop and convertible forms for 1967. *Mike Mueller*

Also new in 1967 were two special handling packages. Front torsion bars and sway bar, ball joints, and rear springs all were beefed up when the Rallye suspension option was checked off. The Dart Rallye group added front disc brakes and D70x14 Red Streak tires on 5.5J rims along with those heavy-duty underpinnings. With these components present, a 1967 GT could handle the road relatively well even if it couldn't really pound it, at least not with the four-barrel 273 small-block. Fortunately, help in that department also arrived mid-year, thanks in part to a little inspiration supplied by Chicago speed merchant Norm Kraus.

Like their counterparts at Plymouth, Dodge engineers couldn't help but hear about General Motors' plans to offer optional big-block power for its new-for-1967 pony car, Chevrolet's Camaro and Pontiac's Firebird. Ford had a big-block Mustang in the works too, leaving the two Chrysler divisions little choice but to retaliate with comparable A-body models. Plymouth people somewhat amazingly managed to stuff a 383 into the 1967 Barracuda, but early experiments with a similar combo in Dodge ranks fell a bit short.

Enter Kraus and his team at Grand-Spaulding Dodge. They built a 383 Dart with nearly no sweat, drove it to Detroit, and showed it to Dodge division head Robert McCurry. Suitably impressed, McCurry suggested to his engineers that if the Grand-Spaulding guys could pull this one off, they could too. So they did, and thus the Dart GTS was born.

05

Right:
Exhaust restrictions translated into a slight power drop for the 325-horsepower, 383-cubic-inch big-block once it nestled into Dodge's A-body platform. Advertised output for the Dart GTS version was 280 horses. *Mike Mueller*

Below:
The transmission breakdown for the 383 GTS in 1967 read 229 four-speeds, 228 automatics. The sport steering wheel seen here, with its simulated wood rim, was an option. *Mike Mueller*

It was quiet delivery to say the least. Save for a low-profile black-and-white magazine ad, no official announcement came from Dodge concerning the midyear appearance of the company's first big-block A-body. Production reportedly began in February 1967, and only 457 were built in hardtop and convertible forms, explaining why all press reports seen 40 years back claimed that the 1968 GTS was the first of the breed. Similar claims continue to make it into print today.

Mating Chrysler's 383-cubic-inch B-series V-8 with Dodge's Dart resulted in a few compromises, one involving the dual exhaust system. Predictably tight confines excluded the free-flowing exhausts used on B-body Mopars in 1967, meaning a few horses were lost in translation due to the use of more restrictive plumbing. As it was in Barracuda applications, the 325-horse 383 was downrated to 280 horsepower for the GTS installation. Under-hood constraints also ruled out the inclusion of power steering, making the 383 GTS more or less a real man's machine.

On top of that big-block was a low-restriction air cleaner that, as ad copy explained, emitted "a low moan that your mother-in-law won't understand and your wife will eventually get used to." Included, as well, was the Rallye suspension package with its front discs and Red Streak rubber. Backing up the 383 was either a four-speed stick or the three-speed Torqueflite. Choices were split down the middle: 229 1967 GTS Darts featured the manual gearbox, 228 the automatic.

1968

GT hardtops and convertibles continued to rely on six-cylinder power in standard trim, but the GTS rolled on into its first full year on the market with eight cylinders or none at all. Two V-8s were available this time: the proven 383 big-block and the new 340-cubic-inch small-block, the latter created by stroking the good ol' 273 LA. Advertised output for the 340 was 275 horsepower, a figure few witnesses trusted. As a *Car and Driver* report explained, "we'd be the last to accuse anyone of underrating, but the underground isn't kidding when they say 340s shoot Darts down the road in a 350-hp fashion." Quarter-mile performance for the small-block GTS was 14.4 seconds at 99 miles per hour. Talk about hauling ass. But there still was no substitute for cubic inches in 1968, and few compacts of the day could kick ass like a 383-powered GTS.

New for the 1968 GTS was a sporty hood with parallel vented (simulated, of course) bulges facing each fender. The heavy-duty Rallye suspension was included, as were Dodge's new Scat Pack tail stripes, which could've been deleted on request. Also available was a longitudinal stripe treatment.

No stripes at all were available for easily the meanest, nastiest Darts yet, created in conjunction with Hurst in 1968. Like a similar run of Hurst-built Barracudas that year, these A-body Dodges were all finished in plain white primer, leaving buyers to add their own paint schemes, not to mention sponsorship decals. Super-stock drag racing was the sole goal in this case, as demonstrated by that big, bad

1968
Dart GTS

Specifications

Model availability	two-door hardtop and convertible
Wheelbase	111 inches
Length	195.4 inches
Width	69.7 inches
Height	52.9 inches
Weight	3,305 pounds
Base Price	$3,189 (with base 340-cubic-inch V-8)
Track (front/rear, in inches)	57.4/55.6
Wheels	14.0×5.5
Tires	D70×14 Red Streak Wide Tread
Construction	unitized body/frame
Suspension	independent A-arms with heavy-duty torsion bars, front; solid axle with longitudinal heavy-duty leaf springs, rear
Steering	recirculating ball
Brakes	four-wheel drums
Engine	275-horsepower, 340-cubic-inch V-8 (383-cubic-inch Magnum V-8 also available)
Bore and stroke	4.04×3.31 inches
Compression	10.5:1
Fuel delivery	single Carter four-barrel carburetor
Transmission	four-speed manual or Torqueflite automatic
Axle ratio	3.23:1
Production (including exports)	8,745 (8,020, domestic)

The GTS rolled over into 1968, again as a hardtop or convertible. A V-8 remained the only power source, and a buyer that year could've picked between the existing 383-cubic-inch R-series big-block or the new 340-cubic-inch LA small-block. *Chrysler LLC Corporate Historical Collection*

By far the hottest Dart ever built was the Hemi-powered super-stock rendition, created in 1968 with help from Hurst. Production was 80, all featuring fiberglass hoods and fenders, acid-dipped steel body parts, and Plexiglas windows. *Mike Mueller*

Chrysler's awesome race Hemi was last used in a factory super-stock application in 1968 when both Dodge and Plymouth offered Hurst-built A-body factory drag cars that year. Twin 650 cfm carbs on a magnesium cross-ram fed this beast. Compression was a molecule-mashing 12.5:1 *Mike Mueller*

race Hemi barely hiding beneath a gaping hood scoop. Output was announced as the same as the street Hemi, 425 horsepower, but one look at those twin 650 cfm four-barrels mounted diagonally on that magnesium cross-ram intake let everyone in on this joke. With crushing 12.5:1 compression, this emissions-illegal beast was by no means suited for the street. No way, no how.

Cramming the humongous Hemi into the space that was barely able to hold Chrysler's RB big-block was, as one might've expected, no easy task. Reworking the shock towers and relocating the brake master cylinder were required, and the battery was moved to the trunk, the latter representing an equally expected racer's trick that would've been done anyway to aid weight transfer during hard launches.

Additional weight adjustments included trading steel for fiberglass for the hood and front fenders, acid-dipping the bumpers and body panels to reduce their gauge, and removing the stock glass in favor of Plexiglas windows. Rear quarter windows were fixed, while operating the doors' Plexi pieces was left up to straps when the heavier regulators also were deleted. Same for amenities like heater, radio, back seat, sound deadener, and body insulation. Stock seating in front was dumped too, replaced by lighter, low-back buckets borrowed from Dodge's A-100 van.

Hooker headers with token mufflers were added at Hurst, as was one of the company's legendary shifters when a four-speed was installed. Automatic Hemi Darts also were built. Total production was 80. As for more important numbers, the Hemi S/S Dart was a 10-second screamer at the dragstrip. Awesome totally wasn't a big enough word.

Known for his trademark cigar, veteran Mopar man "Dandy" Dick Landy campaigned a Hemi Dart in 1968. Hemi Darts were 10-second screamers on the quarter-mile. Landy drove Dodges at the drags, with considerable factory support, from 1964 to 1981. *Chrysler LLC Corporate Historical Collection*

Dart GT hardtops and convertibles again came standard with six-cylinder power in 1969. Available V-8s included the 273- and 318-cubic-inch LA small-blocks. *Chrysler LLC Corporate Historical Collection*

1969
Dart Swinger 340

Specifications	
Model availability	two-door hardtop
Wheelbase	111 inches
Length	195.4 inches
Width	69.6 inches
Height	54.4 inches
Weight	3,310 pounds
Base Price	$2,857
Track (front/rear, in inches)	57.4/55.6
Wheels	14.0×5.5
Tires	D70×14 Red Streak Wide Tread
Construction	unitized body/frame
Suspension	independent A-arms with heavy-duty torsion bars, front; solid axle with longitudinal heavy-duty leaf springs, rear
Steering	recirculating ball
Brakes	four-wheel drums
Engine	275-horsepower, 340-cubic-inch V-8
Bore and stroke	4.04×3.31 inches
Compression	10.5:1
Fuel delivery	single Carter four-barrel carburetor
Transmission	four-speed manual with Hurst shifter
Axle ratio	3.23:1
Production	16,637

1969

Both the GT and GTS carried over into 1969, with either the 340 or 383 again available in the latter's case. Yet another performance choice, the Dart Swinger 340, also debuted that year as a cost-conscious alternative to the GTS in Dodge's Scat Pack pecking order. By cutting back here and there, product planners managed to put the Swinger 340's bottom line at about $2,850. Ads referred to it as "6,000 rpm for less than $3,000."

But where did they cut back? Along with the potent 340 small-block, the long list of standard stuff also included a Hurst-shifted four-speed, the heavy-duty Rallye suspension with its D70 wide treads, and a 3.23:1 rear axle. Both 3.55:1 and 3.91:1 ratios were available at no extra cost when the optional Sure-Grip differential was specified. The GTS hood was standard too, as was a three-spoke steering wheel (with padded hub) and the Scat Pack's ever-present bumblebee stripes around the tail.

Like the 340 GTS, the Swinger 340 seemed to violate physical laws, offering big-block-type performance in a comparatively nimble, easy-to-handle package. "The Swinger's secret was optimum power," claimed a *Car Life* review. "Just what the chassis was capable of handling and no more. The 340 is another of those 'naturals' like the small-block Chevy that breathes and revs well. Most of its power is spread over the upper rpm ranges. This keeps traction-busting torque from overpowering the chassis and blowing a drag run or landing the driver in trouble in a curve."

Car Life's road-testers managed a 14.8-second quarter-mile pass at the wheel of a 1969 Swinger 340, leading the magazine's editors to name this hot little A-body their "Best Compact" that year. "To us, the current crop of compacts offer little of what they are supposed to, anyway. They are not small, they are not economical and they are not very much fun to drive. The Swinger has performance and is fun to drive—a lot more performance and fun than some of the intended performance and fun cars."

05

Above:
As was the case with all Scat Pack cars in 1969, deleting the Dart GTS's bumblebee stripes in back was a customer prerogative. *Mike Mueller*

Above, right:
Base price for a GTS hardtop in 1969 was $3,226. Production (including exports) was 6,285. Domestic deliveries totaled 5,557. Of these, 1,912 had the optional 383 Magnum big-block V-8. *Mike Mueller*

Inset:
The production count for GTS hardtop 340 small-block installations in 1969 was 3,645. Of these, 2,623 were backed by Torqueflite automatics, and 1,022 featured four-speed manuals. *Mike Mueller*

Far right:
A three-spoke steering wheel, again featuring a fake wood rim, was a $32 option in 1969. The Torqueflite automatic was standard for the GTS that year. *Mike Mueller*

Right:
A revised mag-style wheel cover option appeared for the Dart GTS in 1969. *Mike Mueller*

Above:
As you might've guessed, the car's full name was "GT Sport," as this 1969 convertible's tail attests. One of the Scat Pack's three founding members (along with the Charger R/T and Coronet R/T), the Dart GTS of course featured those requisite bumblebee stripes out back. *Mike Mueller*

Left:
A basic GTS convertible cost $3,419 in 1969. Total production was 417, with 345 delivered domestically. Of those 345, 272 had the 340 small-block, and 73 featured the optional 383 Magnum. *Mike Mueller*

Ads referred to the 1969 Swinger 340 as "6,000 rpm for less than $3,000." Base price was $2,836. A heavy-duty suspension was standard, along with the 275-horsepower 340. *Mike Mueller*

Scat Pack stripes were part of the Swinger 340 deal too, as were D70x14 Red Streak tires. A 3.23:1 axle was standard; 3.55:1 and 3.91:1 gears were optional. *Mike Mueller*

The proven 340 LA small-block continued kicking tail and taking names in 1969. Compression was 10.5:1. Every 340 installed from 1968 to 1973 featured a four-barrel carb and dual exhausts. *Mike Mueller*

The division's supreme A-body for 1969 was again created with help from Hurst and, again, Mr. Norm. Along with their 383 swaps, the Grand-Spaulding group also had been toying with 440-equipped Darts dating back to late 1967. Once again, if this A-body combo worked for Plymouth, why not give Dodge customers a similar taste? Kraus' men again did a "prototype," and Chrysler took it from there.

Fitting the 440 into the Dart GTS engine bay required modifying the K-member below, fabricating a motor mount for the driver side, and using the 383 A-body's special left-hand exhaust manifold. A power brake booster—and thus front disc brakes as well—again was out of the question.

Hurst Performance Research in Ferndale, Michigan, handled the "440 Engine Conversion," listed under option code A13 in Dodge paperwork. Hurst took delivery of 1969 Darts equipped with 383 big-blocks, Torqueflite transmissions, and Sure-Grip rear ends, and traded the B engine for the 375-horse RB. Sure-Grip ratios were either 3.55:1 or 3.91:1. A heavy-duty suspension, 14.0x5.5 wheels wearing E70 Red Streak tires, bucket seats, and a console were included too.

The sum of these parts? Differing only a bit compared to Dodge's "factory" GTS 440s, Mr. Norm's 440-equipped "GSS" was capable of breaking into the 12s on the quarter-mile. As many as 640 440 GTS Darts were built.

Dart Swinger 340 domestic production for 1969 was 16,637, with 8,834 of those featuring four-speeds, 7,803 automatics. The GTS count was 5,557 hardtops, 345 convertibles. The engine breakdown for hardtops was 3,645 340 small-blocks, 1,912 383 big-blocks; 272 340s and 73 383s for the rarely seen convertibles.

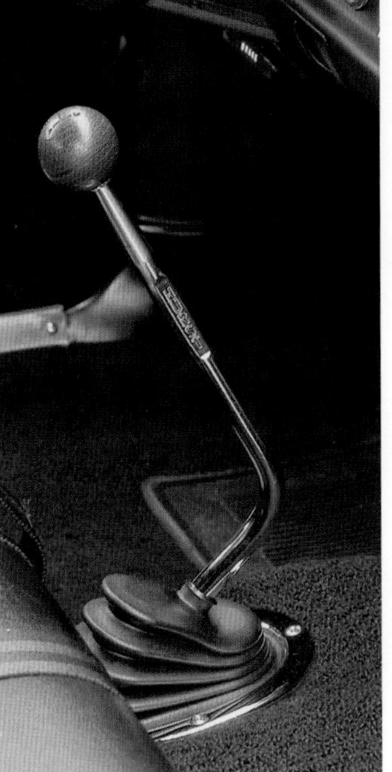

Above:
A Hurst-shifted four-speed manual transmission was standard for Dodge's original Swinger 340. *Mike Mueller*

Left:
A standard front bench helped keep the Swinger 340's bottom line down, just as Dodge people planned. *Mike Mueller*

Above:
Dodge teamed up with Hurst again in 1969 to offer another big-block Dart, this one far better suited for everyday operation compared to the Hemi S/S cars created the year before. In this case, the weapon of choice was Chrysler's 375-horsepower, 440-cubic-inch RB big-block. The option code for the 440 engine conversion was "A13." *Mike Mueller*

Above, right:
At least 640 A13 Darts were built for 1969, all of them hardtops. *Mike Mueller*

Right:
All 440-powered Dart GTS hardtops were built with Torqueflite automatics in 1969. Bucket seats and a console were included too. *Mike Mueller*

1970

The Dart Swinger 340 became even more affordable for 1970 after nearly $200 was cut off the bottom line, thanks primarily to a decision to substitute a mundane three-speed manual for 1969's standard Hurst-shifted four-speed. At least the second-edition Swinger 340 was the only member of the 1970 Scat Pack to offer standard front disc brakes.

Most other standard pieces rolled over from 1969, including those take-'em-or-leave-'em bumblebee stripes out back. Up front was a new hood that incorporated non-functional scoops copped from the Super Bee's optional Ramcharger induction system. Popular options included Rallye wheels, bucket seats, hood pins, and a blacked-out hood.

The GT and GTS models didn't carry over into 1970, nor did any optional big-blocks, by way of Hurst or otherwise. Forget the 440, even the much more palatable 383 was no longer a viable choice for A-body installations considering what insurance companies were by this time charging, by the pound, to cover such high-powered, lightweight muscle machines. For now, all Dodge's eggs went into the Swinger 340's basket.

Domestic deliveries of 1970 Swinger 340s numbered 10,382, with the total (counting exports) being 13,781. Transmission breakdowns for the former figure were 955 base three-speeds, 4,423 four-speeds, and 5,004 automatics.

1970
Dart Swinger 340

Specifications	
Model availability	two-door hardtop
Wheelbase	111 inches
Length	196.2 inches
Width	69.7 inches
Height	53 inches
Weight	3,175 pounds
Base Price	$2,808
Track (front/rear, in inches)	57.4/55.6
Wheels	14.0×5.5
Tires	E70×14
Construction	unitized body/frame
Suspension	independent A-arms with heavy-duty torsion bars, front; solid axle with longitudinal heavy-duty leaf springs, rear
Steering	recirculating ball
Brakes	front discs, rear drums
Engine	275-horsepower, 340-cubic-inch V-8
Bore and stroke	4.04×3.31 inches
Compression	10.5:1
Fuel delivery	single Carter four-barrel carburetor
Transmission	three-speed manual
Axle ratio	3.23:1
Production (including exports)	13,781 (10,382, domestic)

Along with the Torqueflite-backed 440, the A13 package also included a heavy-duty suspension, E70 tires, and a Sure-Grip differential with either 3.55:1 or 3.91:1 gears. *Mike Mueller*

The affordable, yet still sexy, Swinger 340 returned for 1970, this time with a standard three-speed stick to cut costs even further. Base price was $2,808. Still standard were those 275 ponies, supplied again by one of Detroit's hottest small-block V-8s of the day. *Chrysler LLC Corporate Historical Collection*

1971
Demon 340

Specifications	
Model availability	two-door hardtop
Wheelbase	108 inches
Length	192.5 inches
Width	not available
Height	not available
Weight	3,165 pounds
Base Price	$2,721
Track (front/rear, in inches)	not available
Wheels	14.0×5.5
Tires	E70×14
Construction	unitized body/frame
Suspension	independent A-arms with heavy-duty torsion bars, front; solid axle with longitudinal heavy-duty leaf springs, rear
Steering	recirculating ball
Brakes	four-wheel drums
Engine	275-horsepower, 340-cubic-inch V-8
Bore and stroke	4.04×3.31 inches
Compression	10.5:1
Fuel delivery	single Carter four-barrel carburetor
Transmission	three-speed manual
Axle ratio	3.23:1
Production (including exports)	10,089 (7,981, domestic)

Dodge followed Plymouth's lead in 1971 after the latter division had introduced its A-body Duster 340 the previous year. Dodge's knock-off was the Demon 340, introduced in nearly identical fashion right down to its 275-horse heart. *Mike Mueller*

As Major League Baseball people in Florida apparently discovered, naming anything after something found in hell isn't exactly a good idea. Just as the American League champ Tampa Bay Devil Rays simply became the Rays in 2008, Dodge's devilish little muscle car didn't run around long adorned with this imagery once right-thinking Americans took notice. Damn straight; the Demon 340 was offered only for 1971 and 1972. *Mike Mueller*

1971 Demon 340

Although a handful of Swinger 340s reportedly were built for Canadian consumption in 1971, the Dart's high-performance career had ended in this country the previous year. But that's not to say that Dodge didn't offer a hot A-body after 1970. Once Plymouth people proved just how far your bucks could go when shopping for compact Mopar muscle, the Dodge Boys just couldn't resist copying their plan. Hence, following in the 1970 Duster 340's tire tracks was the similarly attired Demon 340. The two shared the same basic fastback body shell, with expectedly differing nose and tail treatments setting the 1971 Demon 340 apart from its Plymouth cousin.

The recipe for success, however, was all but identical. For something like $2,700, a Dodge customer got the still-strong 275-horse 340, a heavy-duty three-speed manual transmission, 3.23:1 gears, the Rallye suspension, 10-inch drum brakes, and E70 wide treads on 14.0×5.5K rims. Inside was a 150-miles-per-hour speedometer, just to remind you where your money was going most.

While compression was falling in all the cars around it, Dodge's 340 LA small-block remained a mean machine in 1971 at 275 horsepower. *Mike Mueller*

If more cash was at hand, a Demon 340 buyer could've added a heavy-duty four-speed (with perhaps a Pistol Grip shifter) or the Torqueflite automatic, a Sure-Grip differential, twin hood scoops, a blacked-out hood, hood pins, a rear spoiler, bucket seats, a console, a Tuff steering wheel, and a 6,000 rpm tach. Even without any options, this devilish Plymouth could run from rest to 60 miles per hour in 6.5 seconds. A quarter-mile went by in 14.5 seconds.

The total Demon 340 domestic tally for 1971 was 7,981, with 998 featuring the standard three-speed manual, 2,051 getting an optional four-speed, and 4,932 coming equipped with the Torqueflite. Including exports, the total count was 10,089.

Dodge offered another Demon 340 in 1972 before deciding to drop the name, not the car. More than one uptight, right-thinking individual had complained about the use of such evil imagery, convincing promotional people to rethink this package. The same basic model itself then returned for 1973 and 1974 bearing the name Dart Sport 340. Total 1972 Demon 340 production, domestic and export, was 10,222, with 8,773 finding homes in this country.

Right:
Base price for the Demon 340 in 1971 was $2,721. Included in this price was a three-speed manual transmission and Dodge's beefed Rallye suspension. *Mike Mueller*

Below, right:
Of the 7,981 Demon 340s delivered domestically in 1971, 998 featured the base three-speed manual transmission. Another 2,051 were fitted with the optional four-speed, and 4,932 had the Torqueflite automatic. *Mike Mueller*

Below:
This heavily loaded 1971 Demon 340 features bucket seats, a sport steering wheel, and a Hurst-shifted four-speed. Also notice the optional cassette tape player/recorder with microphone mounted below the dash in front of the shifter. *Mike Mueller*

Giving in to outside pressure from good folk who couldn't warm up to Dodge's devilish name choice, company officials opted to drop the Demon image after 1972, replacing it with the "Dart Sport 340" moniker. At least the 240-horsepower, 340-cubic-inch V-8 remained standard. *Chrysler LLC Corporate Historical Collection*

06

Dodge Coronet R/T 1967–1970

The Big Bore Hunter

- The first of Dodge's long-running "road and track" legacy, the 1967 Coronet R/T was followed by the Charger R/T in 1968 and the Challenger R/T in 1970.
- One 1967 magazine ad curiously used the term "road runner" in reference to Dodge's new Coronet R/T.
- The upscale Coronet 500 was used as a base for the R/T models.
- Both hardtop and convertible renditions were offered during the short (1967–1970) Coronet R/T run.
- Only two Engines were installed in the Coronet R/T from 1967 to 1969: the standard 440 Magnum or the optional 426 Hemi.
- Magazine ads called the 1968 Coronet R/T "The Silken Snarl."
- A third available Engine, the 390-horse 440 Six Pack, appeared for the 1970 Coronet R/T.

As hot as Dodge's sleek Charger looked in 1966, it still didn't qualify as a direct response to all the Pontiac GTOs and Chevy SS 396s seen smoking up Main Street U.S.A. that year, and even quick-thinking product planner Burt Bouwkamp wasn't ashamed to admit it. After all, the initial plan was to let the Charger compete in Detroit's newly formed specialty car field, not necessarily go nose-to-nose with the likes of Motown's latest, greatest midsized muscle cars. According to Bouwkamp, T-birds and Rivieras were the true targeted rivals, not Goats and Super Sports. Of course a Charger customer could've shelled out considerable cash for optional Hemi power, instantly transforming Dodge's Coronet-based fastback into a real boulevard brute able to beat up on any other big-block on the block. But so few buyers did dig that deep, meaning most first-generation Chargers rolled off the line as mild-mannered daily drivers.

Dropping the 425-horse 426 into Dodge's garden-variety B-body in 1966 also instantly created a monster, but the story in this case remained the same: way too expensive, hence few-and-far-between. Various curbside kibitzers additionally were quick to point out the same way-too-plain reality inherent in Plymouth's Hemi Belvederes and Satellites that year. After testing a 425-horse 1966 Coronet, *Hot Rod* magazine's Eric Dahlquist explained that "people said the Hemi package wasn't distinctive enough, lacked uniqueness, needed a hood scoop; in short, it had to look as fast as it went."

Plymouth people solved their identity crisis with the nicely distinctive GTX, introduced for 1967. Not to be left behind, the Dodge guys tried a similar tack, using the same 375-horse RB-series big-block delivered in base GTX models. Once fitted with a 440 Magnum V-8 and a similarly beefed up foundation as standard equipment, the GTX's corporate cousin needed only a neato name to complete the deal.

Opposite:
Magazine ads called Dodge's original Coronet R/T "The Big Bore Hunter" due to its 440 standard cubes, at that time the most in the muscle car field. Its unique grille was similar to the Charger's except that the headlights did not hide away. *Mike Mueller*

Above:
Dodge product planners based the 1967 R/T on their Coronet 500 model, the division's B-body flagship. Bucket seats were standard inside the 1967 Coronet 500. Note the optional Hemi installed in this hardtop. *Chrysler LLC Corporate Historical Collection*

Opposite:
Early magazine ads in 1967 defined the "R/T" reference for Dodge customers, but also notice the reference that would bring Plymouth buyers running in to their local dealerships the following year. *Chrysler LLC Corporate Historical Collection*

Bouwkamp reportedly handled that task, coming up with "R/T," predictably short for "road and track." Ad guys then took it from there, announcing that the new Coronet R/T was a "dual purpose machine" that was as "sweet as can be on the road. . . . Hot as you want it on the track."

Being based on the Coronet 500, the decked-out flagship in Dodge's B-body lineup, the R/T models (both hardtop and convertible were offered) came standard with sporty bucket seats inside. The Torqueflite automatic transmission also was standard but could've been replaced at no extra cost by a preferred four-speed stick. A heavy-duty Sure-Grip differential (with 3.54:1 gears) was a mandatory option when the manual gearbox was added.

On the outside, the 1967 Coronet R/T was set apart from the B-body pack with prominent badges on all four sides, simulated hood louvers, and a Charger-style grille that featured fixed headlamps instead of hideaway units. Body-side paint stripes were included too, but they could've been deleted on request. Six stripe colors were offered: white, black, dark red metallic, dark blue metallic, light tan metallic, and medium copper metallic.

Dodge dealerships let loose only 10,109 Coronet R/Ts in 1967, compared to the nearly 82,000 Goats that squealed off Pontiac lots that year. Stark statistics, however, didn't necessarily tell the whole story, at least not as far as Eric Dahlquist was concerned. As he concluded in his February 1967 *Hot Rod* review of Dodge's new factory hot rod, "perhaps the R/T's mystique can be understood by the comments of a young parking attendant at the Century Plaza Hotel, where the to-and-from lot route represents a combination of Nurburgring and the Pikes Peak Hillclimb: 'Hey, I like this better than my GTO.' That's got to be the endorsement of the year."

1967
Coronet R/T

Specifications	
Model availability	two-door hardtop, two-door convertible
Wheelbase	117 inches
Length	203 inches
Width	75.3 inches
Height	53.9 inches, hardtop
Weight	3,565 pounds (hardtop); 3,640 pounds (convertible)
Base Price	$3,199 (hardtop); $3,438 (convertible)
Track (front/rear, in inches)	59.5/58.5
Wheels	14.0×5.5 stamped-steel
Tires	7.75×14.00 Red Streak
Construction	unitized body/frame
Suspension	long-arm/short-arm with heavy-duty longitudinal torsion bars and sway bar in front; longitudinal heavy-duty leaf springs in back.
Steering	recirculating ball
Brakes	four-wheel drums, standard; front discs, optional
Engine	375-horsepower, 440-cubic-inch 440 Magnum V-8 (426 Hemi, optional)
Bore and stroke	4.32×3.75 inches
Compression	10:1
Fuel delivery	single Carter four-barrel carburetor
Transmission	Torqueflite automatic, standard; four-speed manual, optional at no extra cost
Axle ratio	3.23:1
Production	10,109 (hardtops and convertibles)

1967

"Hunting for trophy-winning performance that handles beautifully on the road?" asked Dodge ads in 1967. "Check the odds. They're 440 to 1 in favor of the Coronet R/T . . . a balanced automobile engineered for the enthusiast." Along with its standard 440 Magnum, the 1967 Coronet R/T also rolled off the truck with high-performance Red Streak tires and a heavy-duty suspension that included stiffened shocks and a thickened (0.94-inch) sway bar up front. Torsion bars at the nose were toughened too, as were the rear leaf springs, which featured an extra leaf on the right to help handle the Magnum's 480 lbs-ft of torque. Standard at the corners were 3-inch-wide drum brakes, which could've been improved upon by ordering optional front discs.

Popular options included a console, a console-mounted tachometer, a three-spoke fake-wood steering wheel, mag-type wheel covers or five-spoke road wheels, a vinyl roof, and power assists for brakes, steering, and windows. Less popular but still prominent was the ever-present 426 Hemi, priced at $564. Additional mandatory equipment once again nearly doubled the Hemi option's asking price.

The base sticker for a topless Coronet R/T in 1967 read $3,438. Priced at a relatively tidy $3,199, a box-stock 1967 Coronet R/T hardtop represented, in *Super Stock* magazine's words, "one of the best all-around performance packages being offered, [featuring] as much or more performance per dollar than any other car currently available." As for more important numbers, a Coronet R/T coupe could toast the quarter-mile in 14.91 seconds at 93.16 miles per hour, according to *Hot Rod*. Zero to 60 miles per hour required a mere 6.30 seconds.

An optional Hemi installation, of course, promised even more intimidating numbers along with its wallet-wilting bottom line. The choice was yours. "If you like to play it safe and economical, the Magnum's your baby with its friendly price tag and full 5/50

Above:
Base price for a 1967 Coronet R/T hardtop was $3,199. Included in that deal were requisite heavy-duty underpinnings. Standard brakes were hefty drums. *Mike Mueller*

Inset:
Designers apparently didn't want bystanders to miss a new Coronet R/T in 1967. Rear quarter-panel badges were large, to say the least. *Mike Mueller*

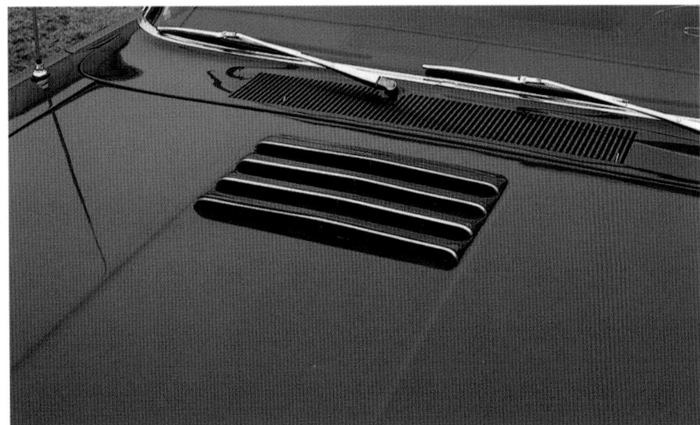

Simulated hood louvers were standard for the 1967 Coronet R/T. *Mike Mueller*

"R/T" identification also appeared on the tail near the passenger-side taillight. *Mike Mueller*

Above, left:
The 1967 Coronet R/T shared its standard power source with Plymouth's equally new GTX. Like Plymouth's Super Commando big-block, Dodge's 440 Magnum produced 375 horses. *Mike Mueller*

Above:
Installing an optional tachometer in a 1967 Coronet R/T meant the customer also had to shell out extra for the console, which served as a mounting place for the $48.70 rev counter, as was the case inside Plymouth's 1967 GTX. *Mike Mueller*

Left:
Bucket seats were included as part of the original Coronet R/T package, but the console was a $52.85 option. The four-speed manual transmission seen here was a no-cost option. The Torqueflite automatic was standard. *Mike Mueller*

Door panels also were adorned with special identification in 1967. *Mike Mueller*

Red Streak tires on conventional 14-inch rims were standard for the 1967 Coronet R/T. A set of five-spoke road wheels cost $97.30. *Mike Mueller*

Dodge's first B-body R/T was available in two body styles, one with a top, the other without. Base price for the convertible model was $3,438 in 1967. *Chrysler LLC Corporate Historical Collection*

warranty," wrote *Motor Trend*'s John Etheridge. "On the other hand, if you're the type that likes to live a little, be the envy of every service station attendant, attract admirers of both sexes when you show up at the local drive-in, and have roughly $600 extra to invest; go ahead and get the Hemi. The warranty is limited, but the dividends are high and paid promptly."

Only 283 Hemi Coronet R/T hardtops and convertibles were built for 1967. The count for the base 440 Magnum models (again for both body styles) was 9,826. Transmission breakdowns amounted to 162 automatics, 121 four-speeds for the Hemi; 8,471 automatics, 1,355 manuals for the 440.

1968

A nicely priced, relatively prestigious performance package, the Coronet R/T still failed to bring horsepower hounds running into Dodge dealerships during its short, still exciting career. Those 10,000 or so coupes and convertibles built for 1967 were followed by 10,491 more domestically delivered examples (the total count, exports included, was 10,849) the second time around. Any chance at increasing these numbers was effectively squelched by the decision to add a fourth member to Dodge's newborn Scat Pack midway through the 1968 model run.

Introduced in February 1968, Dodge's new Super Bee also was based on the Coronet, though on the mundane coupe rendition instead of the stylish pillar-less hardtop. Relying on that simpler foundation, and powered by a standard 383 Magnum instead of the bigger, pricier 440, the Super Bee offered even more performance per dollar than its B-body running mate, and thus helped knock the knees out from under the more expensive Coronet R/T. The R/T's total annual count dwindled markedly each year from there.

Base prices in 1968 were $3,353 for the R/T coupe, $3,613 for its convertible counterpart. Other numbers rose that year too, after Dodge designers subjected their B-body platform to a noticeable makeover. Still rolling on a 117-inch wheelbase, the 1968 Coronet, at 208 inches, measured some five inches more as far as overall length was concerned, and a lowered stance and lessened girth only enhanced nose-to-tail impressions even further. Leading the way for new crisper, cleaner lines was a full-width egg-crate grille that again housed quad headlights. Another full-width panel in back served a similar function for the taillights.

Exterior enhancements for the second-edition Coronet R/T included an aggressive bulging hood that did nothing but look mean. No functional scooping was available. Both ends were treated to blacked-out touches and those now-familiar, still-large "R/T" badges. Similar badging again appeared on the body sides, only this time it was relocated from the rear quarters to the front fenders. Buyers also were presented with a choice between typical side striping or "bumblebee stripes" around the tail, the latter serving to announce Scat Pack membership. A 150-miles-per-hour speedometer and bucket seats again were standard inside, and the former could've been further complemented with optional color-keyed head restraints, which could've been added to the rear seats as well.

All mechanicals basically rolled over, with the standard 440 Magnum and optional Hemi again representing the only choices beneath that bulging hood. As expected, the rare Hemi obviously offered more potential, but not all witnesses were convinced that it was the best choice.

1968 Coronet R/T

Specifications	
Model availability	two-door hardtop, two-door convertible
Wheelbase	117 inches
Length	206.6 inches
Width	76.7 inches
Height	52.5 inches, convertible
Weight	3,845 pounds (convertible)
Base Price	$3,353 (hardtop); $3,613 (convertible)
Track (front/rear, in inches)	59.5/59.2
Wheels	14.0×5.5 stamped-steel
Tires	F70×14 Goodyear WideTread Red Streak
Construction	unitized body/frame
Suspension	long-arm/short-arm with longitudinal heavy-duty torsion bars and sway bar in front; longitudinal heavy-duty leaf springs in back.
Steering	recirculating ball
Brakes	four-wheel drums, standard; front discs, optional
Engine	375-horsepower, 440-cubic-inch 440 Magnum V-8 (426 Hemi, optional)
Bore and stroke	4.32×3.75 inches
Compression	10:1
Fuel delivery	single Carter four-barrel carburetor
Transmission	Torqueflite automatic, standard; four-speed manual, optional at no extra cost
Axle ratio	3.23:1
Production (domestic)	9,963 hardtops; 528 convertibles (10,280 hardtops, 569 convertibles, including exports)

After testing the three 1968 Scat Pack players (340 Dart GTS, 440 Coronet R/T convertible, and Hemi Charger R/T), *Car Life*'s critics came away touting the wedge over the Hemi, which in their humble opinion required too much fine-tuning to perform at its expected best. With no careful handling at all, they concluded, the 440-powered drop-top Coronet "ran like the Hemi should have."

"The old saw about no substitute for cubic inches certainly fits the 440 Magnum," continued *Car Life*'s report. "Acceleration is very rapid, yet the engine never seems to be laboring. The 440's brute torque makes high revving completely unnecessary. Shift points up to 5500 rpm were tried, but 4000 rpm gave the best performance." Quarter-mile time was 14.69 seconds at 97.4 miles per hour. Only 6.60 clicks were needed to run from 0 to 60 miles per hour.

Both hardtop and convertible Coronet R/T renditions returned for 1968, but the 1967 sheet metal didn't. At 208 inches, Dodge's latest B-body shell was some 5 inches longer than its predecessor. *Chrysler LLC Corporate Historical Collection*

Total production for Dodge's Coronet R/T hardtop in 1969 was 6,755, with 6,448 of those delivered domestically. Base price for the hardtop R/T rendition was $3,425. *Chrysler LLC Corporate Historical Collection*

Production breakdowns for 1968 (for domestic deliveries) were 9,963 hardtops and a mere 528 convertibles. The Hemi count was 219 hardtops and only 9 convertibles. Of the latter, 8 had automatic transmissions, and 1 featured the no-cost four-speed. The tallies for the base 440 Magnum was 9,734 hardtops, 519 convertibles. Of the hardtops, 7,751 had automatics, and 1,983 had four-speeds. The 440 Magnum convertible totals read 431 automatics, 88 four-speeds.

Base price for a Coronet R/T convertible in 1969 was $3,643. Total production that year, including exports, was 483. The domestic count was 426, of which 416 featured the standard 440 Magnum V-8. *Mike Mueller*

1969
Coronet R/T

Specifications	
Model availability	two-door hardtop, two-door convertible
Wheelbase	117 inches
Length	206.6 inches
Width	76.7 inches
Height	53 inches, hardtop
Weight	3,601 pounds (hardtop), 3,721 pounds (convertible)
Base Price	$3,442 (hardtop); $3,660 (convertible)
Track (front/rear, in inches)	59.5/59.2
Wheels	14.0×5.5 stamped-steel
Tires	F70×14 Goodyear WideTread Red Streak
Construction	unitized body/frame
Suspension	long-arm/short-arm with longitudinal heavy-duty torsion bars and sway bar in front; heavy-duty longitudinal leaf springs in back.
Steering	recirculating ball
Brakes	four-wheel drums, standard; front discs, optional
Engine	375-horsepower, 440-cubic-inch 440 Magnum V-8 (426 Hemi, optional)
Bore and stroke	4.32×3.75 inches
Compression	10:1
Fuel delivery	single Carter four-barrel carburetor
Transmission	Torqueflite automatic, standard; four-speed manual, optional at no extra cost
Axle ratio	3.23:1
Production (domestic)	6,448 hardtops; 426 convertibles (6,755 hardtops, 483 convertibles, including exports)

1969

Total domestic deliveries of Coronet R/Ts, hardtops and convertibles, fell to 6,874 in 1969, while Super Bee production soared to nearly 26,000, proving perhaps that many stoplight challengers were no longer so willing to put so much money where their mouths were. Of that shrinking total, 6,448 were R/T hardtops, and 426 were convertibles.

Standard equipment once more carried over essentially unchanged, as did the basic Coronet body shell. A new grille up front announced the 1969 model's arrival, and revamped taillights also appeared. In the latter's case, layouts varied, since the base Coronet featured a pair of long, thin lamps reminiscent of that year's Charger's, while the R/T was adorned with what looked like three lenses at the tail. In truth, the unit in the middle was actually a reflector patterned after the taillights located on each side of it.

R/T exterior identification was updated slightly as the front fender badges disappeared in favor of incorporating the name within the bumblebee stripe in back. If the Scat Pack striping was deleted, per a customer's prerogative, appropriate badges were added to the quarter panels. A new option for 1969, simulated air scoops also could've been added to the rear quarters just behind the doors.

A second new option enhanced the 1969 R/T's image up front and also improved performance. Called the "Ramcharger" hood, this fully functional bonnet was easily identified by the two scoops perched atop it in place of that standard, totally useless "power bulge." Beneath those twin scoops on the hood's underside was a fiberglass plenum that sealed directly to a special oval air-cleaner housing. This plumbing allowed the standard 440 Magnum or optional Hemi to suck in

Dodge's 1969 Coronet R/T was given a different taillight treatment compared to that year's garden-variety Coronet, which featured one long, thin lens at each rear corner. The R/T tail incorporated a third "lens" in the middle that actually was a reflector. *Mike Mueller*

Only two engines were installed in the Coronet R/T during its first three years on the market: the standard 440 Magnum or optional 426 Hemi. The Ramcharger hood, with its two functional scoops, was standard with the Hemi, optional atop the 440 in 1969. *Mike Mueller*

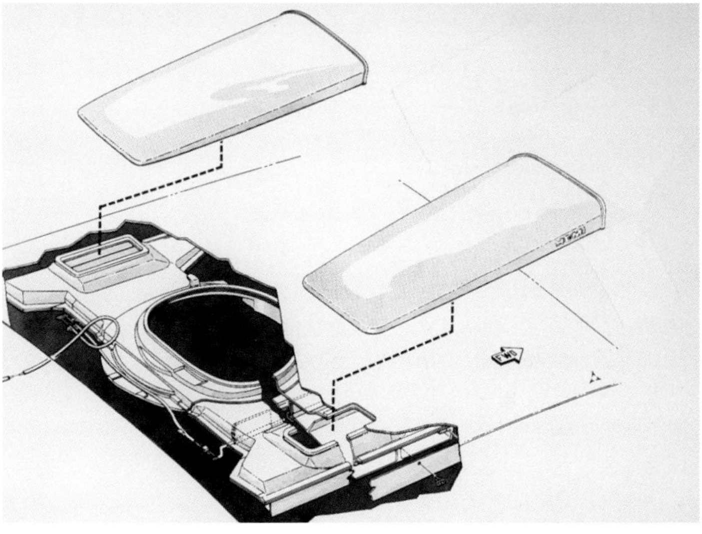

New for 1969 was Dodge's Ramcharger hood option. The N96 Ramcharger lid incorporated a pair of fully functional scoops in place of that symbolic bulge seen on standard Coronet R/T hoods since 1968. Ductwork below was opened and closed mechanically by a cable-operated switch. *Chrysler LLC Corporate Historical Collection*

cooler, denser outside atmosphere whenever the hammer went down, but only after the driver pulled an under-dash knob marked "carb air" that opened those scoops for business. Either engine drew in heated under-hood air during warm-up and typical operation. Included as part of the Hemi package, the Ramcharger hood was a $73.30 option atop the 440 Magnum.

Various aggressive gear ratios also appeared for the 1969 Coronet R/T, as well as its Super Bee cousin, and this equipment was specially grouped with other hot parts to further sweeten the pot. First came the A31 High Performance Axle Package, an option for the Super Bee's 383 Magnum V-8 only. Included were 3.91:1 gears in an 8.75-inch Sure-Grip differential, the heavy-duty Hemi suspension, and "Maximum Cooling" equipment that, among other things, added a seven-blade torque-drive fan.

Next up was the A32 Super Performance Axle Package, available with the 426 Hemi and 440 Magnum V-8s mated to automatic transmissions only. The A32 option was the same as A31 save for the addition of power front disc brakes and the substitution of 4.10:1 gears in a beefy 9.75-inch Dana 60 axle.

Above, left:
Simulated scoops became available for Coronet R/T quarter panels in 1969. These scoops simply bolted in place atop the similarly simulated air vents found on Coronet rear quarters in 1968 and 1969. This option, coded M46, cost $35.80.
Mike Mueller

Above:
Those Scat Pack bumblebee stripes again wrapped around a standard Coronet R/T's tail in 1969 and also could've been deleted by customer request. As in 1968, the stripes came in three colors: red, black, and white.
Mike Mueller

Left:
Adding the Ramcharger hood didn't change the standard 440's advertised output rating in 1969. It remained at 375 horsepower. Notice the air cleaner seal that mated up to the N96 option's under-hood ductwork.
Mike Mueller

The A33 option was offered for Hemis and Magnums with four-speeds and was known as the Track Pack. The Track Pack deal was similar to the A32 package but didn't include power front discs and featured a 3.54:1 ratio instead of the stump-pulling 4.10:1 gears. Another four-speed-friendly option, A34, did include everything from A32 and was called the Super Track Pack. None of these packages—A31, A32, A33, or A34—was compatible with air conditioning.

More civilized was the A36 Performance Axle Package, which was similar to the A31 deal except for 3.55:1 gears in place of the 3.91:1 ratio. A36 was available behind the A-body's 340 small-block V-8, the Super Bee's 383 Magnum (with four-speed or automatics), and Hemi and 440 Magnum big-blocks with automatic transmissions only.

Engine counts for 1969 hardtops were 6,351 440s, 97 Hemis. Of the Hemis, 39 had automatic transmissions, 58 had four-speeds. The 440 Magnum breakdown was 4,810 automatics, 1,541 four-speeds. The convertible numbers were 416 440s, 10 Hemis, with that latter total consisting of 6 automatics, 4 four-speeds. Backing up the 440 Magnums in topless applications were 317 automatics, 99 convertibles.

Right:
A rather mundane three-spoke steering wheel (with a partial horn ring) was standard inside the 1969 Coronet R/T. A deluxe wheel (with full horn ring) and sport unit (with a simulated wood rim) were optional. *Mike Mueller*

The 1969 R/T's standard instrumentation included a 150-miles-per-hour speedometer. The optional 8,000 rpm tachometer, coded N85, shared its location with the optional clock—you could've ordered one or the other, not both. *Mike Mueller*

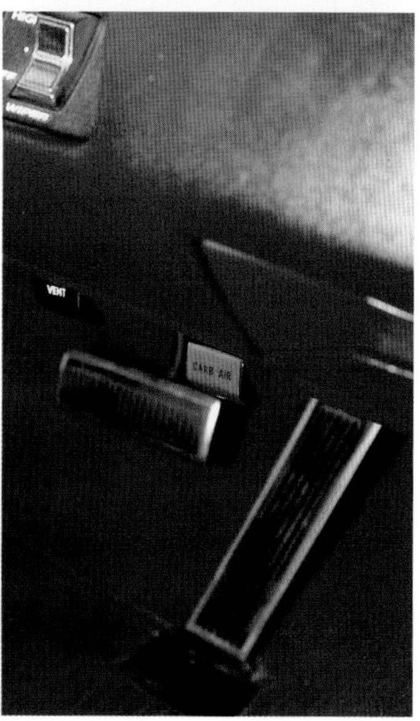

As was the case with the Plymouth Air Grabber system, Dodge's Ramcharger hood (priced at $73.30) was activated by an under-dash knob. *Mike Mueller*

A distinctive split bumper/grille arrangement marked the latest, greatest Coronet R/T's arrival in 1970. New that year was a second optional big-block, the 390-horsepower, 440-cubic-inch Six Pack. *Mike Mueller*

1970
Coronet R/T

Specifications	
Model availability	two-door hardtop, two-door convertible
Wheelbase	117 inches
Length	209.7 inches
Width	76.7 inches
Height	53 inches, hardtop
Weight	3,573 pounds (hardtop), 3,638 pounds (convertible)
Base Price	$3,569 (hardtop); $3,785 (convertible)
Track (front/rear, in inches)	59.7/59.2
Wheels	14.0×5.5 stamped-steel
Tires	F70×14 Goodyear WideTread Red Streak
Construction	unitized body/frame
Suspension	long-arm/short-arm with longitudinal heavy-duty torsion bars and sway bar in front; heavy-duty longitudinal leaf springs in back.
Steering	recirculating ball
Brakes	four-wheel drums, standard; front discs, optional
Engine	375-horsepower, 440-cubic-inch 440 Magnum V-8 (426 Hemi and 390-horsepower 440 Six Pack V-8s, optional)
Bore and stroke	4.32×3.75 inches
Compression	9.7:1
Fuel delivery	single Carter four-barrel carburetor
Transmission	Torqueflite automatic, standard; four-speed manual, optional at no extra cost
Axle ratio	3.23:1
Production (domestic)	2,155 hardtops; 236 convertibles (2,319 hardtops, 296 convertibles, including exports)

1970

Basically nothing changed beneath the skin during the Coronet R/T's short, happy life, which came to an end in 1970—the last year Dodge offered a two-door Coronet. But new on the outside for the breed's final run was a markedly refreshed B-body shell capped up front by a split grille/bumper layout that turned heads with ease. Behind that fully refreshed face on the R/T was a restyled power bulge hood that this time incorporated two large, still non-functional openings.

An "R/T" badge appeared between those twin grilles up front, and another graced the center of the blacked-out rear panel. Body-side "R/T" badges this time were located on simulated scoops in all instances when these pieces became standard features in 1970. The familiar Scat Pack bumblebee striping again brought up the rear, as did new taillights segmented into three sections on each side. The Super Bee taillight for 1970 once more was less ornate to help denote its lower place in the Coronet series pecking order.

The optional Ramcharger hood carried over into 1970 and again traded the familiar power bulge for two fully functional scoops. New for 1970 was a third optional engine, the 390-horsepower, 440-cubic-inch Six Pack, priced at $119.50. Only 210 Six Pack Coronet R/Ts were built for 1970; 194 hardtops, 16 convertibles. Of the latter, 9 featured Torqueflite automatics, 7 four-speeds. The breakdown for the hardtops was 97 automatics, 97 four-speeds.

Above:
Total Coronet R/T production for 1970 was 2,319, including exports. The domestic count was 2,155, 1,948 of which featured the standard 440 Magnum V-8. *Mike Mueller*

Right:
The groovy Pistol Grip shifter, supplied by Hurst, was standard on all four-speed B-bodies beginning in 1970. The transmission breakdown for the base Coronet R/T hardtop's domestic count that year was 1,543 with the Torqueflite automatic, 405 with the four-speed. *Mike Mueller*

The Hemi tally for the last Coronet R/T was 13 hardtops and a mere 1 convertible, which was fitted with a Torqueflite. Of the hardtops, 9 had automatics, 4 four-speeds. The count for base 440 Magnum hardtops in 1970 was 1,948, with 1,543 of these featuring automatics, 405 four-speeds. The 219 Magnum convertibles that year consisted of 203 automatics and 16 four-speeds.

Right:
The total production count for Dodge's 1970 Coronet R/T convertible was 296, with 236 of those finding homes in the United States. Base price was $3,785. *Chrysler LLC Corporate Historical Collection*

Fake quarter-panel air scoops became standard Coronet R/T features in 1970 and this time incorporated one large opening in place of the two seen the previous year. *Mike Mueller*

A revised 440 Magnum air cleaner appeared for the Ramcharger option in 1970. Again, the Ramcharger hood, with its twin functioning scoops, was included whenever the optional Hemi was installed that year. *Mike Mueller*

07

Plymouth Road Runner 1968–1974

Beep-beep, Beep-beep

- All early Road Runners were pillared coupes with flip-out rear quarter glass; a classier hardtop rendition with roll-up rear windows appeared in January 1968.
- Only two V-8s were available in 1968, the standard 335-horsepower 383 and the optional 426 Hemi.
- Plymouth's second-edition Road Runner took home *Motor Trend*'s coveted Car of the Year trophy in 1969.
- Road Runner became Detroit's second-best-selling muscle car in 1969.
- A Road Runner convertible was offered for 1969 and 1970 only.
- The stripped-down, dragstrip-ready 440 Six Barrel Road Runner was a one-hit wonder, built only for 1969.
- Road Runner knock-offs introduced for 1969 included Ford's Fairlane Cobra, Pontiac's GTO Judge, and a post-sedan rendition of Chevrolet's SS 396 Chevelle.
- Road Runners equipped with the optional 440 big-block were tagged with GTX identification from 1972 to 1974.

Opposite:
Plymouth's Road Runner was among Detroit's most popular muscle cars from 1968 to 1974. The 1969 edition (in front) was the industry's second-best-selling performance machine that year. And the 1973 Road Runner (rear) was still no slouch. *Mike Mueller*

The basic plan looked so damned simple when those excitable guys at Pontiac first started stuffing big, bad V-8s into not-so-big, not-so-expensive midsized bodies in 1964. A car as quick as the GTO, or as cool, had never before come this cheap, nor had truly hot horsepower ever been this easy to handle. Hence, the so-called "Goat" sold like those proverbial hotcakes. Furthermore, other automakers just couldn't resist copying the highly profitable idea, with General Motors' own divisions initially doing the bulk of the replication. Oldsmobile's 4-4-2 followed later in 1964, as did Buick's Gran Sport and Chevrolet's SS 396 Chevelle in 1965.

But how soon they forget. Pontiac's original budget-conscious ideal quickly gave way to price hikes as competitive pressures came into play. Sure, performance models weren't exactly collecting dust in showrooms during the sixties. By 1967, however, more and more were turning into rich boys' toys as rivals around Detroit typically fell all over themselves trying to one-up each other. A prime example of just how far a company was willing to go to beat another off the line was Chrysler's Hemi-powered B-body, which offered arguably the industry's biggest bang but for equally loud bucks.

Fortunately, for Average Joey and his buddies, Plymouth people had an even better idea. According to product planner Joe Sturm, the light bulb first went on after he received a phone call from Plymouth's sales division early in 1967. As he explained it during a Society of Automotive Engineers presentation in September 1969, the sales guy had a simple request: "Why not offer a car that has the biggest engine we make as standard equipment; a car that has no rear seats, no floor mats and eliminates every piece of trim and ornamentation?" Sturm bounced this one off fellow planners Jack Smith and Gordon Cherry, and all

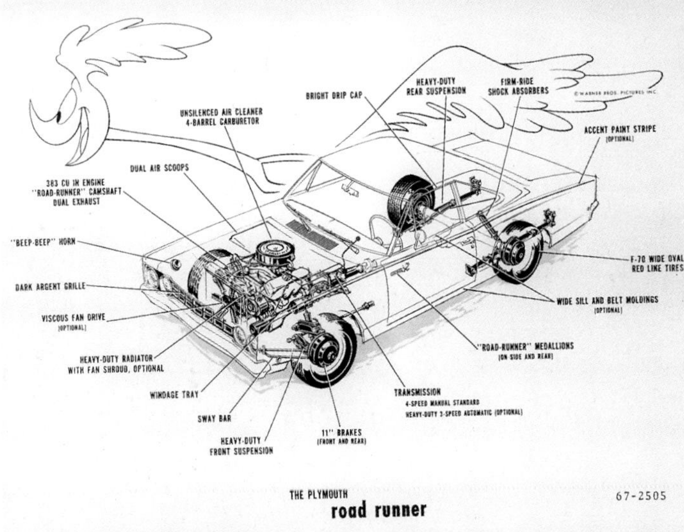

Road Runner designers kept frills to a minimum to help keep the bottom line low. Offering the biggest bang for the buck was the main focus. *Chrysler LLC Corporate Historical Collection*

agreed that such a stripped-to-the-bone machine would never fly—but something considerably less extreme might.

First came some rather serious market research. One study identified five potential target markets, with the most prominent of these including professional racing's top drivers. "While this group is small," said Sturm, "they exert the greatest degree of influence on [all other groups]. Their opinions and actions serve to direct and mold the desires and attitudes of the balance of the enthusiast market."

Next in order of size was the amateur-yet-still-serious racing fraternity, made up of buyers who prioritized real performance over pizzazz. Even larger was the third group, consisting of enthusiasts who may or may not have raced part-time. These fellows generally preferred a car able to run well on the street as well as the strip, and they also valued appearances more than members of the second class. Sturm called those in the fourth category "executive hot rodders" because they really liked hot-looking performance cars and could afford to pay for them.

The fifth group, the so-called "drive-in set," was by far the largest and was home to customers who loved muscle cars but had the least to spend. Due to its sheer size, this club was responsible for many more Plymouth purchases than the four others, leaving Sturm and his team no choice but to focus their efforts here.

Additional market research dealt with possible parameters. "In order to determine what performance level was necessary for this proposed car and what price tag [it] could support, the existing offerings of that time were reviewed in detail," added Sturm. One meaningful reality was instantly discovered: Detroit was offering many factory hot rods in 1967 priced above $3,300 that could run 100 miles per hour in the quarter-mile. Not one so-called performance car costing less, on the other hand, could score triple digits at the end of 1,320 feet. Thus came Plymouth's goal: build a $3,000 car able to do 100 miles per hour at the strip.

"To accomplish this, it was necessary to eliminate some of the more costly appointments that characterized the earlier kinds of super cars," continued Sturm. "The expense of the extra brightwork and high interior trim level was converted to the performance engine and chassis hardware." Mechanicals became the main focus; everything else was simply secondary, as *Car and Driver*'s critics explained while reviewing the concept in 1969:

"If you like the taste of whisky you drink it on the rocks, right? Distilled. There's nothing very complicated about that. But what do you do if you really like the taste of automobiles? We'll tell you what. You order your car with every go, stop, and turn part available, nothing else. No candy coating to kill the flavor because the flavor is the thing. And you haven't pushed the price out of sight with tack-ons, which only serve to confuse the issue anyway. You've got yourself an Econo-Racer and it's sano."

Plymouth people kept the price down on their groundbreaking Econo-Racer by first basing it on a bare-bones Belvedere coupe that featured flip-out rear windows instead of roll-up units. Appointments inside were as plain-Jane as a taxi cab, save for that tall, shiny floor shifter. Per performance demands, a four-speed manual gearbox was standard—no wimpy, column-shifted three-speed would do. As for seating, a mundane bench was standard too, and no pricey buckets were available optionally. Included on the outside were low-buck "dog-dish" hubcaps.

Bottom-line-busting image-conscious frills were left to the other guys, since a blacked-out grille, a hood conveniently borrowed from the upscale GTX, and a few decals made up the bulk of the car's exterior identification. But, though understated, the overall image was hard to miss, thanks to the subject of those small stick-on labels. "Road Runner" was this car's name, catching wily Goats was its game.

Many monikers were considered, but it was timing more than anything that helped make the final decision. According to Sturm, "the name Road Runner had shown up on lists off and on for a couple of years, but apparently neither the product was right, nor had the correct 'sell' job been done to get it considered." Sturm then determined the speedy bird's moment had finally arrived after Smith and Cherry sent him home to watch Saturday morning cartoons.

"We were amazed to find that we could put a hold on the name Road Runner for a car," he said in 1969. "That started the process which eventually led to the Plymouth Division adopting the name for the new car. Subsequently, [an] agreement was reached with Warner

All Road Runners initially were coupes with flip-out rear quarter windows. An upscale hardtop, with typical roll-up glass, appeared in January 1968. Total hardtop production for 1968 was 15,359, with 15,334 of those delivered domestically. *Chrysler LLC Corporate Historical Collection*

Brothers to use their copyrighted cartoon character instead of our own, which we had under development."

Along with their gregarious cartoon character, Warner Brothers also licensed Plymouth to re-create the Road Runner's iconic "beep-beep" sound, achieved by adding a special horn modified with copper windings instead of the aluminum strands normally used. Comedic value also carried over into advertisements, which referred to this new automotive species by its reputed Latin name, "acceleratii rapidus maximus."

Ad copy claimed the 1968 Road Runner was the "private property of the young and aware, priced right." At $2,896, the base model easily ranked among Detroit's biggest bangs for the buck at the time, a plain fact that couldn't be missed by almost anyone with eyes.

"Plymouth figures, and rightly so, that one way to win you over this year is to give you lots of car for your money," began *Car Life*'s conclusion. "In the case of the Road Runner, Plymouth's idea is to give lots of *performance* for the money, and it does this partly by putting gobs of go-goodies into the car, partly by not charging tremendous amounts for it, and partly by keeping things simple." Calling the new Road Runner "the world's fastest club coupe," *Car and Driver* pointed out that "this is the first car since the GTO to be aimed directly at American youth and it very probably is dead on target. But just wait till ol' Nader hears about it."

Luckily, for Plymouth bean counters, young Americans got wind of the Road Runner before consumer advocate and all-around killjoy Ralph Nader could spoil things. Demand for Plymouth's muscle-car-for-the-masses quickly skyrocketed, with 1968's total domestic run surpassing 44,300. Sales for 1969 then went beyond 80,000, making the second-edition Road Runner Detroit's second-best-selling high-performance model behind the market segment's new leader, the Chevelle SS 396 from Chevrolet. The former leader of the pack, the GTO, fell to third that year, surely leaving Pontiac people wondering what had just hit them.

No, it wasn't an ACME anvil.

1968
Road Runner

Specifications	
Model availability	two-door coupe and hardtop
Wheelbase	116 inches
Length	202.7 inches
Width	76.4 inches
Height	53.1 inches
Weight	3,405 pounds (coupe), 3,400 pounds (hardtop)
Base Price	$2,896 (coupe), $3,034 (hardtop)
Track (front/rear, in inches)	59.5/59.2
Wheels	14.0×5.5 (15-inch rims with Hemi option)
Tires	F70×14 Wide Tread
Construction	unitized body/frame
Suspension	independent A-arms with heavy-duty torsion bars, front; solid axle with longitudinal heavy-duty leaf springs, rear
Steering	recirculating ball
Brakes	four-wheel drums
Engine	335-horsepower, 383-cubic-inch V-8, standard (426 Hemi, optional)
Bore and stroke	4.25×3.38 inches
Compression	10:1
Fuel delivery	single Carter four-barrel carburetor
Transmission	four-speed manual
Axle ratio	3.23:1
Production (including exports)	29,240 coupes, 15,359 hardtops

Only two engines were available in the 1968 Road Runner: the standard 335-horsepower 383 R-series big-block and the optional 426 Hemi. Hemi coupe production that year was 840. *Mike Mueller*

1968

The original Road Runner coupe was joined in January 1968 by a comparatively upscale hardtop rendition that featured roll-up rear windows. Base price for this "pillar-less" model was $3,034. Domestic production for the hardtop was 15,359, compared to 28,978 for the original coupe.

Standard mechanicals in both cases included a beefed suspension accompanied by warmly welcomed F70 wide-tread tires wrapped around conventional steel rims measuring 14 inches in diameter. Full wheel covers, done in "deluxe" style or simulated-mag "sport" form, were optional, as were Chrysler's attractive five-spoke road wheels, which also stood 14 inches tall. Heavy-duty 11-inch drum brakes were standard, while a front disc brake option, with mandatory power assist, cost $72.95. Image-conscious customers additionally could've accented those two parallel hood bulges with a blacked-out paint patch, a popular $17.55 addition.

Beneath that bonnet was the star of the show, a big-block V-8 that represented a clever combination of passenger-car power source and hot-off-the shelf hardware. Plymouth engineers began with Chrysler's yeoman 383-cubic-inch B-series big-block, then added the cylinder heads, intake manifold, cam, and windage tray belonging to the 375-horsepower, 440-cubic-inch RB V-8 introduced along with the GTX in 1967. On top went a large Carter four-barrel sucking air in through an unsilenced air cleaner, and low-restriction dual exhausts went on at the other end of the process. The sum of these parts amounted to 335 rather cheaply corralled horses, just what the original budget-conscious plan required.

The standard gear ratio was 3.23:1. Various ratios were predictably optional, as was a preferred Sure-Grip differential. Chrysler's ever-present, bullet-proof Torqueflite automatic was a $38.95 option, and the High Performance Axle Package cost $87.50. Included in the

A blacked-out grille was standard for the Road Runner from the get-go, as was the GTX's hood with its twin simulated vents. *Mike Mueller*

A deluxe steering wheel with partial horn ring also was included in the Decor Group deal in 1968. *Mike Mueller*

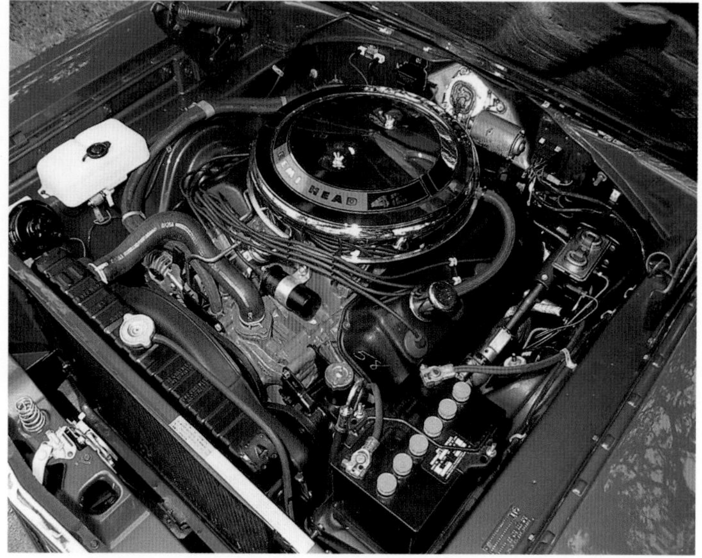

The Hemi V-8 alone cost an extra $714.30 in 1968. Additional mandatory equipment hiked up a Hemi-powered Road Runner's price even higher that year. Notice the horn (located near the wiper fluid reservoir on the passenger-side inner fender), which was done in basic black paint in 1968. *Mike Mueller*

Coupe production (exports included) for 1968 was 29,240. The domestic count was 28,978. The bright trim on this Hemi coupe's tail was included as part of the Decor Group option. *Mike Mueller*

Along with a bright trim accent in back, 1968 Road Runners fitted with the Decor Group package also were treated to stainless-steel trim on each window pillar. *Mike Mueller*

latter deal was a heavy-duty 3.55:1 Sure-Grip rear end, a slip-drive fan with shroud, and a wider heavy-duty radiator.

The only optional power source was the 426 Hemi, which was updated enough for 1968 to earn the designation "Stage II." A slightly hotter cam and recalibrated carburetors made up the main modifications, while compression, at 10.25:1, carried over from 1967, as did that familiar 425-horsepower output tag. Both transmissions, Torqueflite and four-speed, were beefed up extra tough-like when bolted up behind the Hemi.

The Hemi was a $714.30 option for the 1968 Road Runner, but boosting the bottom line didn't stop there when the 425-horse 426 was specified. Mandatory, at least for four-speed cars (it was optional with automatics), was the super-heavy-duty Dana 60 rear axle with Sure-Grip differential and 3.54:1 gears, a package priced at $139. All Hemi Road Runners also featured their own special "K-member" subframe and extra-heavy-duty suspension, improved cooling, and big 15-inch wheels and tires.

Though it clearly defeated Plymouth's original cost-conscious purpose, Hemi power transformed a plain-Jane Road Runner into one of Detroit's meanest, nastiest muscle cars in 1968. Quarter-mile passes in the low-13-second range were no problem, inspiring *Motor Trend*'s Eric Dahlquist to claim later that this machine represented "probably the fastest production sedan made today."

Domestic Hemi production was 840 coupes, 169 hardtops. Another 20 Hemi coupes and 6 Hemi hardtops went to Canada. Transmission breakdowns for the coupes read 449 four-speeds, 391 Torqueflites; 108 four-speeds and 61 automatics for the hardtops.

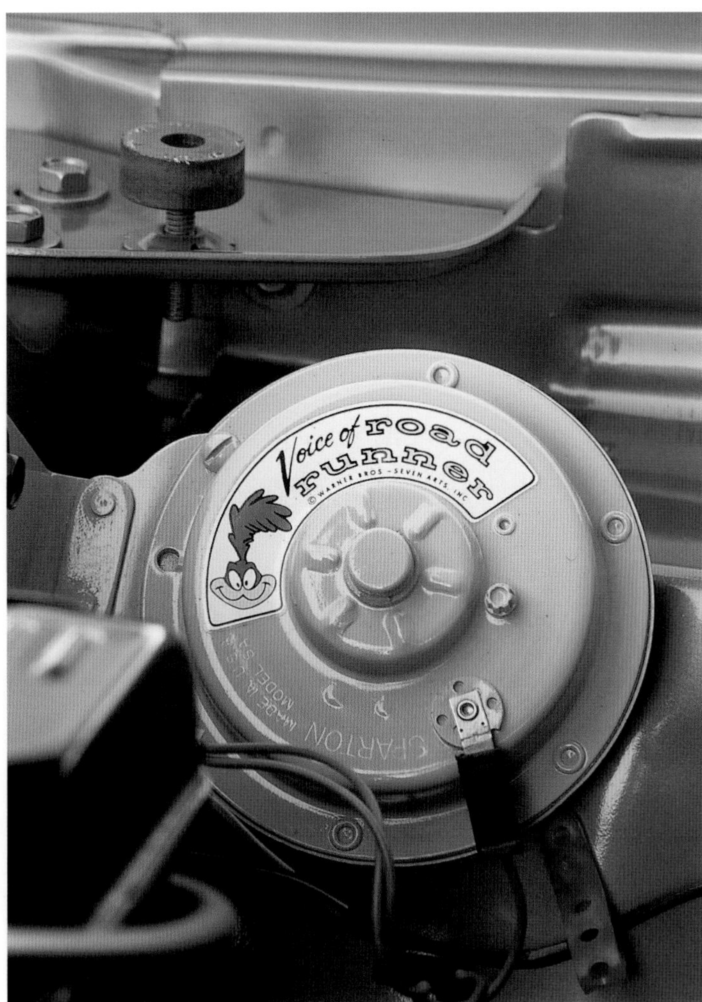

The Road Runner's cute "beep-beep" horn was treated to a special decal and eye-catching purple paint in 1969. *Mike Mueller*

1969
Road Runner

Specifications	
Model availability	two-door coupe, hardtop, and convertible
Wheelbase	116 inches
Length	202.7 inches
Width	76.4 inches
Height	53.1 inches
Weight	3,435 pounds (coupe), 3,450 pounds (hardtop), 3,790 pounds (convertible)
Base Price	$2,945 (coupe), $3,083 (hardtop), $3,313 (convertible)
Track (front/rear, in inches)	59.5/59.2
Wheels	14.0×5.5 (15-inch rims with Hemi option)
Tires	F70×14 WideTread
Construction	unitized body/frame
Suspension	independent A-arms with heavy-duty torsion bars, front; solid axle with longitudinal heavy-duty leaf springs, rear
Steering	recirculating ball
Brakes	four-wheel drums
Engine	335-horsepower, 383-cubic-inch V-8, standard (426 Hemi, optional)
Bore and stroke	4.25×3.38 inches
Compression	10:1
Fuel delivery	single Carter four-barrel carburetor
Transmission	four-speed manual
Axle ratio	3.23:1
Production (including exports)	33,743 coupes, 48,549 hardtops, 2,128 convertibles

1969

A convertible joined the Road Runner lineup in 1969, just in time to help Plymouth's Econo-Racer soar to all-time heights. Total domestic production for all three body styles reached 81,125 (export deliveries bumped that figure up to 84,420), putting Plymouth's high-flying B-body second only to Chevy's Chevelle SS 396 in Detroit's high-performance sales race by only a couple grand. The market segment's former leader, Pontiac's GTO, fell to third, more than 10,000 units behind the Road Runner.

Customers weren't the only ones impressed. *Motor Trend* staffers picked the 1969 Road Runner as their annual Car of the Year, a somewhat surprising announcement that publisher Ray Brock defended with all his might. "We anticipate letters from many readers saying that we've pulled the biggest goof of all time because we didn't select this car, or that car, but those of us who voted cast the largest number for Road Runner. We made the decision and we're proud of it!

"Just what is there about Plymouth's Road Runner that influenced us to choose it?" he continued. "First of all, the original concept of the Road Runner was one of combining a low-priced two-door sedan body with a strong but docile-running engine. Add on a firm suspension and good brakes, throw in some simple ornamentation, a silly bird emblem, a beep-beep horn and you have a reasonably priced automobile that performs like something that usually costs half again as much."

Hardtop Road Runners outsold their coupe counterparts by nearly 50 percent in 1969. Hardtop production (exports included) that year was 48,549. The domestic count was 46,868. *Mike Mueller*

Above:
How to tell a 1969 Road Runner apart from a 1968 at a quick glance? No problem: the hood's simulated vents faced outward in 1968, upward in 1969. These vents are also functional thanks to the addition of the Air Grabber system, a new option for 1969. *Mike Mueller*

Right:
Apparently Road Runner customers preferred rolling their own—windows, that is—in 1969. Base price for the hardtop model that year was $3,034, compared to $2,896 for the basic coupe. *Mike Mueller*

Far right:
As in 1968, plain-Jane stamped-steel wheels with ho-hum "dog-dish" hubcaps were standard fare for Plymouth's second-edition Road Runner in 1969. *Mike Mueller*

Bucket seats and a console were optional for the 1969 Road Runner, as was the sport steering wheel with its simulated wood rim. Notice the red Air Grabber activation knob below the dash. *Mike Mueller*

The Road Runner's standard 383-cubic-inch big-block again made 335 horsepower in 1969 thanks to the addition of the 440 RB V-8's cam, intake manifold, and cylinder heads. Adding Air Grabber induction, a $55.30 option, didn't change advertised output. *Mike Mueller*

The Road Runner's Air Grabber air cleaner, which sealed to ductwork on the functional hood's underside, was specially identified with "Coyote Duster" graphics. *Mike Mueller*

The basic Bird rolled over mechanically unchanged from 1968. Minor exterior updates included a revised grille, recessed taillights, and hood vents that this time faced upward instead of outward. Like the 1969 GTX, the second-edition Road Runner also could've been equipped with Plymouth's new Air Grabber system, which made those vents fully functional. In the Road Runner's case, the air cleaner lid was adorned with "Coyote Duster" artwork when this fresh-air equipment was installed. In both applications, GTX and Road Runner, the Air Grabber ductwork was activated by an under-dash knob.

07

Above:
Installing the optional Hemi in an early Road Runner certainly defeated the whole cost-conscious purpose. But the end result was out-of-this-world performance. A *Car and Driver* test of a 1969 Hemi Road Runner produced a quarter-mile time of 13.54 seconds. *Mike Mueller*

Right:
Hemi coupe production in 1969 was 356. Another 421 hardtops also were fitted with the 426 Hemi that year. *Mike Mueller*

The Road Runner convertible's base price was $3,313 in 1969. *Mike Mueller*

A convertible Road Runner appeared for 1969 and was built through 1970 only. Total drop-top production for 1969 was 2,128, with 1,889 of those delivered domestically. *Mike Mueller*

Another silly bird emblem was added to the steering wheel inside, joining the cartoon characters still found on the instrument panel's far right side, as well as on the doors and deck lid outside. Plain and simply done in black in 1968, the beep-beep horn beneath the hood was repainted in a light purple shade for 1969 and was adorned further with a decal announcing it was "The Voice of the Road Runner."

Sporty bucket seats and a console debuted on the Road Runner options list in 1969, as did the same beefed-up rear end parts that debuted that year for the GTX: the Performance Axle Package, Super Performance Axle Package, Trak Pack, and Super Trak Pack. Again, these deals included, among other things, improved cooling equipment and the extra-heavy-duty Hemi suspension. A carryover from 1968, the High Performance Axle Package, with its 3.91:1 Sure-Grip differential, was available only with the Road Runner's base 383 V-8.

That big-block and the optional Hemi again represented the only available power choices for 1969, at least early on during the model run. The domestic Hemi count that year was 356 coupes (plus 22 Canadian), 421 hardtops (14 Canadian), and 10 convertibles (2 Canadian). Of the 356 coupes, 194 had four-speeds, and 162 had automatics. The breakdown for the 421 hardtops was 234 four-speeds, 187 automatics. And the tally for the super-rare convertibles read 4 four-speeds, 6 automatics.

Above:
Fourteen-inch, chromed, styled-steel road wheels were Road Runner options in 1968 and 1969. The price in 1969 was $86.15.
Mike Mueller

Right:
New for 1969 was the V21 "Performance Hood Paint" option, which added parallel black bands in exchange for an extra $18.05.
Mike Mueller

Above:
Additional Road Runner identification appeared in the steering wheel hub in 1969.
Mike Mueller

Right:
The Hemi engine's price rose to $813.45 in 1969. As was the case when installed along with the base 383 V-8, the optional Air Grabber did not change the Hemi's 425-horse advertised output figure. *Mike Mueller*

1969 1/2
Road Runner 440 Six Barrel

Specifications	
Model availability	two-door coupe and hardtop
Wheelbase	116 inches
Length	202.7 inches
Width	76.4 inches
Height	53.1 inches
Weight	not available
Base Price	440 Six Barrel Engine package cost $462.80
Track (front/rear, in inches)	59.5/59.2
Wheels	15×6 (no hubcaps included)
Tires	G70×15 Goodyear Polyglas
Construction	unitized body/frame
Suspension	independent A-arms with heavy-duty torsion bars, front; solid axle with longitudinal heavy-duty leaf springs, rear
Steering	recirculating ball
Brakes	four-wheel, heavy-duty, 11-inch drums
Engine	390-horsepower, 440-cubic-inch V-8
Bore and stroke	4.32×3.75 inches
Compression	10.1:1
Fuel delivery	three Holley two-barrel carburetors
Transmission	four-speed manual or Torqueflite automatic
Axle ratio	4.10:1 gears in a 9.75-ich Dana 60 rear end
Production	615 coupes, 797 hardtops

Mounted on an Edelbrock aluminum manifold, those three Holleys more than doubled the intake flow compared to the 375-horsepower 440's lone Carter four-barrel. *Mike Mueller*

1969 1/2 440 Six Barrel

A third Road Runner engine appeared in the spring of 1969, a new 440-cubic-inch RB big-block rated at 390 horsepower, 15 more ponies than the GTX's Super Commando V-8. Credit for that power boost primarily went to three Holley two-barrel carburetors mounted on an aluminum Edelbrock intake. A 650 cfm four-barrel fed fuel/air to the 375-horsepower 440; those Holleys more than doubled that flow rate for what Plymouth people called their 440 Six Barrel V-8.

On the inside, the four-barrel 440 and its triple-carb cousin were identical as far as cam specs and compression were concerned, but the 390-horse rendition was built to withstand higher revolutions. Stiff Hemi valve springs, beefed rocker arms and connecting rods, molybdenum-filled piston rings, and flash-chromed valves were used, while cam lobes and lifter surfaces were specially machined to equalize excessive wear typically encountered with higher valve spring pressures. Chrysler engineers earlier had discovered that heavy-duty Hemi springs shortened a cam's life in short order, with some owners flattening lobes after only 10,000 miles. As the cam lobes bumped them, the Six Barrel's lifters would rotate, distributing wear more evenly.

The 440 Six Barrel V-8 was packaged up rather tidily with various purposeful pieces in what Chrysler called its "Engine Conversion Package." Coded A12, this option appeared midyear in 1969 for both

Above:
Like hood hinges, hubcaps also weren't offered for the 440 Six Barrel Road Runner in 1969. Its 15x6 wheels were adorned only with chrome lug nuts. *Mike Mueller*

Right:
A third Road Runner engine became available in the spring of 1969 and brought various race-ready components along with it. The 1969 1/2 440 Six Barrel model featured, among other things, a lift-off fiberglass hood with an enormous functional scoop. *Mike Mueller*

Below, right:
Like its 440 Six Pack Super Bee cousin, the 440 Six Barrel Road Runner was available as a coupe and hardtop in 1969. Production of the former (shown here) was 615. Another 797 hardtop models also were built. *Mike Mueller*

Left:
Most sources in 1969 referred to the removal of the 440 Six Barrel Road Runner's fiberglass hood as a two-man affair, but the job wasn't all that tough for one guy if you knew the trick. *Mike Mueller*

Below, left:
The 440 Six Barrel V-8 was pumped up to 390 horsepower, primarily by trading the 375-horsepower 440's single Carter four-barrel carburetor for three Holley two-barrels. A special valvetrain gear better suited for high-rpm operation also was incorporated. *Mike Mueller*

the Road Runner and Super Bee, with the latter identified in Dodge terms as a 440 Six Pack model. In either case, the A12 parts list was the same: a fully beefed Hemi suspension went underneath, 4.10:1 Sure-Grip gears in a 9.75-inch Dana 60 rear end appeared out back, and G70×15 Goodyear Polyglas tires on 15x6 wheels were bolted on at the corners. No wheel covers were included, not even those humble dog-dish hubcaps. The A12 package's black-painted 15-inch rims were simply adorned with chrome lug nuts, nothing else.

A lightweight fiberglass hood also was included, but hinges were deemed unnecessary: this lid simply lifted off by hand after four chrome-plated locking pins were removed. "All very racy, but we're sure the novelty of the two-man hood would wear off quickly," observed *Car Life* in reference to the same equipment seen on Dodge's Six Pack Super Bee.

This lift-off hood also featured a huge scoop that directed cooler outside air into an air cleaner sealed to the hood's underside by a large rubber doughnut. That scoop, again in *Car Life*'s words, "gapes wide open, seemingly ready to ingest all that gets near it including water, dirt, or birds." Special drain tubes handled any excess moisture that might've splashed into the air cleaner; birds in search of a bath did so at their own risk.

In a *Super Stock* road test, a 440 Six Barrel Road Runner averaged 13.50 seconds at 109.31 miles per hour for the quarter-mile. Hemi-style performance at an un-Hemi price, such a deal! As *Hot Rod*'s Steve Kelly explained further, "if the price and temperament of a hemi-head engine haven't been enough to thoroughly discourage street-driving performance-car buyers from ordering the 426 in their new Dodge (or Plymouth), then the new 390-horsepower Mopar Six-Pack option will deal the final blow."

Six Barrel Road Runner production was 615 coupes, 797 hardtops. The transmission breakdowns for the coupe count read 388 four-speeds, 227 automatics. The hardtop tally was 422 four-speeds, 375 automatics.

1970 Road Runner

Specifications	
Model availability	two-door coupe, hardtop. and convertible
Wheelbase	116 inches
Length	204 inches
Width	76.4 inches
Height	53.0 inches
Weight	3,450 pounds (coupe), 3,475 pounds (hardtop), 3,550 pounds (convertible)
Base Price	$2,896 (coupe), $3,034 (hardtop), $3,289 (convertible)
Track (front/rear, in inches)	59.5/59.2
Wheels	14×6 (15-inch rims with Hemi option)
Tires	F70×14
Construction	unitized body/frame
Suspension	independent A-arms with heavy-duty torsion bars, front; solid axle with longitudinal heavy-duty leaf springs, rear
Steering	recirculating ball
Brakes	four-wheel drums
Engine	335-horsepower, 383-cubic-inch V-8, standard (426 Hemi, optional)
Bore and stroke	4.25×3.38 inches
Compression	10:1
Fuel delivery	single Carter four-barrel carburetor
Transmission	three-speed manual
Axle ratio	3.23:1
Production (including exports)	15,716 coupes, 24,944 hardtops, 824 convertibles

Plymouth restyled its B-body Belvedere for 1970, with the results pleasing most Road Runner fans. Base prices for all three models went down that year due to the inclusion of a three-speed manual in place of the four-speed used previously in base applications.
Mike Mueller

1970

An attractively restyled B-body shell served as the base for Plymouth's third-edition Road Runner, which once more shared its hood with its pricier GTX brethren. Three body styles—traditional coupe, cooler hardtop, and sexy convertible—were offered for the last time. Base prices were $2,896, $3,034, and $3,289, respectively. Each of these bottom lines went down slightly from 1969's figures thanks to a switch from the familiar four-speed to a heavy-duty three-speed on the standard equipment list. Predictably few frugal customers opted to stick with the low-buck gearbox; production was only 1,330 for coupes, 584 for hardtops, and a mere 13 for the convertible. Total 1970 domestic production for the three body styles was 14,782 coupes, 23,371 hardtops, and 658 convertibles.

Like the $227 Torqueflite automatic, the four-speed manual was a 1970 option (priced at $197.25) behind the base 335-horse 383. Two extra-cost engines again were offered, the wallet-wilting Hemi and not-so-expensive 440 Six Barrel. The former carried an $841.05 price tag, the latter a humble $249.55. Modifications made to the two optional big-blocks included a less-expensive cast-iron intake for the Six Barrel and hydraulic lifters for the Hemi. The 440 Six Barrel option (code E87) this time included the engine alone, no strip-ready extras, thus explaining the precipitous drop in price. Gas-station-attendant-friendly hood hinges and fashionable wheel covers were now part of the plan when the 390-horse 440 was installed.

Like the 440 Six Barrel, the 426 Hemi once again could've been mated only to the Torqueflite or four-speed—weak-kneed three-

A base Road Runner hardtop cost $3,034 in 1970. The bottom lines for the coupe and convertible were $2,896 and $3,289, respectively. *Mike Mueller*

The 440 Six Barrel big-block returned as a Road Runner option on its own for 1970 without all the strip-ready extras seen the year before. Output remained at 390 horsepower. *Mike Mueller*

speeds needed not apply. Included, as well, in the Hemi's case was the same tough supporting cast, beginning with a super-strong Dana 60 axle. Suspension was also strengthened by adding thicker front torsion bars, much stiffer shocks, and beefed rear leaf springs with six leaves on the right and five (plus two halves) on the left.

Hemi models also came standard with a redesigned Air Grabber hood, a boss bonnet that both functioned well and formed an even groovier image for the already too-cool-for-school Road Runner. Flicking an under-dash switch activated the new Air Grabber's vacuum-controlled flap in the center of the Road Runner's bulging hood. When opened up for business, this flap showed off a snarling, toothy grin reminiscent of the nose art used in World War II on fighter aircraft like Curtiss' P-40 Warhawk. In non-Hemi applications, the gnarly Air Grabber option cost $65.55.

Among other options introduced for 1970 were Chrysler's popular Rallye wheels, available in 14.0×5.5 and 15.0×7.0 sizes, with the latter argent-colored rims wrapped in fat F60 rubber. A new "Gold Dust" accent stripe option, priced at $15.55, added a dust trail behind the running Road Runner decal located at the leading edge of each front fender. This trail blew backward into the simulated brake scoops added to the Plymouth B-body's rear quarters as part of its 1970 makeover. Also new for 1970 was a wide array of extra-cost exterior colors with quasi-clever names like Vitamin C Orange, Lemon Twist, Lime Light, Tor-Red, and In Violet.

07

It always shared hoods with its upscale GTX cousin, so the Road Runner also informed its driver of what was cooking beneath that bulging lid in 1970. *Mike Mueller*

Plymouth's Air Grabber option was revised for 1970, with one central flap replacing the dual vents seen the previous year. When opened, that flap showed off a toothy grin. *Mike Mueller*

Revised Coyote Duster graphics appeared for the 1970 Road Runner's optional Air Grabber equipment. *Mike Mueller*

Hemi counts for 1970 were 74 coupes, 75 hardtops, and 3 convertibles. The numbers for 440 Six Barrel installations were 651 coupes, 1,130 hardtops, and 34 convertibles. Reportedly one 440 four-barrel 1970 Road Runner hardtop, fitted with an automatic transmission, is known.

Transmission breakdowns went like this: Hemi coupes: 44 four-speeds, 30 automatics. For the Hemi hardtops: 59 four-speeds, 16 automatics. For the Hemi convertibles: 1 four-speed, 2 automatics. For the Six Barrel coupes: 429 four-speeds, 222 automatics. For the Six Barrel hardtops: 697 four-speeds, 433 automatics. For the Six Barrel convertibles: 20 four-speeds, 14 automatics.

Above:
Charger-style instrumentation became standard inside the Road Runner in 1970. Notice the optional combination clock/tachometer in the large left-hand “pod.” A 150-miles-per-hour speedometer remained part of the basic package. *Mike Mueller*

Left:
Activated by cable in 1969, Plymouth’s Air Grabber hood switched to vacuum operation the following year. This toggle allowed engine vacuum to open that snarling hood flap. *Mike Mueller*

07

This whimsical promotional pose shows off a new option for 1970, the Dust Trail tape stripe. This golden accent curled backward to the simulated rear-quarter scoop from a dashing decal located at the front fender's leading edge. *Chrysler LLC Corporate Historical Collection*

Plymouth's Superbird made its NASCAR debut at Riverside International Raceway in California on January 18, 1970. Driving for Petty Enterprises, Dan Gurney's 'Bird started on the pole that day, but victory went to A. J. Foyt's Ford. The King himself, Richard Petty, placed his Superbird fifth at Riverside's Motor Trend 500 that year. *Chrysler LLC Corporate Historical Collection*

1970
Superbird

Specifications	
Model availability	two-door hardtop
Wheelbase	116 inches
Length	218 inches
Width	76.4 inches
Height	53.0 inches
Weight	3,841 pounds
Base Price	$4,298
Track (front/rear, in inches)	59.5/59.2
Wheels	14×6 (15-inch rims with Hemi option)
Tires	F70×14
Construction	unitized body/frame
Suspension	independent A-arms with heavy-duty torsion bars, front; solid axle with longitudinal heavy-duty leaf springs, rear
Steering	recirculating ball
Brakes	four-wheel drums
Engine	375-horsepower, 440-cubic-inch V-8, standard (440 Six Barrel and 426 Hemi V-8s, optional)
Bore and stroke	4.32×3.75 inches
Compression	10.1:1
Fuel delivery	single Carter four-barrel carburetor
Transmission	four-speed manual or Torqueflite automatic
Axle ratio	3.23:1
Production	1,935

1970 Superbird

Easily the biggest news concerning 1970 introductions involved a new Road Runner model, this one created solely with NASCAR racing in mind. Following in the slipstream of Dodge's Charger Daytona, built only for 1969, Plymouth's Superbird was conceived in June 1969, temporarily cancelled in August, then quickly prepared for the 1970 NASCAR season. Looking very much like its Daytona cousin, the Superbird also wore a long, pointed nose and tall towel-rack spoiler in back, both added to help Plymouth join stock-car racing's 200-miles-per-hour club, a group founded the year before by the aero-conscious Charger.

As Dodge did in 1969, Plymouth rolled out street-going Superbirds to meet NASCAR's homologation standards. Though Chrysler's latest winged warrior looked a lot like its forerunner from Dodge at a glance, the two high-flying models in truth differed in many ways. First off, the Road Runner front clip wouldn't mate up to the aerodynamic nose graft as easily as the 1969 Charger's did, leaving designers no choice but to steal a hood and front fenders from Dodge's Coronet line for this Plymouth application.

The two metal noses also differed in various ways, beginning with the fact that the Superbird's front cap swept upward slightly while the Daytona's didn't. The Plymouth unit additionally carried a continuation of the hood's center crease, which Dodge's pointed snout didn't. The chin spoilers below were the same, but the air inlets were located differently.

Other measurements differed too, including those involving the rear wing, which in the Superbird's case was taller, wider, and raked back farther than the Daytona's. Pedestals for the Superbird's wing also were wider, and no striping was applied. Daytona wings featured three-piece tape stripes done in three contrasting shades: red, white, or black.

Base price for the 1970 Superbird was $4,298. Adding that pointed prow brought overall length to nearly 18 1/2 feet. The color appearing here is Lime Light, one of seven available shades. *Mike Mueller*

The highest-flying Road Runner of all was the NASCAR-inspired Superbird, built for 1970 only. Production was 1,935, all featuring aerodynamic nose extensions and tall "towel-rack" spoilers in back. *Mike Mueller*

Differences appeared atop each fender as well. Commonly called "air extractors" on the street cars, the fender scoops added to both the Daytona and Superbird in NASCAR configurations actually were intended to allow extra clearance for the enormous tires required in stock-car competition. Yes, the flat-topped scoops on stock Daytonas covered a meshed opening meant to allow trapped air an exit from the front wheel wells. But the Superbird's rounded scoops were for looks only. They did absolutely nothing but sit there.

Finally, unlike Daytonas, all Superbirds featured vinyl roofs, which were put on as a quick fix to hide the seams required by the modified rear-window-mounting plug. Hand leading those seams was not considered this time to save both time and money, since conservation became a major issue in 1970 thanks to new NASCAR rules. The homologation standard that year was increased to either 1,000 regular-production models or a number equal to half of the company's dealers, whichever was higher. This meant Plymouth had to create nearly four times as many Superbirds as Dodge did Daytonas in 1969.

The final count was 1,935; 1,084 with 440 four-barrels, 135 with 426 Hemis, and an additional 716 with the 440 Six Barrel V-8. Transmission breakdowns for the Hemi Superbirds were 58 four-speeds, 77 automatics. For the 440 four-barrel models: 458 four-speeds, 626 automatics. For the Six Barrel cars: 308 four-speeds, 408 automatics.

On NASCAR tracks in 1970, Chrysler's two aero racers took command after Ford began backing off on its motorsports program that year. Superbirds won eight races, Daytonas four, and another win was managed by a Charger 500. Ford Motor Company's tally was four wins apiece from Ford's long-nose Talladega and its Mercury clone, the Cyclone Spoiler II. Henry Ford II threw in the towel completely late in 1970, and NASCAR mogul Bill France then stepped in to put a lid on these 200-miles-per-hour screamers, first instituting a carburetor restrictor plate rule (sound familiar?) for the winged Mopars. These restrictions, in turn, inspired Chrysler officials to kill off Plymouth's Superbird. Like the Daytona, it only took flight for one year before retiring.

The Superbird's rear wing was larger and swept back more compared to the unit used by the Charger Daytona in 1969. Daytona wings also featured special stripes; the Superbird's did not. *Mike Mueller*

All Superbirds featured vinyl roofs—not for enhanced aesthetics, but as a cost-conscious shortcut to hide the bodywork required to add a special rear window into the wind-cheating mix. Time-consuming, costly handwork was performed to achieve this end in the Charger Daytona's case. *Mike Mueller*

Superbirds were fitted with three engines: the 375-horse 440, the 390-horse 440 Six Barrel (shown here), and the 426 Hemi. The production tally was 1,084, 716, and 135, respectively. *Mike Mueller*

The transmission breakdown for 440 Six Barrel Superbirds read 308 four-speeds (shown here) and 408 automatics. Power steering and power front disc brakes were standard. *Mike Mueller*

1971

Exciting, truly fresh "fuselage styling" appeared for Plymouth's mid-sized models in 1971, as did a new 115-inch wheelbase for the line now named Satellite after the Belvedere badge was dropped at 1970's end. A widened rear track (to 62 inches) also came along in the package to enhance ride stability. On the clean side, the 1971 Satellite was a certified head-turner with its soft, rounded contours, purposeful wheel-house bulges, and full-loop chrome bumper up front.

Both the GTX and Road Runner were offered only as top-shelf hardtops in 1971, and they shared a hood once more, this one featuring twin, outward-facing simulated scoops. Ordering the optional Air Grabber added a flap similar to the one seen the previous year with its snarling graphics, and this equipment was housed in a special hood featuring one bold bulge in the center. Plymouth also offered a rear spoiler option, and this wing could've been complemented with a two-part front spoiler available by way of dealer installation.

Additional new options included rear window louvers, a partial "canopy" vinyl roof, black-out tape treatment for the rear valance, a color-keyed elastomeric front bumper, and a prominent appearance

Another new B-body arrived for 1971, the year the Road Runner lineup was reduced to one model, a hardtop. Base price that year was $3,120. An optional small-block, the 275-horsepower 340, appeared for the first time. *Chrysler LLC Corporate Historical Collection*

1971
Road Runner

Specifications	
Model availability	two-door hardtop
Wheelbase	115 inches
Length	203.2 inches
Width	79.1 inches
Height	52.7 inches
Weight	3,640 pounds
Base Price	$3,147
Track (front/rear, in inches)	60.1/62.0
Wheels	14×6
Tires	F70×14
Construction	unitized body/frame
Suspension	independent A-arms with heavy-duty torsion bars, front; solid axle with longitudinal heavy-duty leaf springs, rear
Steering	recirculating ball
Brakes	four-wheel drums
Engine	300-horsepower, 383-cubic-inch V-8, standard (340, 440 Six Barrel, and 426 Hemi V-8s, optional)
Bore and stroke	4.25×3.38 inches
Compression	8.5:1
Fuel delivery	single Carter four-barrel carburetor
Transmission	three-speed manual
Axle ratio	3.23:1
Production (including exports)	14,218 (13,664, domestic)

The Hemi and 440+6 big-blocks didn't return for 1972, but a still-hot Road Runner did. Standard that year was a 400-cubic-inch big-block net-rated at 255 horsepower. *Chrysler LLC Corporate Historical Collection*

package consisting of strobe striping that ran from each rear wheel opening up over the roof. Inside, the optional bucket seats this year could've been done in various color combos, the wildest being a two-tone black with blaring orange inserts.

Also new for 1971 was the Road Runner's first available small-block V-8, the 275-horsepower 340, an addition made with cost savings in mind. The hot little 340 was much easier to insure than Plymouth's brutish big-blocks. Other mechanicals rolled over in familiar fashion: a heavy-duty suspension, beefy brakes, and F70×14 tires were standard, as was a mundane three-speed manual transmission.

The equally familiar 383-cubic-inch B-series V-8 remained standard but lost a few horses in 1971 thanks to toughening safety regulations and emissions standards. Compression ratios dropped slightly in most available Plymouth engines that year, and the Road Runner's 383 was no exception: a cut to 8.5:1 translated into a 330-horse rating. The optional triple-carb RB, now called the "440+6" V-8, also lost 5 ponies, while the unstoppable Hemi remained at its familiar 425 advertised horses.

Motor Trend's Jim Brokaw tested two 1971 Road Runners, one with the standard 383, the other with the 385-horsepower 440+6 big-block. Curiously, the 383 ran a 14.84-second quarter-mile (at 94.50 miles per hour), while its triple-carb cousin posted a 15.02-second (at 96.00 miles per hour) run.

Road Runner popularity sagged dramatically in 1971 as the final domestic tally read only 13,644, down from 41,116 for 1970. Clearly the end was near. Additionally only 55 Hemi models (plus 4 Canadians) were built: 28 with four-speeds, 27 with automatics. The count for the 440+6 Road Runner was 246: 137 with four-speeds, 109 with automatics. Plymouth rolled out 1,681 of the new cost-conscious 340 cars: 1,243 with automatics, 438 with four-speeds.

1972

Once true performance went on the wane, Plymouth people, like most of their counterparts at rival companies, began concentrating more on image and less on muscle. They basically had to, after both the Hemi and 440+6 were cancelled as the 1971 run came to a close. Reportedly, a few triple-carb RB B-body installations did sneak out early in 1972 before the final axe fell. Neither of Chrysler's beastly big-blocks would've been able to meet new Environmental Protection Agency emissions standards, so that was that.

Compression ratios continued to drop in 1972, as did available horsepower, albeit thanks partly to Detroit's new net-rating system. Standard that year for the Road Runner was a new 400-cubic-inch big-block, created by boring the old 383. Net output for this four-barrel-fed V-8 was 255 horsepower. Options included a 240-horsepower, 340-cubic-inch small-block and 280-horsepower, 440-cubic-inch four-barrel. Adding the 440 also brought along "GTX" identification on the fenders and deck lid, creating a combo similar to Dodge's Charger Super Bee of 1971. GTX-tagged 440 Road Runners were offered up through 1974.

A rear sway bar joined the standard heavy-duty suspension package in 1972, and the Air Grabber hood remained an option for one last year. Two high-profile tape treatment options were offered for 1972, hopefully to distract customers' attention away from what was going on beneath the skin.

Road Runner sales again fell dramatically for 1972, dropping by more than 50 percent to 6,861. The total count, including exports, was 7,628. The 440 GTX tally was 672: 219 four-speeds, 453 automatics. Of the 2,360 340-equipped 1972 Road Runners built for domestic consumption, 192 had the base three-speed manual, 329 had four-speeds, and 1,839 had automatics. The transmission breakdown for the 3,828 standard models (with the 400 V-8) was 1,433 three-speeds, 906 four-speeds, and 1,489 automatics.

1972
Road Runner

Specifications	
Model availability	two-door hardtop
Wheelbase	115 inches
Length	203.2 inches
Width	79.1 inches
Height	52.7 inches
Weight	3,495
Base Price	$3,080
Track (front/rear, in inches)	60.1/62.0
Wheels	14×6
Tires	F70×14
Construction	unitized body/frame
Suspension	independent A-arms with heavy-duty torsion bars, front; solid axle with longitudinal heavy-duty leaf springs, rear; sway bars in front and back
Steering	recirculating ball
Brakes	manual front discs, rear drums (power front discs, optional)
Engine	240-horsepower, 340-cubic-inch V-8, standard (400- and 440-cid V-8s, optional)
Bore and stroke	4.04×3.31 inches
Compression	8.5:1
Fuel delivery	single Carter four-barrel carburetor
Transmission	three-speed manual (not available with 440 V-8)
Axle ratio	3.23:1
Production (including exports)	7,628 (6,861, domestic)

Total production for 1973 was 19,056. The domestic count was 15,928, including 5,384 with the optional 340 small-block, shown here. *Mike Mueller*

The bottom line for a 1973 Road Runner began at $2,987. A tame 318-cubic-inch small-block V-8 was standard. *Mike Mueller*

07

1973
Road Runner

Specifications	
Model availability	two-door hardtop
Wheelbase	115 inches
Length	210.8 inches
Width	79.1 inches
Height	52.7 inches
Weight	3,525 pounds
Base Price	$3,115
Track (front/rear, in inches)	60.1/62.0
Wheels	14×6 Rallye
Tires	F70×14
Construction	unitized body/frame
Suspension	independent A-arms with heavy-duty torsion bars, front; solid axle with longitudinal heavy-duty leaf springs, rear; sway bars in front and back
Steering	recirculating ball
Brakes	manual front discs, rear drums (power front discs, optional)
Engine	170-horsepower, 318 cubic-inch V-8, standard (340, 400, and 440 cid V-8s, optional)
Bore and stroke	3.91×3.31 inches
Compression	8.6:1
Fuel delivery	single two-barrel carburetor
Transmission	three-speed manual (not available with 440 V-8)
Axle ratio	3.23:1
Production (including exports)	19,056 (15,928, domestic)

At least the 1973 Road Runner's non-functional hood looked cool. Optional engines included the 340 small-block and two big-blocks, the 400 and 440. *Mike Mueller*

1973

"Only the strong survive" was the ad slogan chosen to promote Plymouth's Road Runner in 1973, but let's be real, folks. A mild-mannered 318-cubic-inch small-block topped by a two-barrel carb? Net-rated at 170 clearly lame horses? Strong? Dual exhausts remained part of the standard package. Options included the 340 small-block (240 horsepower) and two big-blocks, the 260-horse 400 and 280-horse "GTX" 440. The three-speed manual was limited to the base 318, and only the Torqueflite was offered behind the 440-cubic-inch four-barrel V-8. Both the Torqueflite and four-speed manual were optional behind the other three V-8s.

Additional standard equipment included front disc brakes and 14-inch Rallye wheels. The standard foundation from 1971 rolled over, as did the optional Performance Axle Package with its 3.55:1 Sure-Grip axle, 26-inch high-performance radiator, and torque-drive slip fan. Reportedly that fan taxed 5 to 8 horsepower less than Plymouth's conventional unit, an important bit of conservation considering how increasingly tough it was to keep horses hanging around during the early seventies.

Nose and tail revisions to the Satellite shell in 1973 added a whopping seven inches in total length to that year's Road Runner. The big loop bumper seen up front since 1971 was dropped to cut costs, leaving Plymouth's B-body with a more conventional facade. New stripes—available in black, white, or red—were standard, running along the top of each body side and meeting on top at the roof's trailing edge. These stripes could've been deleted on request, and additional striping was optionally available for the hood in this case.

Above, left:
Graphics became more important as performance waned during the seventies. The 1973 Road Runner's body-side stripes ran up and over the roof in dramatic fashion. *Mike Mueller*

Above:
Though detuned and decompressed, Plymouth's 340 small-block (a $153 Road Runner option) was still a player in 1973. Compression was 8.5:1. Net-rated output was 240 horsepower. *Mike Mueller*

Left:
The transmission tally for 340-equipped Road Runners in 1973 was 4,428 automatics (shown here) and 956 four-speeds. The base three-speed manual was not available behind the 340. *Mike Mueller*

Above:
Plymouth's last midsized B-body Road Runner appeared for 1974 looking all but exactly like its 1973 predecessor. Total production in 1974 was 11,555. Of these, 9,646 were delivered domestically. *Chrysler LLC Corporate Historical Collection*

Right:
A Road Runner image package was offered for Plymouth's Volare Super Coupe from 1977 to 1980. A 1977 example is shown here. *Chrysler LLC Corporate Historical Collection*

Although sales more than doubled for 1973, the days for Plymouth's once-popular Road Runner were clearly numbered. That year's count for the 440 GTX models was 749. Base 318 cars numbered 7,056, the 340 total was 5,385, and the tally for 400-equipped 1973 Road Runners was 2,740.

1974
Road Runner

Specifications	
Model availability	two-door hardtop
Wheelbase	115 inches
Length	212.4 inches
Width	79.1 inches
Height	52.7 inches
Weight	3,616 pounds
Base Price	$3,545
Track (front/rear, in inches)	60.1/62.0
Wheels	14×6 Rallye
Tires	F70×14
Construction	unitized body/frame
Suspension	independent A-arms with heavy-duty torsion bars, front; solid axle with longitudinal heavy-duty leaf springs, rear; sway bars in front and back
Steering	recirculating ball
Brakes	manual front discs, rear drums (power front discs, optional)
Engine	170-horsepower, 318 cubic-inch V-8, standard (360, 400, and 440 cid V-8s, optional)
Bore and stroke	3.91×3.31 inches
Compression	8.6:1
Fuel delivery	single two-barrel carburetor
Transmission	three-speed manual (not available with 440 V-8)
Axle ratio	3.23:1
Production (including exports)	11,555 (9,646, domestic)

New for 1974 was an optional 360-cubic-inch small-block V-8. Net-rated output for this 340 descendant was 245 horsepower. *Mike Mueller*

1974

Standard power again was supplied by a 318-cubic-inch small-block, net-rated at 150 horsepower, for Plymouth's 1974 Road Runner, which looked all but identical to its 1973 forerunner. The options list also again featured one small- and two big-block V-8s, but this time the former was Plymouth's new 360, rated at 245 net horses. Output ratings for the 400 and "GTX" 440 were 250 and 275, respectively.

Even more emiles per hourasis on imagery demonstrated that the muscle car era was all but over. Instead of promoting Road Runner performance, Plymouth people concentrated all their efforts on touting exterior color choices and interior options. Standard inside the 1974 Road Runner was the Rallye instrument cluster.

Total domestic production was 9,648 for what most consider the last "real" Road Runner. The nameplate rolled over into 1975, but with the midsized Satellite platform's cancellation that year, the once-proud Bird was moved up into the luxury-conscious Fury lineup for one final appearance as an individual model. That it just wasn't the same went without saying.

A Road Runner trim package appeared for the F-body Volare coupe in 1976, but again the message appeared clearly lost. This combo continued on the market until the Volare was discontinued at the end of 1980.

08

Dodge Super Bee 1968–1971

What's the Buzz?

Dodge's Scat Pack included only three members when it was first announced in magazine ads in the fall of 1967: Dart GTS, Coronet R/T, and Charger R/T. A fourth then appeared shortly after the turn of the year: yet another B-body that, according to those ever-present ad guys, offered "Scat Pack performance at a new low price." First seen in showrooms in February 1968, Dodge's latest muscle machine was meant to follow in the Road Runner's tire tracks and thus echoed many of the tightwad touches that helped make that bad bird a high-flying success right out of the nest. Back to basics was again more or less the main part of the plan, explaining why a rather mundane Coronet coupe, with flip-open rear quarter windows, was used as a base.

"Plymouth pioneered the idea," began an early-1969 *Car and Driver* test of this newborn breed, which focused on minimizing unneeded frills while still maximizing tire-melting thrills. "The division realized it wasn't doing its big engines any favors by stuffing them into cars already overweight with gadgets and glitter, and after much introspection it produced the Road Runner. Road Runner logic forthwith became impossible to argue with—as all of Detroit discovered—when in the first year, 19.8 percent of the intermediate-size Plymouths were Road Runners. Dodge, which is always somewhere on the same lap with Plymouth, [then] joined the movement."

Like Plymouth's midsized muscle-car-for-the-masses, Dodge's counterpart also was given a cartoonish name, this one obviously intended to play up on that whole Scat Pack thing. If a bumblebee could use V-8 power to run around on drag slicks instead of legs, it definitely was no mere mortal insect, right? It was—class?—a "Super Bee," a no-brainer that apparently suited Dodge's variation on *Car and Driver*'s Econo-Racer theme to a T, or at least as far as company men were concerned. Curbside critics, on the other hand, weren't quite so sure. "A kind of inverse kinky name, but no less a real car," went *Car Driver*'s initial impression. According to a *Road Test* review of a 1969 model, "the Super Bee is a good looking [automobile] even with the insect carrying the banner on each rear fender."

- "Rumble Bee" was the nickname Dodge ads used for the new Super Bee in 1968.
- All Super Bees were based on Coronet coupe bodies (with flip-out rear quarter windows) in 1968.
- Dodge's B-body platform used a 117-inch wheelbase from 1968 to 1970, while Plymouths relied on a shorter 116-inch hub-to-hub stretch.
- No Super Bee convertibles were ever offered.
- A pillar-less hardtop (with roll-up rear quarter glass) joined the original coupe in the Super Bee lineup for 1969.
- The race-ready 440 Six Pack Super Bee was offered for 1969 only.
- Super Bees built from 1968 to 1970 were based on Coronet coupes and hardtops and featured big-block power only.
- A three-speed manual Transmission became standard Super Bee fare in 1970 in place of the previously used Hurst-shifted four-speed.
- Dodge's original Super Bee package reappeared for one last year in the Charger model lineup for 1971.

Opposite:
Dodge people took one look at Plymouth's Road Runner and rapidly rushed their own "Econo-Racer," the Super Bee, into production midyear in 1968. They kept costs down by first basing this new muscle machine on the division's yeoman Coronet coupe. *Mike Mueller*

Above:
Dodge truck designers created two high-profile pickups in 2004 using a pair of Mopar muscle cars as inspiration. New that year were the Hemi GTX and Rumble Bee Rams, the latter shown here with its striping and motorized insect reminding many of the Coronet-based Super Bee born in 1968. Like the GTX Ram half-ton, the 2004 Rumble Bee came standard with Dodge's 345-horsepower, 5.7-liter Hemi V-8. *Mike Mueller*

Left:
An early magazine ad announcing the new Super Bee also promoted various bits of Scat Pack paraphernalia. A shiny quarter was all that was needed to obtain a complete catalog of Scat Pack goodies in 1968. *Chrysler LLC Corporate Historical Collection*

Not only did the 1968 Super Bee get a helmet-wearing, goggle-eyed, buzzing bug in decal form at the trailing edge of each rear quarter panel, it also was treated to a small die-cast likeness on its black-accented cove panel in back. Predictably standard as well, wrapped around the tail, was the tape treatment already made relatively famous by the original Scat Pack trio—after all, these were "the cars with the bumblebee stripes." Completing exterior enhancements was a blacked-out grille and the Coronet R/T's hood with its central bulge sporting non-functional vents.

Clearly the Super Bee stood a bit taller in the "glitter" department relative to its desert fowl cousin, and this excess imagery, working in concert with a few more standard features, helped Dodge's superior bug take a bigger bite out of a customer's back pocket compared to the Road Runner. The latter, in bare-bones coupe form, cost $2,896 in 1968, compared to $3,027 for the Super Bee. Looking a bit less economical than the Road Runner, the Super Bee never did reach similar heights on the popularity scale. Road Runner sales dwarfed Super Bee results by more than five times for 1968, and the Dodge model's zenith, attained the following year, was a comparatively tidy 25,994. The Road Runner's production peak, also put up in 1969, was 81,125.

Mechanically the two were nearly identical, with the Super Bee sharing the same 335-horsepower, 383-cubic-inch big-block created especially for the Road Runner application. Shared, too, was a standard four-speed tranny, but included in Dodge's basic package was a preferred, yet costlier, Hurst shifter. Helping defeat the cost-

Left:
The heart of the 2007–2008 Super Bee was Dodge's 6.1-liter Hemi V-8, rated at 425 horsepower. *Mike Mueller*

Below:
A new and vastly improved Super Bee, done only in Detonator Yellow paint, appeared for 2007 based on Dodge's Charger SRT-8. A second-edition reborn Bee, this time painted only in Blue Pearl Coat, a shade highly reminiscent of Richard Petty's favorite color, showed up the following year. Only 1,000 2008 Super Bees were built. *Mike Mueller*

conscious purpose a bit further was the Bee's Charger-sourced Rallye dash (featuring full instrumentation and a 150-miles-per-hour speedometer), a standard inclusion that plainly represented a paradox paired up with the Coronet's yeoman bench-seat interior.

Easily the greatest paradox involved the optional installation of the expensive Hemi option, the only other powertrain choice for the 1968 Super Bee. Costing at least a grand more than its 383 Magnum counterpart, a Hemi Bee obviously didn't qualify as an Econo-Racer in anyone's book, but those 425 horses definitely helped put the Scat in Scat Pack in a majorly serious way. A third extra-cost engine, the 390-horsepower triple-carb 440, then appeared in 1969 and, like the 383 and top-shelf Hemi, could've been backed by either the standard four-speed or optional Torqueflite automatic.

Dodge offered its midsized Super Bee for four years only, with the Coronet serving as a base from 1968 to 1970. After 7,841 "pillared" coupe models were built that first year, a classier hardtop coupe—with conventional roll-up rear windows in place of the budget-conscious flip-out units—was added into the mix in 1969. Of the 25,994 Super Bees built for 1969, 7,633 were low-buck coupes, and 18,361 were upscale hardtops. The breakdown for 1970 was 3,630 coupes, 10,507 hardtops.

The Super Bee was left seemingly without a leg to stand on after Dodge decision-makers transformed the Coronet into a luxury-conscious family car, with four doors only on a lengthened 118-inch wheelbase, in 1971. Fortunately the Charger—redesigned on a shortened 115-inch wheelbase—was still around, and this sleek sports coupe became the new foundation for the final Super Bee.

A similar buzz wouldn't be heard again for another 36 years.

08

1968
Super Bee

Specifications	
Model availability	two-door coupe
Wheelbase	117 inches
Length	206.6 inches
Width	76.7 inches
Height	54.1 inches
Weight	3,765 pounds
Base Price	$3,027
Track (front/rear, in inches)	59.5/59.2
Wheels	14.0×5.5 inches
Tires	F70×14
Construction	unitized body/frame
Suspension	independent A-arms with heavy-duty torsion bars and stabilizer bar, front; solid axle with longitudinal heavy-duty leaf springs, rear
Steering	recirculating ball
Brakes	four-wheel drums
Engine	335-horsepower, 383 Magnum V-8, standard (426 Hemi V-8, optional)
Bore and stroke	4.25×3.38 inches
Compression	10:1
Fuel delivery	single Carter four-barrel carburetor
Transmission	four-speed manual, standard; Torqueflite automatic, optional
Axle ratio	3.23:1
Production	7,841

Like the original Road Runner, the 1968 Super Bee initially was only offered as a plain-Jane coupe with cost-conscious flip-out rear quarter windows in place of roll-up units. No convertible versions were ever offered. *Mike Mueller*

1968

After watching Road Runners dash off into the marketplace like nobody's business, Dodge product planners surely felt they couldn't lose with their intra-corporate knock-off. All they had to do, they probably thought, was let the world know a Super Bee invasion was on the way. It was then left to the ad men, who put the buzz out there like nobody's business early in 1968. If it was a magazine about cars, it contained a full-page, gloriously colorful promotion for the fourth Scat Packer. And demonstrating that affordability was meant to be a main attraction, publicity wizards also reportedly ran black-and-white ads in nearly 250 college newspapers.

"Why sit there dreaming when you could be running?" asked one ad titled "Rumble Bee." "Beware of the Super Bee," announced another pitch, "proof you can't tell a runner by the size of his bankroll." Save for the aforementioned minor excesses (relative to the Road Runner), the 1968 Super Bee still ranked among Detroit's more economical muscle cars in 1968, certainly so in base form. Even chrome exhaust tips were optional, as were dress-up items where the rubber burnt the road. Typically dull "dog-dish" hubcaps on conventional stamped-steel rims were standard.

Standard mechanicals, however, included much of the stuff speed demons' dreams were made of back in the sixties. Along with the four-speed-backed 383 Magnum, that list featured a free-flowing exhaust system (low-restriction mufflers and 2.25-inch tailpipes), big brakes, and suspension components of the heavy-duty variety. Bringing those 335 ponies back to rest was left up to 11-inch drums at all four corners, with power front discs available at extra cost for a little more whoa-ability. Among beefed underpinnings were stiffer shocks, stronger six-leaf springs in back, beefed 0.90-inch torsion

Above:
First appearing in showrooms in February 1968, Dodge's original Super Bee, of course, instantly joined the Scat Pack, bringing the count for "the cars with the bumblebee stripes" to four. Notice that this particular 1968 Super Bee was ordered sans stripes 40 years back. *Mike Mueller*

Inset:
Yes, as was the case with the Coronet R/T, those standard wraparound stripes (done in parallel wide bands with thin pinstripe outlining in 1968) could've been deleted by customer prerogative. Fortunately, the cute Super Bee decal remained on each rear quarter panel, regardless of that choice. *Mike Mueller*

Both the Road Runner and Super Bee shared the same standard engine in 1968: the 335-horsepower, 383-cubic-inch B-series big-block. Of the 7,841 Super Bees built for 1968, 7,716 featured the 383 Magnum. The other 125 were equipped with the optional 426 Hemi. *Mike Mueller*

An appropriate die-cast emblem appeared on the 1968 Super Bee's tail only—no comparable identification was added to the grille as one might've expected. *Mike Mueller*

Standard inside the 1968 Super Bee was a front bench seat and the Charger's sporty dash featuring Rallye instrumentation. Included in the Rallye package were a 150-miles-per-hour speedometer and real readouts (from left to right) for fuel level, coolant temperature, oil pressure, and alternator. Bucket seats weren't even offered optionally. *Mike Mueller*

bars at the nose, and a healthy 0.94-inch sway bar in front. F70×14 Goodyear redline tires on widened rims went on at the corners.

Again, only two engine choices existed for the 1968 Super Bee coupe, with production breakdowns reading 7,716 for the standard 383, a mere 125 for the big-buck 426 Hemi. Another 3 Hemi Super Bees were delivered through Canadian dealerships that year. Of the domestic Magnum count, 4,783 were backed by the optional Torqueflite, 2,933 by the four-speed. The U.S.-delivered Hemi count went 94 automatics, 31 four-speeds.

08

1969
Super Bee

Specifications	
Model availability	two-door coupe and hardtop
Wheelbase	117 inches
Length	206.6 inches
Width	76.7 inches
Height	54.1 inches
Weight	3,765 pounds (coupe)
Base Price	$3,059, coupe; $3,121, hardtop
Track (front/rear, in inches)	59.5/59.2
Wheels	14.0×5.5 inches
Tires	F70×14
Construction	unitized body/frame
Suspension	independent A-arms with heavy-duty torsion bars and stabilizer bar, front; solid axle with longitudinal heavy-duty leaf springs, rear
Steering	recirculating ball
Brakes	four-wheel drums
Engine	335-horsepower, 383 Magnum V-8, standard (426 Hemi V-8, optional)
Bore and stroke	4.25×3.38 inches
Compression	10:1
Fuel delivery	single Carter four-barrel carburetor
Transmission	four-speed manual, standard; Torqueflite automatic, optional
Axle ratio	3.23:1
Production (including exports)	8,202 coupes, 19,644 hardtops

The same 14-inch Magnum 500 road wheels available for the Coronet R/T in 1968 were offered optionally for Dodge's first Super Bee. The Red Streak tires were standard. *Mike Mueller*

1969

Next to nothing changed mechanically as far as the second-edition Super Bee was concerned, at least in standard form. New options, however, made rather big splashes, especially so in the case of the new triple-carb 440, detailed further on page 203. Of note, as well, were the same high-performance axle packages (Track Pak, Super Track Pak, etc.) introduced to Coronet R/T and Road Runner customers in 1969. And like the R/T, a 1969 Super Bee also could have been fitted with the Ramcharger fresh-air hood, which replaced the ornamental bulge that carried over from 1968 with twin functional scoops that funneled cooler ambient air directly into the 383's single four-barrel below. Ramcharger scoops and ductwork were included as part of the deal when a Super Bee buyer forked over the ample green required to install a 426 Hemi.

All Coronets were treated to new taillights in 1969, but that year's Super Bee carried only two lenses in back, compared to the upscale R/T's three. Both hopped-up Coronets also could've been adorned with simulated rear-quarter air scoops, applied in pairs below each window in back. Eagle-eyes (or not) might've also noticed a revised bumblebee stripe for 1969 that featured one thick band framed by a pair of light pinstripes. New that year, too, was a die-cast, tire-smoking "Rumble Bee" character added up front to the grille near the driver-side headlight.

Above:
The Super Bee decal remained the same for 1969, but the standard striping—which once more could've been deleted—was redone, with one thick band outlined by thin pinstripes. As in 1968, this tape treatment came in white, black, or red. *Mike Mueller*

Above, left:
A classy hardtop Super Bee, with passenger-friendly roll-up rear windows, joined the original coupe rendition for 1969. Base price for the new hardtop that year was $3,121. *Mike Mueller*

Left:
The Super Bee's standard hood for 1968 and 1969 featured a centrally located bulge with simulated air vents on each side. A second hood, with two functional scoops, appeared as part of Dodge's new Ramcharger fresh-air option for 1969. *Mike Mueller*

Dodge's second-edition Super Bee was treated to appropriate die-cast identification in its grille. Total hardtop production in 1969 was 19,644, including 18,361 delivered domestically. *Mike Mueller*

Let's not forget 1969's new body style. Though slightly more expensive ($3,121, compared to $3,059) than the existing coupe, the new pillar-less Super Bee outsold its established brethren by a wide margin: domestic production was 18,361 for the airy hardtop, 7,633 for the comparatively mundane coupe. The difference must have been that easier-to-use roll-up quarter glass.

Engine production totals in the coupe class read 7,122 of the 383 Magnums and just 91 Hemis. Base 383s were backed by 3,695 Torqueflites, 3,427 four-speeds. The Hemi breakdown was 53 automatics, 38 four-speeds. Twelve other Hemi coupes ended up in Canada. The figures for the hardtop group went 16,709 383s, 165 Hemis, and another 12 Canadian Hemis. Transmission counts for the domestic Hemi hardtops were 93 four-speeds, 72 automatics. The base 383 figures were 9,346 automatics, 7,363 four-speeds.

Bucket seats were a $100.85 option for the Super Bee in 1969. A console, priced at $54.45, was also available. *Mike Mueller*

The two scoops on the optional Ramcharger hood were painted to match the body unless basic black was specified. Also notice the optional hood locks on this 1969 Super Bee. *Mike Mueller*

Above:
Ramcharger fresh-air induction was a $73.30 option atop the Super Bee's standard 383 Magnum V-8 in 1969. Total production of base-engine hardtops that year was 16,709: 9,346 with Torqueflite automatic transmissions, 7,363 with four-speed manuals. *Mike Mueller*

Left:
Like Plymouth's Air Grabber in 1969, Dodge's original Ramcharger system was mechanically activated, via cable, by yanking this under-dash knob. *Mike Mueller*

1969
440 Six Pack Super Bee

Specifications	
Model availability	two-door coupe and hardtop
Wheelbase	117 inches
Length	206.6 inches
Width	76.7 inches
Height	53 inches
Weight	3,845 pounds (hardtop)
Base Price	440 Six Pack package cost $468.80
Track (front/rear, in inches)	59/59
Wheels	15×6 inches (no hubcaps included)
Tires	G70×15 Goodyear Polyglas
Construction	unitized body/frame
Suspension	independent A-arms with heavy-duty torsion bars and stabilizer bar, front; solid axle with longitudinal heavy-duty leaf springs, rear
Steering	recirculating ball
Brakes	four-wheel, heavy-duty, 11-inch drums
Engine	390-horsepower, 440-cubic-inch V-8
Bore and stroke	4.32×3.75 inches
Compression	10.1:1
Fuel delivery	three Holley two-barrel carburetors
Transmission	four-speed manual or Torqueflite automatic
Axle ratio	4.10:1 gears in a 9.75-inch Dana 60 rear end
Production (including exports)	420 coupes, 1,487 hardtops

Above:
A fiberglass hood sporting an enormous, wide-open scoop was standard for the Six Pack Super Bee. No hinges were used; this lightweight hood simply lifted off by hand once tie-down pins were pulled at each corner. *Mike Mueller*

Below:
Conventional steel wheels, measuring 15x6 inches, were standard for the Six Pack Super Bee, as were G70 Goodyear tires. No hubcaps were included, just chrome lug nuts. *Mike Mueller*

1969 440 Six Pack

Readers with enough fingers and toes might have already noticed that the production breakdowns their eyes (eagle or otherwise) just passed over don't add up as far as 1969's individual engine totals are concerned. Such cipherin' works out once we take into account the aforementioned third engine option introduced for both the Road Runner and Super Bee that year. Known as the 440 Six Barrel in Plymouth terms, this 390-horsepower RB big-block was tagged 440 Six Pack by the Dodge guys. The Six Pack Super Bee count for 1969 was 420 coupes, 1,487 hardtops. Of the coupe total, 267 featured four-speeds, 153 automatics. The hardtop split read 826 four-speeds, 661 automatics.

The 440 Six Pack Super Bee, of course, offered everything its Road Runner counterpart did, beginning with that hinge-less, blacked-out, fiberglass hood crowned by an enormous, wide-open scoop. Familiar, as well, were those black-painted 15x6 steel wheels, adorned only with chrome lug nuts. Additional standard equipment included heavy-duty brakes, an A833 Hemi four-speed or Torqueflite automatic, a 9.75-inch Dana 60 rear end with 4.10:1 Sure-Grip gears, a 26-inch maximum cooling radiator, a seven-bladed torque-drive fan, and G70 Goodyear Polyglas rubber.

Plain and simply meant to run right to the strip with next to no fuss or muss, the Six Pack Super Bee could scorch the quarter-mile with the best of them in 1969: 13.8 seconds at 104.2 miles per hour, according to *Car Life*. Such performance was comparable to a Hemi Bee, a notable achievement considering the Six Pack model didn't bust the bank like its 425-horse alternative. The whole Six Pack deal cost about $470, a palatable price that fit the Econo-Racer ideal rather nicely. Comparatively speaking, that is.

A third engine choice, the 440 Six Pack, appeared midyear for 1969 as part of a purpose-built package meant to go right to the strip. Priced at $468.80, the 440 Six Pack deal was available for both the hardtop and coupe Super Bees. *Mike Mueller*

Production breakdown for the Six Pack Super Bee was 1,487 hardtops (shown here) and 420 coupes. Of the latter, 267 had four-speeds, 153 had automatics. *Mike Mueller*

The basic Six Pack Super Bee interior was as spartan as the car itself. The transmission count for the hardtop renditions read 826 four-speeds, 661 automatics (shown here). *Mike Mueller*

The 440-cubic-inch Six Pack was rated at 390 horsepower. A large rubber seal mated the Six Pack's air cleaner to that fiberglass hood's underside. *Mike Mueller*

Three Holley two-barrel carburetors on an Edelbrock aluminum intake fed the 440 Six Pack V-8. Special rev-conscious valvetrain gear (that improved durability as well) was also part of the package. *Mike Mueller*

The 1970 Super Bee coupe's bottom line also went down predictably to $3,012. Total coupe production, including exports, was 3,966, compared to 11,540 for the hardtop version. *Mike Mueller*

1970
Super Bee

Specifications	
Model availability	two-door coupe and hardtop
Wheelbase	117 inches
Length	209.7 inches
Width	76.7 inches
Height	53 inches
Weight	3,425 pounds (coupe); 3,390 pounds (hardtop)
Base Price	$3,012, coupe; $3,074, hardtop
Track (front/rear, in inches)	59.7/59.2
Wheels	14×6 inches
Tires	F70×14
Construction	unitized body/frame
Suspension	independent A-arms with torsion bars, front; solid axle with longitudinal leaf springs, rear
Steering	recirculating ball
Brakes	four-wheel, heavy-duty, 11-inch drums
Engine	335-horsepower, 383 Magnum V-8
Bore and stroke	4.25×3.38 inches
Compression	9.5:1
Fuel delivery	single Carter four-barrel carburetor
Transmission	three-speed manual, standard
Axle ratio	3.23:1
Production (including exports)	3,966 coupes, 11,540 hardtops

1970

New for 1970 was a radically refreshed Coronet body, graced up front by a dramatic split-grille nose. New for the Super Bee was an equally bold, bulging hood that this time incorporated two aggressive openings and appropriate model-name script. Those non-functional vents again could've been replaced by the dual-scooped Ramcharger hood seen in 1969, and this fresh-air-fed feature once more was included along with the optional 426 Hemi. In non-Hemi applications, the Ramcharger deal cost $73.

A base Super Bee's price actually dipped slightly in 1970 due to the substitution of a yeoman floor-shifted three-speed in place of the previously standard Hurst-shifted four-speed. High-profile magazine ads referred to this switch as "a triumiles per hourantly backward idea" while pointing out that "most performance car prices have gone up." "Naturally, last year's four-speed job costs more," continued Dodge's promotional copy, "but don't think the whole idea of the new Super Bee is getting less." Indeed, those helpful ad guys were more than willing to point out all the great stuff a Super Bee buyer still got for his hard-earned dough in 1970, most specifically the heavy-duty suspension and 335-horse 383 Magnum big-block.

Base prices were $3,012 for the third-edition Super Bee coupe, $3,074 for the hardtop, which translated into a $46 price cut for the former, $64 for the latter. "New 1970 Dodge Super Bee for $64 less," concluded those advertisements in reference to the Bee family's latest "hot dog hardtop." "We think you just might buy the idea." Production totals were 3,631 coupes, 10,507 hardtops. Of these, only 385 coupes and 284 hardtops were built with the base three-speed.

Returning the four-speed back into its rightful place behind the familiar 335-horse 383 was as simple as doling out an additional $197.25. Helping raise the ante further were popular options like those R/T-style body-side scoops, bright exhaust tips, Rallye wheels, a vinyl roof, a trendy rear-deck spoiler, and bucket seats with console.

Black-out treatments front and rear and those cute die-cast bumblebees at both ends again were standard in 1970. New on the

The "upscale" hardtop Super Bee outnumbered its less expensive coupe running mate by nearly a three-to-one margin in 1970. The hardtop's base price that year went down slightly to $3,074 due to the inclusion of a three-speed manual transmission in the standard package. Only 284 three-speed hardtops were built, along with 385 three-speed coupes. *Chrysler LLC Corporate Historical Collection*

options list that year was an alternative tape stripe treatment. Instead of wrapping around the tail bumblebee-style, these reverse "C stripes" complemented the restyled Coronet body's rear quarter contours from each door jam back to the rear bumper. These longitudinal stripes were offered in five body-contrasting colors: black, white, red, green, and blue.

While the Six Pack Super Bee model didn't return for an encore, the engine option itself did, and dropping all those extra goodies (lift-off fiberglass hood, etc.) seen in 1969 translated into some major cost cutting: adding the 390-horse 440 in 1970 required "only" $249.55. Additional changes in the 440 Six Pack's case involved trading the aluminum Edelbrock intake for a cast-iron Chrysler unit, adding a dual-point distributor, and making a few internal tweaks to improve high-rpm operation. Helping out in the latter case were new items like stiffer Hemi valve springs, beefed-up rocker arms and connecting rods, and flash-chromed valves.

Of the 3,630 1970 coupes delivered in America, 3,431 were fitted with the standard 383 Magnum V-8. This Top Banana example is one of only 196 built with the optional 440 Six Pack. Of those, 109 had four-speed transmissions, and 87 had Torqueflites. *Mike Mueller*

The 1970 Super Bee also could've been treated to Dodge's new Rallye wheel option, offered in two sizes that year. Most common were the 14.0x5.5 variety. Much more rare were the big 15x7 Rallye rims, which could've been shod in F60x15 tires. *Mike Mueller*

The optional 440 Six Pack V-8, priced at $249.55 for Super Bee applications, continued to pump out 390 horsepower in 1970. The chrome valve covers seen here are not stock original. *Mike Mueller*

08

The 440 Six Pack's three little Holleys returned for 1970, but the costly Edelbrock intake didn't. It was replaced by an in-house cast-iron piece. *Mike Mueller*

A die-cast Super Bee emblem again appeared up front in 1970. *Mike Mueller*

Two tape treatments were available for the 1970 Super Bee, the traditional bumblebee wrap around the tail and an optional "reverse-C stripe." Color choices numbered five in either case: black, white, red, green, and blue. The familiar Super Bee decal remained in place regardless of which striping was applied. *Mike Mueller*

The bucket seats, console, and sport-type wood-grain steering wheel were Super Bee options in 1970. Charger-style Rallye instrumentation remained standard that year. *Mike Muellerv*

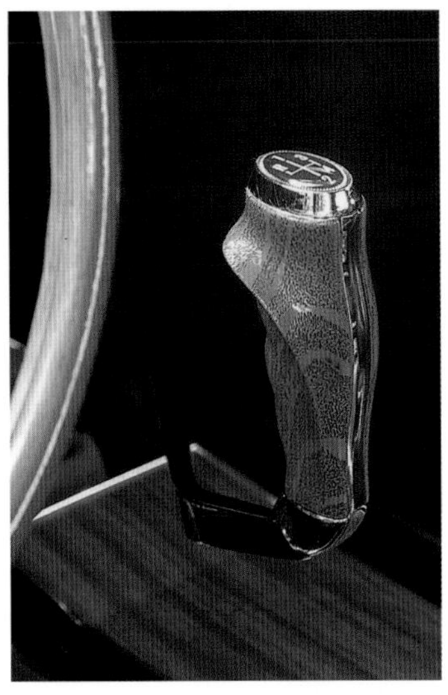

Hurst's high-arching Pistol Grip shifter for 1970 featured a tidy shift pattern on its upper reach. *Mike Mueller*

Engine totals in coupe applications were 3,431 383s, 196 440 Six Packs, and a mere 4 Hemis, all 4 fitted with four-speeds. Optional transmission breakdowns (for coupes) read 1,336 four-speeds and 1,710 automatics in the 383's case, 109 four-speeds and 87 automatics in the 440 Six Pack's. Hardtop figures were 9,404 383s, 1,072 440 Six Packs, and 32 Hemis. Hardtop transmission splits for 383 models were 3,383 four-speeds and 5,737 automatics; 599 four-speeds and 473 automatics for 440 Six Pack models; and 21 four-speeds, 11 automatics for the mighty Hemi Super Bees.

Like the Charger R/T, the Super Bee came standard in 1971 with an aggressively domed hood incorporating simulated vents and engine identification. Optional Bee engines that year included the 340 small-block, 440 four-barrel, 440 Six Pack, and 426 Hemi. *Mike Mueller*

1971
Charger Super Bee

Specifications	
Model availability	two-door hardtop
Wheelbase	115 inches
Length	205.4 inches
Width	79.1 inches
Height	52.7 inches
Weight	3,425 pounds (coupe); 3,390 pounds (hardtop)
Base Price	$3,271
Track (front/rear, in inches)	60.1/62.0
Wheels	14×6 inches
Tires	F70×14
Construction	unitized body/frame
Suspension	independent A-arms with torsion bars, front; solid axle with longitudinal leaf springs, rear
Steering	recirculating ball
Brakes	four-wheel, heavy-duty, 11-inch drums
Engine	330-horsepower, 383 Magnum V-8, standard (340 small-block, 426 Hemi, 440 four-barrel, and 440+6 V-8s, optional)
Bore and stroke	4.25×3.38 inches
Compression	8.5:1
Fuel delivery	single Carter four-barrel carburetor
Transmission	three-speed manual, standard
Axle ratio	3.23:1
Production (including exports)	5,054

1971

With the revised four-door Coronet no longer a viable source for a muscle car foundation after 1970, Dodge's restyled 1971 Charger was left to serve as a hive for Dodge's little hyperactive insect for one final year. Placed midway in that year's three-tiered Charger pecking order, the Charger 500 lineup proved to be the perfect home for the latest, and last, Super Bee.

Sexy enough on its own, the curvaceous 1971 Charger hardtop turned heads even further once treated to the Super Bee touch. A bad-to-the-bone bulging hood was standard and featured a black-out treatment that incorporated the familiar Super Bee character in a prominent circle up front. Additional tape striping ran over the cowl and down the Coke-bottle body sides. Spoilers at both ends were optional, as were trendy color-keyed bumpers. A bench seat remained standard inside, but sporty buckets were again available at extra cost.

08

Opposite, top:
With the Coronet gone after 1970, the Super Bee migrated into Charger ranks for one final appearance in 1971. Black tape striping on the hood, across the cowl, and down the body sides was part of the Super Bee deal that year. Rallye rims or five-spoke road wheels were optional. *Mike Mueller*

Opposite, below:
Base price for Dodge's last Super Bee was $3,271. Production (including exports) was 5,054. The domestic tally was 4,325, of which 3,858 featured the base 383 Magnum big-block. *Mike Mueller*

Right:
The Super Bee's standard 383 Magnum V-8 was rated at 300 horsepower in 1971. Compression was 8.5:1. *Mike Mueller*

Below, right:
A bench seat was again standard inside the 1971 Super Bee. Bucket seats were a $105.95 option that year. Also notice the Tuff steering wheel, itself a $20.10 option. *Mike Mueller*

Below:
An appropriate badge graced the passenger side of the 1971 Charger Super Bee's dash. *Mike Mueller*

The 426 Hemi, also in its last year, was a formidable option for Dodge's final Super Bee in 1971. The 425-horsepower 426 alone cost $883.55 when stuffed between Super Bee fenders. *Mike Mueller*

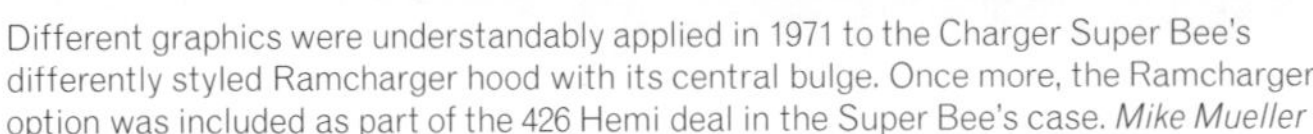
Different graphics were understandably applied in 1971 to the Charger Super Bee's differently styled Ramcharger hood with its central bulge. Once more, the Ramcharger option was included as part of the 426 Hemi deal in the Super Bee's case. *Mike Mueller*

Notice the different graphics applied to the Ramcharger hood flap in 1971. Hemi Super Bee production that year was a mere 22: 13 with Torqueflites, 9 with four-speeds. *Mike Mueller*

Standard power came from a three-speed-backed, toned-down, 383-cubic-inch Magnum, now rated at 300 horsepower. A four-speed and the Torqueflite automatic remained on the options list, as did the 426 Hemi and 440 Six Pack big-block V-8s. New for 1971 was the Super Bee's first available small-block, the 275-horsepower, 340-cubic-inch V-8 (priced at $45.90) and the four-barrel, 440-cubic-inch Magnum, rated at 370 horsepower.

Supporting cast members included the Rallye Suspension Package, which typically stiffened all torsion bars, springs, and shocks, and added a beefy sway bar up front. Heavy-duty brakes (11.0×3.0 inches up front, 11.0×2.5 in back) and F70×14 tires completed the basic package.

Domestic 1971 Super Bee production was 4,325, of which 320 featured the 340 small-block, 3,858 the 383 Magnum, 99 the 440 Six Pack, 26 the 440 four-barrel, and 22 the 426 Hemi. Base three-speed manual installations, behind the standard 383 Magnum, totaled 203. Hemi transmission breakdowns read 13 Torqueflites, 9 four-speeds.

09

BFGoodrich
Radial T/A

340
DUSTER

340
FOUR BARREL
340

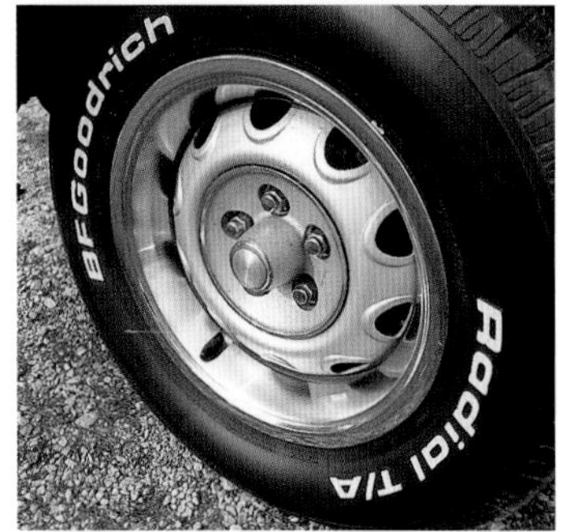

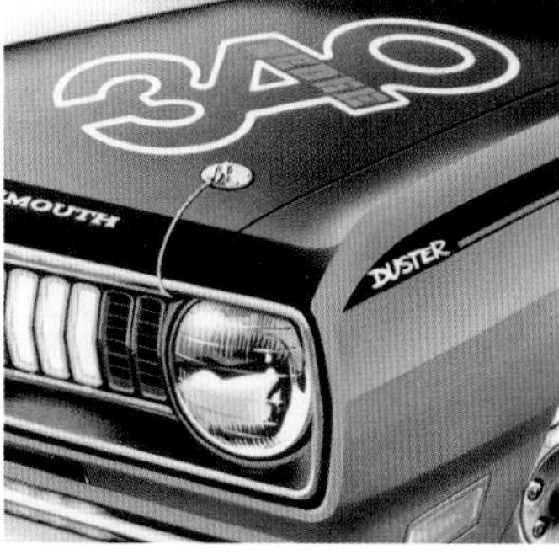

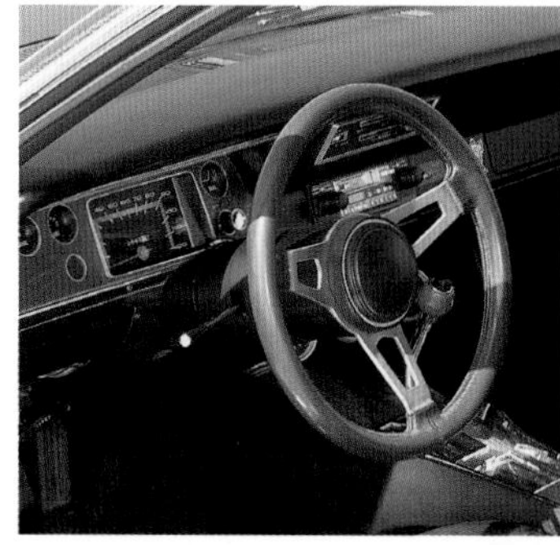

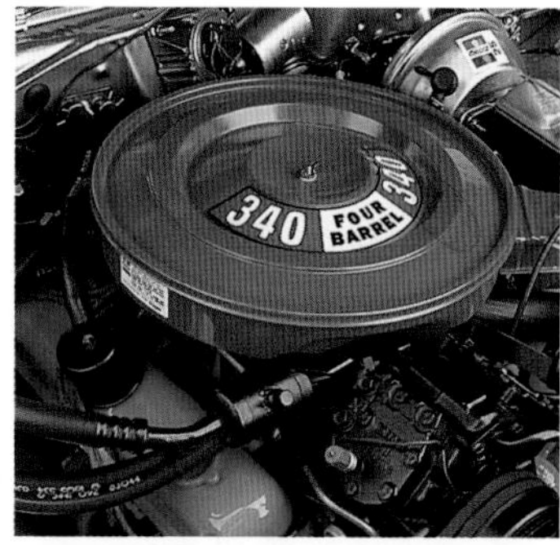

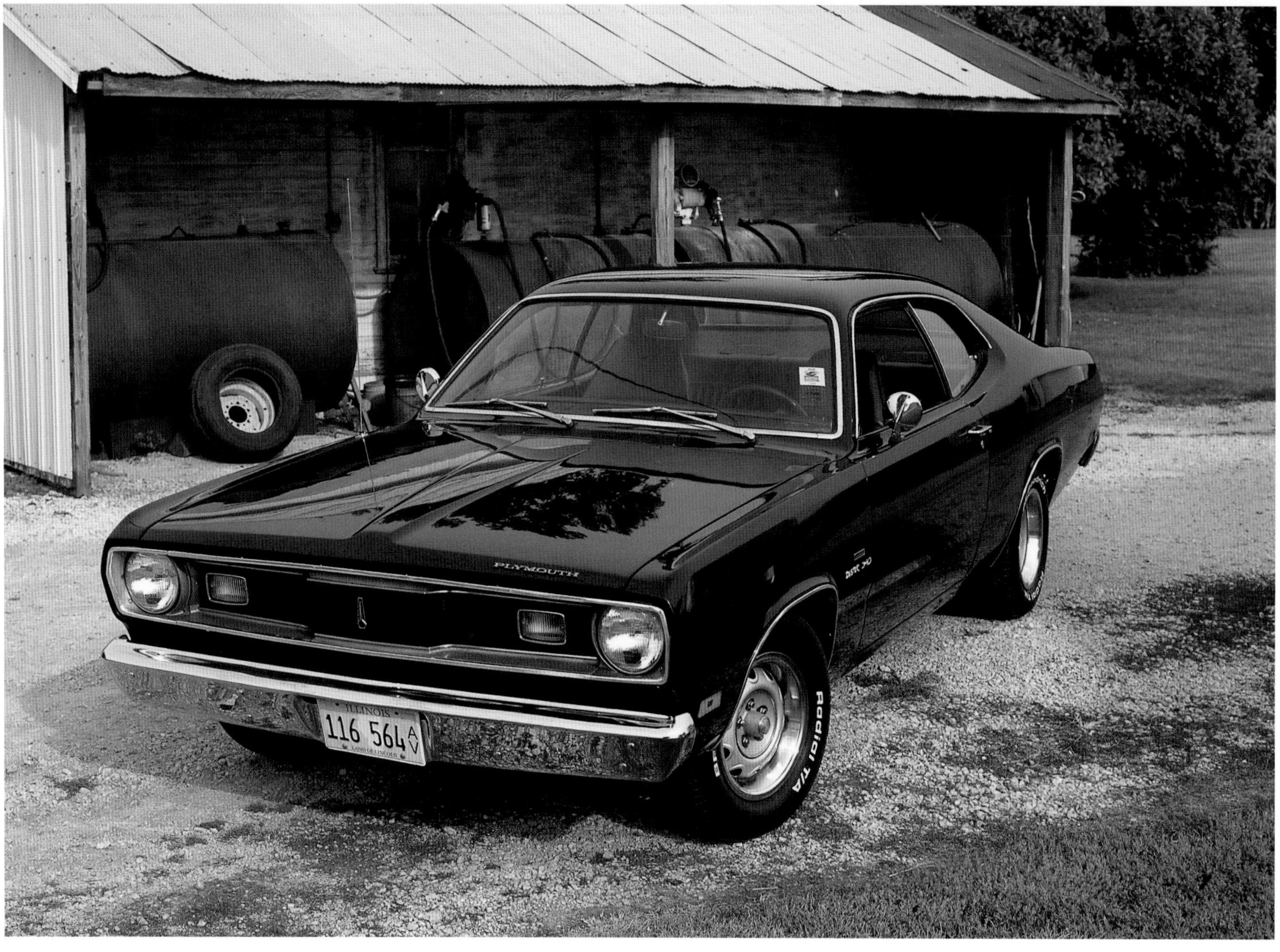
PLYMOUTH
ILLINOIS
116 564 AV
Radial T/A

Plymouth Duster 340 1970–1972

Nothing to Sneeze At

- A concept car, based on Plymouth's Road Runner, made the auto show rounds in 1969 wearing the "Duster I" nameplate.
- Plymouth's original Duster was offered from 1970 to 1976, based on the division's A-body Valiant platform.
- The new Duster 340 became one of five members of Plymouth's equally new Rapid Transit System in 1970.
- Magazine advertisements called the 1970 Duster 340 "the little car that could."
- A Duster trim package reappeared for the Volare sport coupe in 1979 and 1980.
- Another Duster dress-up option was offered for the front-wheel-drive sub-compact Turismo hatchback from 1985 to 1987.
- A Duster trim option showed up again for V-6-powered Sundance models built from 1992 to 1994.

When Plymouth product planners opted to relocate the Barracuda from the foundation it formerly shared with both Valiant and Dodge's Dart over onto Chrysler's exciting new E-body platform for 1970, they inadvertently created a rather noticeable hole in the division's lineup. With a playful A-body two-door coupe apparently no longer available from Plymouth after 1969, what would a Mopar man in dire need of a little affordable sportiness do?

Not wanting to see their customers cross the street to a Dodge lot to look at a Dart Swinger or—gasp!—jump the fence to a Chevy dealership to shop for a Nova SS, Plymouth's best and brightest immediately went scrambling to fill this gap at the last second even as their redesigned E-ticket pony car was making its way to market midway in 1969.

According to Plymouth styling vice-president Dick Macadam, a quick fix was rushed through approval processes in a scant few weeks, thanks mostly to the rapid-fire efforts of designer Neal Walling, who alone performed all the sketch work prior to things taking shape in clay. The name chosen for this hastily created new model was "Duster," a tag previously used (with a Roman numeral "I" suffix) in 1969 for a topless show car based on Plymouth's popular Road Runner.

Much like the division's original Barracuda six years before, the Duster came about more or less by mating a sweeping roofline to Plymouth's ever-mundane Valiant, which was mildly updated for 1970 with a new grille. Only Walling's transformation involved a bit more than simply reshaping the latest A-body's profile. Sure, the Duster's nose was all Valiant, as was its windshield. But from the cowl back, the new sport coupe featured fresh, nicely rounded sheet metal that contrasted notably with Plymouth's typically boxy A-body lines. The end result was a machine that bought like a compact but impressed like few other low-priced rides Detroit then had to offer.

Opposite:
Plymouth's new Duster looked a little sporty in 1970; it was left to the hopped-up Duster 340 to truly play the part of fun machine that year. As the name implied, the only available engine was the 275-horsepower, 340-cubic-inch small-block V-8. *Mike Mueller*

Above:
Plymouth people must've really liked Saturday morning cartoons. Two years after they borrowed Warner Brothers' Road Runner image, they came back with a logo that reminded more than one TV fan of that whirling dervish from down under, the Tasmanian Devil. *Mike Mueller*

Right;
Plymouth introduced its sporty, affordable Duster to relatively rave reviews in 1970. More than 195,000 of these attractive fastback coupes were sold that first year. *Chrysler LLC Corporate Historical Collection*

"Look out little economy cars, here comes Valiant Duster," went Plymouth's televised promotion for its new, certainly sporty, not-so-compact compact. Though not quite as big and heavy as its Nova rival from Chevrolet, the Duster did dwarf its competition from Ford, Maverick, which rolled on a 103-inch wheelbase, compared to 108 for the A-body Plymouth. At 2,919 pounds, Chevy's 1970 Nova used a 111-inch wheelbase. Curb weight for a garden-variety Duster in 1970 was 2,790 pounds. Dearborn's basic Maverick, created with much tighter budgets in mind, tipped the scales at 2,411 pounds that year.

From an aesthetic perspective, most critics liked what Plymouth did to its good old Valiant, although some couldn't quite get a handle on their feelings concerning the Duster makeover. "Is it simply another case of brain fade in [Chrysler styling chief] Elwood P. Engle's office, or is it a complex plot by that company's sociological engineering department to play off truth against beauty in every Plymouth showroom?" asked *Car and Driver* magazine's curbside kibitzers rather cryptically. Plymouth customers then tried to answer this puzzler, at least in part, by shelling out for more than 195,000 Dusters during the model's first year on the market.

The attraction echoed much of what brought so many Mustang buyers galloping into Ford dealerships in April 1964. On one hand, the 1970 Duster was an affordable budget buggy with cost-conscious flip-out rear-quarter glass and a predictably dull bench seat inside. Priced at a tidy $2,172, the base version came standard with a plainly frugal 198-cubic-inch slant-six, rated at a scant 125 horsepower. Behind that six, again predictably, was a yeoman three-speed manual transmission.

On the flipside, however, this cool-looking swoopy coupe offered just enough flair to help completely hide its plebian roots. Also standard inside was the 1969 Barracuda's somewhat sporty dash, which could have been complemented with optional high-back bucket seats and a rather large console with floor shifter.

Enhancing things outside were decals that this time copied a Warner Brothers cartoon character instead of borrowing one: most couldn't miss the resemblance between that googly eyed whirling dust storm and Saturday morning television's hell-raising Tasmanian Devil. And if kicking up a little more dust was the goal, both Plymouth's 145-horse, 225 cid slant-six and 230-horse, 318 cid V-8 were available on the options list.

Yet another available V-8 clearly constituted the eye of the storm. Of course, if the 318-cubic-inch LA small-block fit between Duster fenders, the same obviously was true for Plymouth's proven 340-cube screamer. Hence the Duster 340, the supreme expression of A-body sportiness in Plymouth terms for 1970.

The Duster legacy was reborn again in 1985, this time in the form of an options package for Plymouth's tiny front-wheel-drive Turismo sub-compact. Turismo Duster hatchbacks were offered up through 1987. *Chrysler LLC Corporate Historical Collection*

The Duster name was—dare we say it—dusted off in 1979 and used for a trim package offered for Plymouth's Volare sport coupe. A Volare Duster also appeared for 1980. *Chrysler LLC Corporate Historical Collection*

Light on its feet, and thus deceptively quick thanks to its 275 standard ponies, the Duster 340 basically redefined the term "sleeper." *Car and Driver* called it "a pocket Road Runner," a perfect comparison considering Plymouth's bodacious B-body had just two years before emerged as the epitome of affordable supercars. Many around Detroit simply couldn't believe that so much muscle was available in exchange for so little money as the seventies opened for business. The 1970 Duster 340's base price was an easy $2,547, making it the cheapest member of Plymouth's new Rapid Transit System.

According to *Hot Rod* magazine, Duster 340s were "inflation fighters." "If the Plymouth Duster doesn't fit a logical category, such as compact or something like that, it at least qualifies as one of the best, if not the best, dollar buy in a performance car," added *HR* magazine's Steve Kelly. Pricing wasn't available when *Car and Driver* posted its first Duster review in its September 1969 issue, but that didn't deter the following prognostication: "We believe that the Duster 340 will offer more performance per dollar than any other car in Detroit—or the world for that matter."

Though only around for four years, the Duster 340 still has its fond followers, drivers who know a little about making their dollars go a long way—and go a long way in a hurry.

09

1970
Duster 340

Specifications

Model availability	two-door sport coupe
Wheelbase	108 inches
Length	188.4 inches
Width	71.7 inches
Height	52.1 inches
Weight	3,110 pounds
Base Price	$2,547
Track (front/rear, in inches)	58.2/65.3
Wheels	14.0×5.5 stamped-steel
Tires	E70×14 fiberglass-belted bias-ply
Construction	unitized body/frame
Suspension	long-arm/short-arm with heavy-duty torsion bars and 0.88 sway bar in front; longitudinal heavy-duty leaf springs in back
Steering	recirculating ball
Brakes	front discs, rear drums
Engine	275-horsepower, 340-cubic-inch V-8
Bore and stroke	4.04×3.31 inches
Compression	10.5:1
Fuel delivery	single Carter four-barrel carburetor
Transmission	three-speed manuals, standard; four-speed manual and Torqueflite automatic, optional
Axle ratio	3.23:1
Production	21,799, domestic (22,117, including exports)

The Duster 340's Valiant roots were rather proudly advertised in 1970, put product planners opted to drop the reference the following year. *Mike Mueller*

1970

"And so it came to pass, from the System that generated Road Runner, the country's first low-cost Supercar—a new scheme, another mind-blowing plan. Plymouth would introduce Duster 340, the industry's first real Super Compact." Such was the claim made by Rapid Transit System advertisements touting "the little car that could" late in 1969. Who cared that more than one witness didn't necessarily consider the Duster 340 to be a compact? That was Plymouth people's story, and they were stickin' to it.

RTS brochures for 1970 couldn't say enough about the car that ran with the big dogs but didn't empty out the wallet like one. "We think Supercars should be affordable," began those brags. "Heck, what's the sense of liking anything if you have to wait until you're pushing 30 and your second million to enjoy it? With that in mind we set about to do an encore to Road Runner and create the industry's lowest-priced high performance car. Better yet, we decided to make it a sleeper that would blow the doors off hulking, pretentious behemoths twice its size."

Morphing a mild-mannered Duster into that "sleeper" was simply a matter of mating Plymouth's 275-horsepower, 340-cubic-inch small-block up with a decent collection of high-performance hardware, beginning with a free-flowing dual exhaust system made up of 2.25-inch pipes. Standard behind the 340 V-8 was a heavy-duty three-speed manual transmission, heavy-duty driveshaft and U-joints, and 3.23:1 rear gears. Options included a requisite four-speed manual (with that super-cool Pistol Grip shifter), a Torqueflite automatic, and a Sure-Grip differential with either 3.55:1 or 3.91:1 gears.

Also part of the deal was a reinforced suspension with a thickened 0.88-inch front sway bar, stiffer 0.87-inch torsion bars (with a spring rate of 106 pounds per inch), beefed shocks, and rear springs with

Plymouth's Rapid Transit Caravan toured the country in 1970 and 1971 with a collection of customized machines, including this groovy Duster 340. *Chrysler LLC Corporate Historical Collection*

At $2,547, the base 1970 Duster 340 was the cheapest member of Plymouth's Rapid Transit Authority. Ads claimed this A-body hot rod was "the little car that could." *Mike Mueller*

Right:
A 1969 Barracuda owner would've recognized the 1970 Duster dash—the two vehicles shared the same instrumentation layout. *Mike Mueller*

Above:
Plymouth's new Rallye wheels, measuring 14.0x5.5 inches, were standard for the 1970 Duster 340. Thoroughly modern rubber has long-since replaced the original E70 tires in this case. *Mike Mueller*

All Dusters were cost-conscious coupes with flip-out rear quarter glass instead of roll-up windows. *Mike Mueller*

six leaves instead of five. Front disc brakes were standard, making this the only member of the Rapid Transit System to include these preferred stoppers as part of the base package. Included, as well, were 10.00x1.75-inch rear brake drums and E70 rubber on 14.0x5.5 Rallye wheels. Full instrumentation was added inside.

Even with tasty options like a four-speed stick and Sure-Grip axle (with 3.91:1 gears), the 1970 Duster 340 tested by *Hot Rod* magazine's Steve Kelly still cost only $3,300, a figure that qualified as equally palatable. But Kelly's test results—a 15.38-second quarter-mile run topping out at 91.55 miles per hour—left even him scratching his head. Remember Rapid Transit System membership required time slips in the 14-second range. Kelly concluded that a balky clutch and persnickety transmission in a car that rolled right off the showroom floor onto Irwindale Raceway might've been to blame.

Plymouth's own NHRA-certified flogging produced a best quarter-mile pass of 14 flat. That test's top trap speed was 100.33 miles per hour, all this coming from a 1970 Duster 340 equipped identically to the car Kelly experienced.

U.S. deliveries of Duster 340s in 1970 totaled 21,799. Including exports, the count was 22,117. Of the domestic total, 11,008 featured automatics, 7,390 had four-speeds, and 3,401 were released with the base three-speed.

A blacked-out hood with major graphics was a snazzy new option for 1971. *Chrysler LLC Corporate Historical Collection*

1971
Duster 340

Specifications	
Model availability	two-door sport coupe
Wheelbase	108 inches
Length	188.4 inches
Width	71.7 inches
Height	52.1 inches
Weight	3,140 pounds
Base Price	$2,703
Track (front/rear, in inches)	58.2/65.3
Wheels	14.0×5.5 stamped-steel
Tires	E70×14 fiberglass-belted bias-ply
Construction	unitized body/frame
Suspension	long-arm/short-arm with heavy-duty torsion bars and 0.88 sway bar in front; longitudinal heavy-duty leaf springs in back
Steering	recirculating ball
Brakes	four-wheel drums; power front discs, optional
Engine	275-horsepower, 340-cubic-inch V-8
Bore and stroke	4.04×3.31 inches
Compression	10.3:1
Fuel delivery	single Carter ThermoQuad four-barrel carburetor
Transmission	three-speed manual, standard; four-speed manual and Torqueflite automatic, optional
Axle ratio	3.23:1
Production	10,478, domestic (12,886, including exports)

1971

The most affordable member of the Rapid Transit System returned for 1971 in nearly identical fashion save for some slight image enhancement on the outside and a Carter Thermo-Quad four-barrel in place of the AVS carburetor under the hood. Having proven able to stand tall on its own, Plymouth's so-called super compact was no longer identified as a Valiant variant. Exterior labels simply read "Duster" or "Duster 340." New, too, for 1971 were a truly snazzy grille and some serious body-side stripes. New on the options list that year was a blacked-out hood featuring eye-catching "340 Wedge" graphics with the word "Wedge" incorporated within the number "4." Righteous.

The 340-cubic-inch small-block still advertised at 275 horsepower despite a minor dip in compression, the addition of slightly more restrictive exhaust manifolds, and the new inclusion of the evaporative control system seen before only on California-sold models. Most mechanicals carried over from 1970 save for front disc brakes, which were moved onto the options list in 1971. Four-wheel drums became the norm on a base Duster 340 that year.

Clearly proving it still qualified for RTS membership, a 1971 Duster 340 ran the quarter in 13.90 seconds at 100.8 miles per hour in a *Speed & Supercars* test. Hot parts on this test car included the Torqueflite automatic and 3.91:1 Sure-Grip rear gears.

Total Duster 340 production (exports included) for 1971 was 12,889. The domestic count was 10,478, consisting of 6,213 with automatic transmissions, 4,265 with manuals.

The Twister package appeared midyear for 1971 to offer much of the Duster 340's pizzazz without its performance. A 198-cubic-inch six or 318-cubic-inch V-8 was standard, and the only under-hood option was the 225 cid six. "It's youth-oriented, it's low prices, and it's insurable," was Plymouth's promotional claim. *Chrysler LLC Corporate Historical Collection*

09

SECTION 09: NOTHING TO SNEEZE AT

Plymouth officials placed more emiles per hourasis on the second-edition Duster 340, sprucing up its grille and adding more noticeable striping. Base price was $2,703 in 1971. Front disc brakes—standard items in 1970—became options that year. *Chrysler LLC Corporate Historical Collection*

Domestic production for 1971 was 10,478. Of those, 6,213 featured Torqueflite automatic transmissions, and 4,265 had manuals. *Chrysler LLC Corporate Historical Collection*

High-profile hood graphics appeared again on the Duster 340's options list for 1972.
Mike Mueller

1972
Duster 340

Specifications	
Model availability	two-door sport coupe
Wheelbase	108 inches
Length	188.4 inches
Width	71.7 inches
Height	52.1 inches
Weight	3,175 pounds
Base Price	$2,728
Track (front/rear, in inches)	58.2/56.3
Wheels	14.0×5.5 stamped-steel
Tires	E70×14 fiberglass-belted bias-ply
Construction	unitized body/frame
Suspension	long-arm/short-arm with heavy-duty torsion bars and 0.88 sway bar in front; longitudinal heavy-duty leaf springs in back
Steering	recirculating ball
Brakes	four-wheel drums; power front discs, optional
Engine	240-horsepower (net-rated), 340-cubic-inch V-8
Bore and stroke	4.04×3.31 inches
Compression	8.5:1
Fuel delivery	single Carter ThermoQuad four-barrel carburetor
Transmission	three-speed manual, standard; four-speed manual and Torqueflite automatic, optional
Axle ratio	3.23:1
Production	13,802, domestic (15,681, including exports)

1972

The Duster 340's bold body-side stripes that were added in 1971 were updated the following year with additional whirling dervish cartoon work at their trailing ends. This was the easiest way to tell the two models apart at a glance.

Changes beneath the hood, however, couldn't be missed as industry-wide compression cuts (down to 8.5:1 for the 340 V-8) helped cut back power outputs, which were now rated in net fashion, as opposed to the gross figures seen up through 1971. The 1972 Duster 340's small-block offered 240 net-rated horses. Also contributing to this drop was the substitution of the 360 two-barrel V-8's wimpy heads in place of the excellent big-valve 340 units. While exhaust valve size remained the same (at 1.60 inches), the intake unit shrank from the 340's generous 2.02 inches to a tame 1.88. On a positive note, Chrysler's electronic ignition system became standard for the 1972 340 small-block.

With real muscle on the way into the archives, busting into the 14-second bracket was no longer a possibility for the latest Duster 340. The best *Car and Driver* testers could manage was a 15.6/89.5 quarter-mile pass. Then again, this test vehicle was loaded down with options, including expensive (and heavy) air conditioning.

The total production count for 1972 was 15,681, with 13,802 delivered in this country. The transmission breakdown included 8,530 automatics, 2,871 four-speeds, and 2,401 three-speeds.

09

The base price for a 1972 Duster 340 was $2,728. Total production, exports included, was 15,681. The domestic count was 13,802. *Mike Mueller*

A dust-trailing whirling dervish was added to the Duster 340's body-side stripes in 1972. A compression cut and new net ratings cut the 340 small-block down to 240 horsepower that year. *Mike Mueller*

As in 1970, bucket seats and a center console were options for the Duster 340 in 1971. *Mike Mueller*

Plymouth's popular Tuff steering wheel was a Duster 340 option from the beginning. *Mike Mueller*

1973
Duster 340

Specifications	
Model availability	two-door sport coupe
Wheelbase	108 inches
Length	188.4 inches
Width	71.7 inches
Height	52.1 inches
Weight	3,175 pounds
Base Price	$2,822
Track (front/rear, in inches)	58.2/56.3
Wheels	14.0×5.5 stamped-steel
Tires	E70×14 fiberglass-belted bias-ply
Construction	unitized body/frame
Suspension	long-arm/short-arm with heavy-duty torsion bars and 0.88 sway bar in front; longitudinal heavy-duty leaf springs in back
Steering	recirculating ball
Brakes	four-wheel drums; power front discs, optional
Engine	240-horsepower (net-rated), 340-cubic-inch V-8
Bore and stroke	4.04×3.31 inches
Compression	8.5:1
Fuel delivery	single Carter ThermoQuad four-barrel carburetor
Transmission	three-speed manual, standard; four-speed manual and Torqueflite automatic, optional
Axle ratio	3.23:1
Production	11,841, domestic (15,731, including exports)

Still a relatively formidable force—certainly so compared to what was left in Detroit's muscle car market—the Duster 340 returned for its encore in 1973. Base price was $2,822. *Mike Mueller*

1973

Plymouth's final Duster 340 remained a decent performer for the money, relatively speaking that is. Nowhere near as hot as its forerunners, the 1973 Duster 340 still was more fun to drive than most of its bigger, flashier rivals. Total production that last year was 15,371, including 11,841 domestic issues. Of these, 1,492 had the standard three-speed manual transmission, 2,037 had four-speeds, and 8,312 had automatics. A Duster 360 appeared for 1974, but it plain and simply represented a mere shadow of the Plymouth performance compact's former self.

Above:
The Duster's tail and nose were restyled for 1973, and the A-body's front suspension was beefed a bit. Duster 340 production (including exports) that year was 15,731. Of those, 11,841 were delivered domestically. *Mike Mueller*

Above, right:
Plymouth's 240-horsepower, 340-cubic-inch V-8 appeared one last time between A-body fenders in 1973. Compression was 8.5:1. *Mike Mueller*

Right:
A bench-seat interior with a ho-hum steering wheel was standard inside all Duster 340s. But, as in previous years, buckets, a console, and that image-enhancing Tuff steering wheel remained just an options list away in 1973. *Mike Mueller*

Above:
While the Duster 340 didn't return for 1974, at least the Duster 360 remained around to keep the legacy alive, however feebly. The 360-cubic-inch small-block V-8 was net-rated at 245 horsepower that year. *Chrysler LLC Corporate Historical Collection*

Left:
Flashy tape stripes were standard for the 1975 Duster 360. This package didn't roll over into 1976, but an optional 360 V-8 did for Plymouth's last A-body duster. Notice the optional sunroof. *Chrysler LLC Corporate Historical Collection*

10

POLYGLAS

FUEL

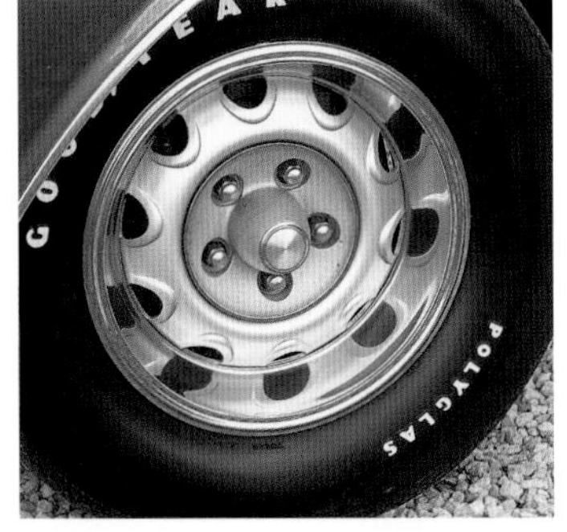

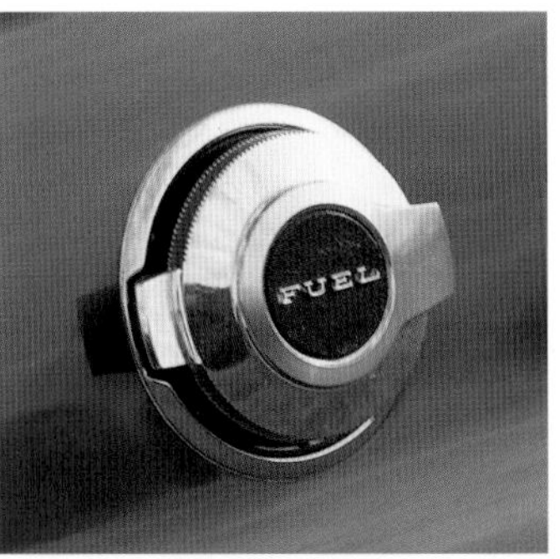

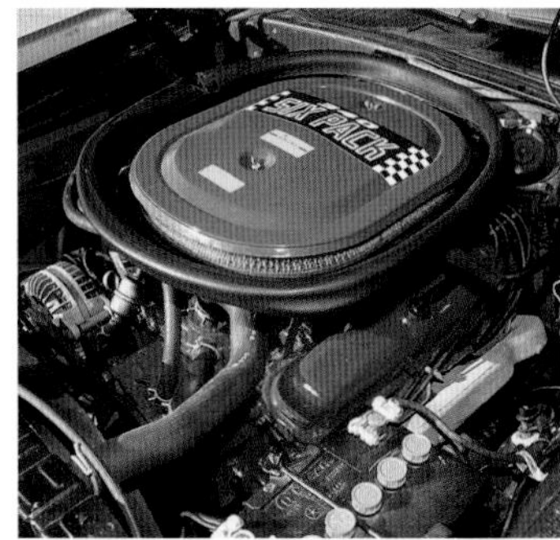

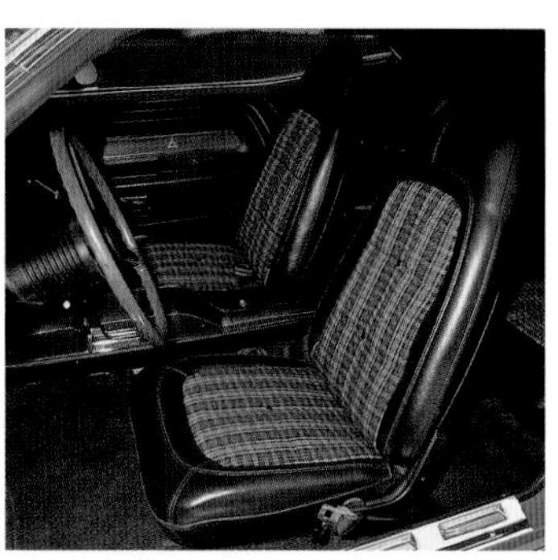

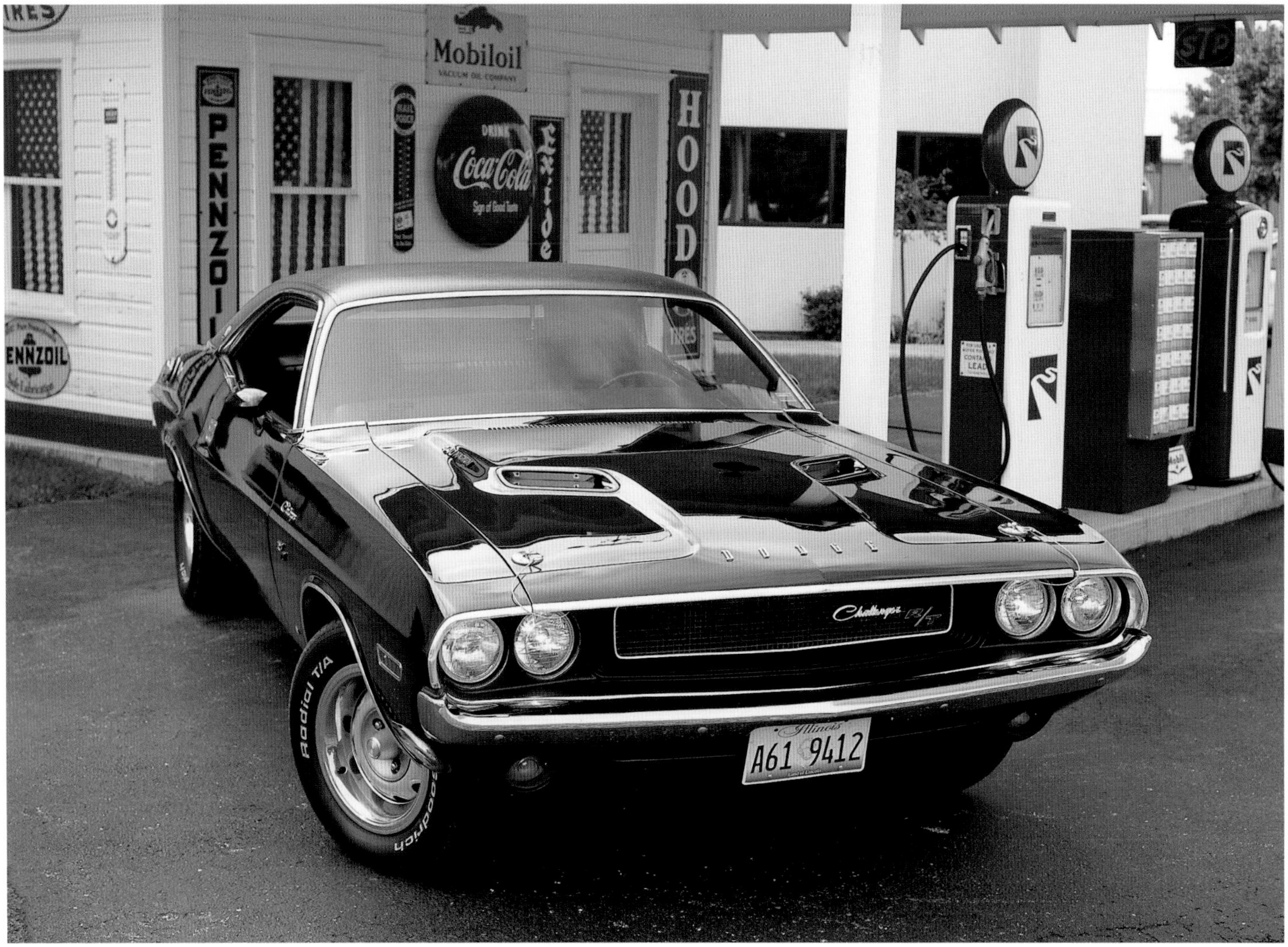
Mobiloil
VACUUM OIL COMPANY
PENNZOIL
Coca-Cola
Sign of Good Taste
Exide
HOOD
TIRES
STP
Challenger R/T
Radial T/A
Illinois
A61 9412

Dodge Challenger 1970 – 1974

E-Ticket Ride

- Challenger convertibles and R/T models were offered only for 1970 and 1971.
- Challenger R/T convertibles were offered only for 1970.
- Dodge's variation on Plymouth's AAR 'Cuda Trans-Am pony car theme, the Challenger T/A, was introduced for 1970 and built for one year only.
- The highest finish for a Dodge Challenger in Trans-Am racing was Sam Posey's fourth at Road America in Wisconsin on May 9, 1970.
- Dodge offered a second-generation Challenger, based on its Mitsubishi-sourced Galant Lambda coupe, from 1978 to 1983.
- Dodge's retro-styled, Hemi-powered Challenger concept car began drawing raves on the auto show circuit in January 2006.
- The dream became reality in 2008 as a regular-production reborn Challenger hit the streets armed with a 425-horsepower, 6.1-liter Hemi V-8.

Talk about your time machines. When the Dodge Boys unveiled their new Challenger concept vehicle at the North American International Auto Show in Detroit in January of 2006, they took many a middle-aged Mopar muscle maven on a backward ride to fondly recalled days gone by. Three years before, on practically the same stage, Ford also had demonstrated that at least some things old can be new again while introducing a comparable concept, in this case a thoroughly modern Mustang that looked an awful lot like one (or more) of that breed's famed forerunners. So what if Dodge simply copied the idea? Rave reviews in January 2006 proved there was more than enough room left over in Detroit's time tunnel to allow Dodge customers to enjoy a similar nostalgic ride. And when the Challenger dream car became a showroom reality in the summer of 2008, it immediately helped many critics forget all about Dearborn's retro-styled pony car, itself ushered into the mainstream as a 2005 model.

Based on a shortened version of the present Charger's LX platform, the 2008 Challenger SRT-8 was powered by a 6.1-liter Hemi, a 425-horse monster that easily qualified as "sw-e-e-e-et" in anyone's book. But there was much more to this saccharine attraction than 13-second bursts down the quarter-mile. Looks were every bit as tasty. *Motor Trend* called the new Challenger a "Big Thumper Reborn" in obvious recognition of Dodge designers' attempts to rival Ford's latest Mustang with their own pony car reincarnation.

Most who set eyes on the 2008 Challenger surely thought it was 1970 all over again. According to *Road & Track* guest scribe Sam Posey, "its styling recalls both the earlier Challenger and its sibling, the Plymouth Barracuda, having the flowing character line of the former and the latter's short overhangs, front and rear." A blast from the past himself, Posey definitely was the right man to compare old and new, thanks to the time he spent putting his spurs to a Sublime Challenger on SCCA Trans-Am tracks nearly 40 years

Opposite:
Dodge offered its original Challenger in a three-tiered pecking order in 1970, beginning with the base six-cylinder models. Next up was the V-8 Challenger, followed by the high-performance R/T. All three lines featured three body styles: hardtop, Special Edition hardtop, and convertible. A top-shelf R/T SE, fitted with the optional 440 Magnum V-8, appears here. *Mike Mueller*

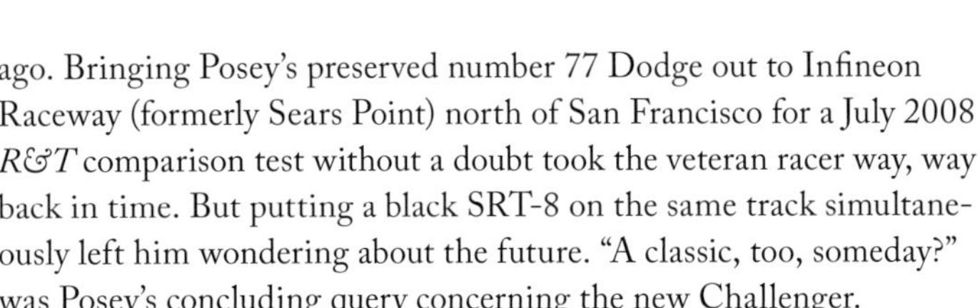

Above:
Dodge introduced its latest Challenger in concept car form at the Detroit auto show in January 2006. Its SRT-8 regular-production version then started hitting the streets in the summer of 2008. *Mike Mueller*

Right:
The Challenger's trademark beltline crease—yet another touch intended to help set Dodge's E-body noticeably apart from Plymouth's—takes shape in this clay mockup. Eagle-eyes might notice the Mercury Cougar hiding behind this clay for comparison purposes. *Chrysler LLC Corporate Historical Collection*

ago. Bringing Posey's preserved number 77 Dodge out to Infineon Raceway (formerly Sears Point) north of San Francisco for a July 2008 *R&T* comparison test without a doubt took the veteran racer way, way back in time. But putting a black SRT-8 on the same track simultaneously left him wondering about the future. "A classic, too, someday?" was Posey's concluding query concerning the new Challenger.

Even casual witnesses not particularly interested in Chrysler products can sometimes be heard these days calling the first-edition Challenger—built all too briefly from 1970 to 1974—a modern classic of sorts, thanks mostly to looks often considered somewhat timeless, even more so now that they've been dusted off 38 years after the initial fact. Sweet simply isn't a sugary enough word, at least from a nostalgic perspective. Some critics back in the day did turn a little sour after first trying Dodge's new pony car on for size. In *Car and Driver*'s words, "there's no doubt the [1970] Challenger is a handsome car but it also has a massive feeling—which stems from a full five inches more width than a Mustang and a need to sign up with Weight Watchers—that is totally unwelcome in a sporty car."

Maybe so, but Dodge officials from the outset fully intended to help make their customers feel right at home in a new brand of bigger, more prestigious pony car. A direct copy of the Barracuda was out of the question and had been from the get-go. When Chrysler execs offered Dodge people that option after Plymouth's fighting-fish-car made its humble splash in 1964, the division's decision-makers chose instead to focus their attentions on a new sporty mid sized model based on the corporation's 117-inch-wheelbase B-body, with the result being the sleek 1966 Charger, primarily styled by a young Bill Brownlie protégé, Carl Cameron.

A full-fledged Dodge pony project didn't really start running until after the Charger was ready for market. Harry Cheeseborough, senior vice president of styling and product planning, was the man put in charge of this project in the fall of 1966, and he turned to Brownlie's studio to fashion the form. While the original plan did include sharing Chrysler's new compact E-body platform with the upcoming 1970 Barracuda, the machine Cheeseborough and crew had in mind took shape as a longer, larger little horse meant to compete with Mercury's upscale Cougar, not Ford's shorter, more mundane Mustang. Initial specifications included using a relatively lengthy 111-inch wheelbase, same as the A-body Dart's. But in the end it was a 110-inch stretch—still two inches longer than the developing

Dodge's idea from the beginning involved offering a little more prestige in its E-body package, and this was accomplished mainly by stretching the Challenger's wheelbase to 110 inches, compared to the 108 inches for Plymouth's 1970 E-body Barracuda. *Chrysler LLC Corporate Historical Collection*

Topless Challenger models were offered only in 1970 and 1971. A convertible R/T appeared only for 1970. Quad headlights were included from the get-go to further help upstage the E-body Barracuda, which used only one lamp on each side in 1970. *Chrysler LLC Corporate Historical Collection*

E-body Plymouth's—that was approved, thanks to Carl Cameron's strong suggestion. As for the name, reportedly Brownlie leaned toward Challenger as a suitable complement to the existing Charger nameplate.

Like its E-body corporate cousin, the 1970 Challenger seemingly violated physical laws. Comparatively compact overall, the car nonetheless incorporated a truly spacious engine bay thanks to the inclusion of the larger B-body's wide cowl structure. From the cowl forward rested more than enough room to house even the monstrous Hemi comfortably without any shoehorning, something that definitely couldn't have been said when Plymouth engineers started stuffing B-series V-8s beneath A-body Barracuda hoods in 1967. Behind all that potential powerplant was a bit more interior space thanks to those two extra clicks on the wheelbase meter.

While the two E-bodies shared front and rear tracks and all glass, that was about it as far as direct carryovers were concerned. The Challenger's profile and roofline looked a lot like the E-ticket Plymouth's, but Brownlie's body featured a prominent beltline crease (mentioned earlier on these pages by Sam Posey) that arched up over the rear wheel openings, a touch that further enhanced the Dodge's longer lines. Four headlights appeared up front instead of two, and a markedly different taillight treatment in back also made sure that even casual witnesses couldn't mistake a Challenger for a Barracuda.

Challengers came in a wide range of flavors from the start, topped off by the truly scrumptious Hemi rendition. Hot packages were available early on with both big- and small-block power, but the attraction started cooling considerably after the Challenger was limited to the latter after 1971. Though the available 340 small-block remained fun, many buyers simply couldn't overlook an age-old truth: in those days, there really was no substitute for cubic inches. A slight sales surge in 1973 did little to erase the handwriting on the wall, and the original Challenger was history by the close of the following year.

The badge did return in definitely compact fashion from 1978 to 1983, but it clearly wasn't the same. Some Dodge devotees surely even felt it a crime to call a four-cylinder Mitsubishi Galant a Challenger. Fortunately, the legacy was repackaged again 25 years later, this time to the utter delight of time travelers everywhere. As *Popular Mechanics'* Jim Dunne suggested after witnessing the Challenger concept's debut in 2006, "DaimlerChrysler management better not screw up the production version of this car or there's gonna be hell to pay."

Sure looks like they hit the nail square on the head.

1970 Challenger R/T

Specifications	
Model availability	two-door hardtop, Special Edition formal roof, and convertible
Wheelbase	110 inches
Length	191.3 inches
Width	76.1 inches
Height	50.9 inches
Weight	3,402 pounds (hardtop), 3,437 pounds (SE), 3,467 pounds (convertible)
Base Price	$3,266 (hardtop), $3,498 (SE), $3,535 (convertible)
Track (front/rear, in inches)	59.7/60.7
Wheels	14×6
Tires	F70×14 raised-white-letter
Construction	unitized body/frame
Suspension	independent A-arms with heavy-duty torsion bars, front; solid axle with longitudinal heavy-duty leaf springs, rear
Steering	recirculating ball
Brakes	four-wheel, heavy-duty, 11-inch drums
Engine	335-horsepower, 383 Magnum V-8, standard (440 Magnum, 440 Six Pack, and 426 Hemi V-8s, optional)
Bore and stroke	4.25×3.38 inches
Compression	9.5:1
Fuel delivery	single Carter four-barrel carburetor
Transmission	three-speed manual
Axle ratio	3.23:1
Production (all three body styles, including exports)	19,938 (18,602, domestic)

Standard R/T features also included beefed brakes and suspension and Wide Tread F70x14 rubber in 1970. Larger 15-inch wheels and tires were typically included when the optional Hemi was installed. The rear spoiler was a $34.80 option. *Mike Mueller*

1970

The Challenger lineup for 1970 began at the bottom with a basic model featuring Dodge's yeoman 225 cid slant-six engine backed by a three-speed manual transmission. This 145-horse six could've been wrapped up in three different bodies: hardtop, convertible, or "Special Edition" sports hardtop. Then in March this trio was joined by "The Deputy," a truly affordable hardtop that featured, among other things, fixed rear quarter glass and a truly frugal 198 cid six-cylinder. On the other side of the coin, the definitely dressy SE featured leather bucket seats; an upscale vinyl roof with a smaller, "opera"-type rear window; and an overhead console that housed warning lights for low fuel, door ajar, and unfastened seat belts. SE customers averse to cowhide could've substituted (at a credit) those standard buckets for cloth and vinyl seats.

Next up the pricing pecking order was the V-8 Challenger, offered in the same three body styles with the dependable 318 cid small-block supplying standard power. V-8-equipped Deputy models were built too, but that sorta defeated the purpose behind this cost-cutting ideal.

Optional V-8s included the 275-horse, 340 cid small-block and two 383 big-blocks: a 290-horse two-barrel version and its four-barrel-

Base price for a Challenger R/T hardtop in 1970 was $3,266. Dodge's 335-horsepower, 383-cubic-inch Magnum big-block was standard beneath the R/T's long hood. *Mike Mueller*

An R/T Challenger could've been adorned in 1970 with familiar bumblebee stripes around its tail or this longitudinal tape treatment. *Mike Mueller*

The competition-style gas cap on Plymouth's A-body Barracuda had been located on the driver side. Dodge design chief Bill Brownlie reportedly relocated the Challenger's fuel filler to the passenger's rear quarter panel to make running out of gas a safer situation. Drivers filling their tanks alongside a road would be out of harm's way away from traffic. Both this stylish pop-open cap and a conventional twist-off unit, painted to match the body, were available on 1970 Challengers. *Mike Mueller*

A bulging hood with twin scoops was standard R/T fare in 1970. Available for the R/T only in Dodge's E-body ranks, the 440 Magnum V-8 was a $130.55 option. *Mike Mueller*

Rallye wheels, available in 14- and 15-inch diameters, were optional for the 1970 Challenger. The price was $43.10. *Mike Mueller*

fed big brother. The hot little 340 was offered as part of a package that also included 15x7 Rallye wheels wearing E60 tires. Later in the model run the Shaker hood also became an option for 340-powered Challengers.

Three-speed manuals were again standard behind these V-8s, save for the 383 two-barrel, which was mated to the Torqueflite automatic only. Automatics were optional in other applications, as was a four-speed manual behind all engines except for the aforementioned 290-horsepower 383 and the base slant-six. A lengthy options list included everything from a vinyl roof (with normal-sized rear glass) to wire wheel covers. Also new from Dodge for 1970 was a delightful paint palette that included such radiant shades as Plum Crazy, Go-Mango, and Sam Posey's fave (Sublime).

The only choice as far as muscle heads were concerned was the top-shelf Challenger R/T, also available in hardtop, convertible, and SE forms. Power choices for the R/T included the base 383 Magnum and three options: the 375-horse 440, 390-horsepower 440 Six Pack, or 426 Hemi. Both of the 440s and the Hemi were only available in R/T models—no other Challenger could put on so much muscle. A three-speed stick was once more standard for a base R/T, with the preferred four-speed and the tough Torqueflite both predictably optional. R/T customers opting for the ever-expensive Hemi or one of the 440s could've picked either the four-speed or the Torqueflite only, and rightly so.

Standard, as well, for the R/T were Dodge's Rallye suspension, heavy-duty drum brakes, and Wide-Tread F70x14 rubber. Typically included on Hemi models were larger 15-inch wheels and tires. Exterior identification consisted of familiar "R/T" badges and either a longitudinal stripe or Dodge's popular bumblebee tail treatment. The Rallye instrument cluster, optional on other Challengers, was included inside as part of the R/T deal. This equipment included a simulated wood-grain dash panel; 150-miles-per-hour speedometer; tachometer; trip odometer; clock; gauges for fuel, oil, and temperature; ammeter; and three-speed variable wipers.

Popular R/T options included Rallye wheels and the groovy Shaker hood scoop, which as mentioned was only seen early on atop the 440 Six Pack and 426 Hemi V-8s. Midway into 1970 this massive, fully functional feature became available with any Challenger V-8 fed by a four-barrel carburetor. Shakers were done in four complimentary colors—red, blue, silver, or black—depending on the exterior finish chosen.

Dodge promotional people turned to various pro racers to tout the division's 1970 lineup, and drag racing's Don "Big Daddy" Garlits was given the Challenger R/T to review. "Now Dodge has gone and done

The 375-horsepower, 440-cubic-inch Magnum RB big-block was one of three optional V-8s offered for the 1970 Challenger R/T. The 440 Six Pack and 426 Hemi also could've been installed. *Mike Mueller*

Along with an 8,000 rpm tachometer and gauges for fuel level, oil pressure, coolant temperature, and alternator, the Challenger's Rallye dash also featured a 150-miles per hour speedometer. *Mike Mueller*

Optional on other Challengers in 1970, Dodge's Rallye instrument cluster was standard for the R/T. A simulated wood-grain panel, a clock, a trip odometer, and variable-speed wipers were included in the Rallye package. *Mike Mueller*

A three-speed manual transmission was standard for basic R/Ts in 1970. The optional four-speed came with Hurst's image-enhancing Pistol Grip shifter. *Mike Mueller*

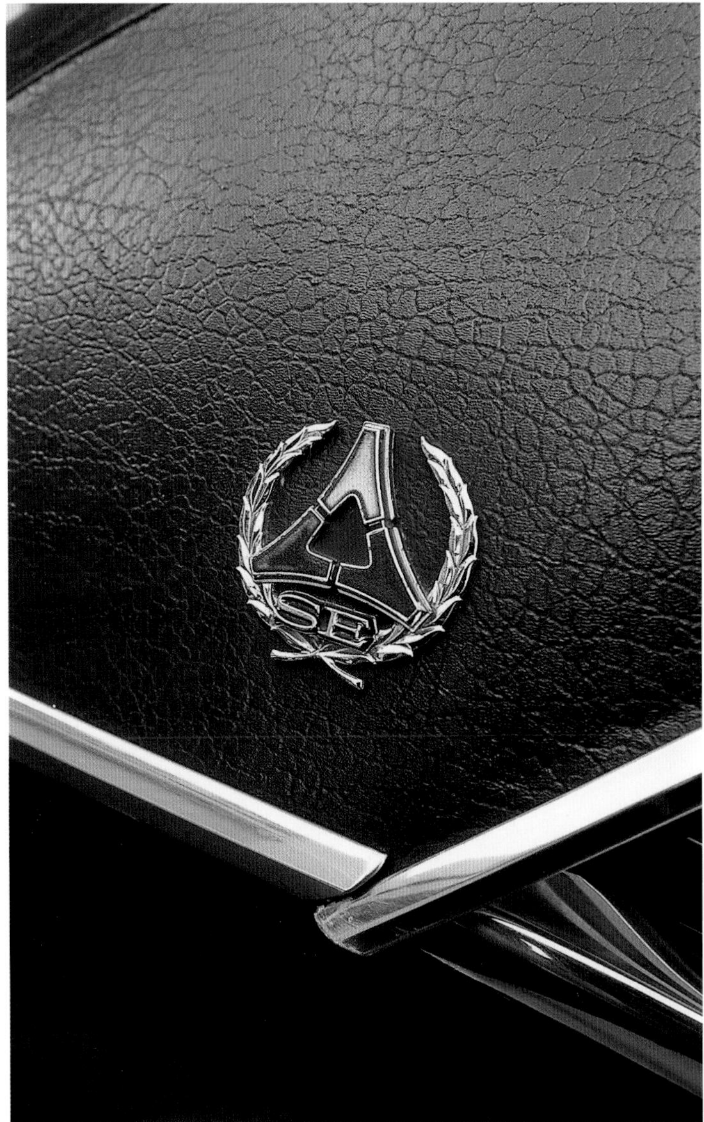

Base price for a Challenger R/T SE in 1970 was $3,498. Total R/T SE production (including exports) that year was 3,979. The domestic count was 3,741. *Mike Mueller*

A downsized rear window was included as part of the Challenger's Special Edition package in 1970. According to *Car and Driver*, this fashion-conscious reduction of rearward visibility transformed the new Challenger into a "park-by-ear car." *Mike Mueller*

the real thing," concluded the Large Father in company ads. "They watched the whole pony car thing develop, then built their own super-tough version. Compact like a Dart. Wide like a Charger. Just the right size for anyone who likes his own personalized backyard bomb. Dodge should sell a million of 'em."

Well, maybe not quite that many. The short-lived Challenger's best year was its first, with more than 80,000 produced for both domestic and export markets. But again, so what? Garlits' tongue-in-cheek production prediction might've fallen flat, but his "backyard bomb" description surely rang true.

A *Sports Car Graphic* road test claimed a 440 Magnum R/T could reach the far side of the quarter-mile in 14.7 seconds, topping out at 95 miles per hour. *SCG* staffers also liked the way the 375-horse R/T looked as hot as it ran yet still felt as cool as a cucumber from

A vinyl roof and leather-accented bucket seats were standard for the Special Edition Challenger hardtop in 1970. The count for Hemi-powered R/T SE models (shown here) that year was 59. *Mike Mueller*

An overhead console was included in the Special Edition package. This unit incorporated warning lights for a door ajar, low fuel, and unlatched seat belts. *Mike Mueller*

Of that meager 1970 Hemi R/T SE count, 37 were fitted with Torqueflite automatics (demonstrated here), 22 with four-speed manuals. *Mike Mueller*

behind the wheel. "Hey fella, you want to buy a body that'll upstage your 42-D girlfriend in a see-through? Could you use a street-stock, smooth-idling mill that'll pull the hide off a rhinoceros? How would you like a two-door outdoor living room that pampers you like an anxious stewardess?" If all three answers were yes, the car for you, in *SCG*'s colorful opinion, was the 440 Magnum–equipped Challenger R/T.

Hemi R/T performance, of course, represented the top of the heap. A *Car and Driver* report listed quarter-mile numbers of 14.1 seconds at 103.2 miles per hour. Zero to 60 required only 5.8 ticks.

R/T domestic deliveries for 1970 totaled 13,668 hardtops, 955 convertibles, and 3,979 SE hardtops. Hemi installations included 287 hardtops, 9 convertibles, and 59 Special Editions. The count for the 440 Six Pack read 1,604 hardtops, 99 convertibles, and 296 SE hardtops. Tallies for the440 Magnum were 2,802 hardtops, 163 convertibles, and 875 SE models.

As in Plymouth's case, Dodge's supreme E-body for 1970 featured the optional Hemi. A *Car and Driver* test produced a 14.1-second quarter-mile time for a 425-horse Challenger R/T. *Mike Mueller*

Body-side tape treatments announced the Challenger T/A's presence. *Mike Mueller*

1970
Challenger T/A

Specifications	
Model availability	two-door hardtop
Wheelbase	110 inches
Length	191.3 inches
Width	76.1 inches
Height	not available
Weight	not available
Base Price	T/A package cost $865.70
Track (front/rear, in inches)	59.7/60.7
Wheels	15×7
Tires	Goodyear, E60×15 in front, G60×15 in back
Construction	unitized body/frame
Suspension	independent A-arms with heavy-duty torsion bars and thickened stabilizer bar, front; solid axle with longitudinal heavy-duty leaf springs, rear
Steering	recirculating ball
Brakes	power front discs, rear drums
Engine	290-horsepower, 340-cubic-inch V-8
Bore and stroke	4.04×3.31 inches
Compression	10.5:1
Fuel delivery	three Holley two-barrel carburetors
Transmission	A-833 four-speed manual (with Hurst shifter) or 727 Torqueflite automatic
Axle ratio	3.55:1 ratio in 8.75-inch Sure-Grip differential
Production	2,400

1970 T/A 340 Six Pack

Another variation on Dodge's E-body theme appeared in March 1970 after the division's counterpart to Plymouth's AAR 'Cuda appeared. Called the Challenger T/A, this street racer also was created to homologate track-ready versions for SCCA Trans-Am road racing. New Trans-Am rules for 1970 required a minimum production run of 2,500 units, but Dodge rolled out only 2,400 or so Challenger T/As during a brief three-month run. Though a little short of the mark, that effort still qualified as being in compliance as far as SCCA governing moguls were concerned, meaning Dodge was back in Trans-Am racing after a two-year hiatus.

On the track, SCCA-spec Challenger T/As, built by Ray Caldwell Autodynamics, used a destroked 305 cid version of Dodge's potent 340 cid V-8 to stay within a specified 5-liter limit. Chrysler's road racing team manager Pete Hutchinson managed to coax 440 haughty horses out of this maxed-out small-block relying on a single four-barrel carburetor. On the street, the civilized Challenger T/A featured the familiar (to AAR 'Cuda drivers) 290-horse, triple-carb, 340-cubic-inch small-block, available in Dodge-land only in the T/A Challenger. Behind the 340 Six Pack was either a 727 Torqueflite automatic or a specially prepared close-ratio four-speed with Hurst shifter.

As expected, the rest of the T/A package mimicked Plymouth's AAR parts list. Most prominent again was that special cool-air fiberglass hood, which fed the three Holleys via an innovative snorkel scoop and large oval air cleaner that sealed directly to the hood's underside. Designers discovered that raising the scoop's opening an inch or so above the hood helped circumvent the induction-inhibiting boundary layer of slow-moving air that naturally develops at speed. This little trick reportedly was worth 10 to 15 addition horsepower at 80 miles per hour.

Right:
The commonly accepted number for Challenger T/A Six Pack production is 2,400, an estimation at best. Some sources claim the exact total was 2,399 in 1970.
Mike Mueller

Below:
Mismatched tire sizes and reworked rear springs gave the Challenger T/A a noticeable forward rake in 1970. Standard front treads (long since replaced here) were E60×15 Goodyears, while G60 rubber originally brought up the rear. *Mike Mueller*

Left:
A convoluted exhaust system allowed the Challenger T/A's spent gases to exit directly in front of its rear wheels. Notice the standard rims with small hubcaps on this example. *Mike Mueller*

Below, left:
Appropriate identification went onto the Challenger T/A's rear spoiler, which was standard. A chin spoiler up front was optional. *Mike Mueller*

The same circuitous exhaust system found beneath the AAR 'Cuda also exited directly ahead of the Challenger T/A's fat G60×15 Goodyear tires. Increasing the camber of the heavy-duty rear leaf springs was again required both to supply ample ground clearance for those exhausts and allow a suitable fit for the mismatched rear rubber. Stiff front and rear sway bars and beefed shocks also carried from AAR to T/A, as did an 8.75-inch Sure-Grip differential with 3.55:1 or 3.91:1 gears. Steering chores were handled by either a 24.0:1 manual box or a quick 14.2:1 power-assisted unit.

Throw in blacked-out touches for the hood and grille, hood pins, bold "TA 340 Six Pack" graphics down the body sides, and a competition-type pop-open fuel filler (optional on other Challengers), and this racy E-body simply couldn't lose, at least not on the Saturday night cruise circuit. Enhancing the image further was a standard ducktail spoiler in back. A front chin spoiler was optional. Most Challenger T/As you see today have the optional Rallye wheels; standard was a 15×7JJ wheel with a small center cap and trim ring. Bucket seats; console; simulated wood-grain touches on the steering wheel, dash, door panels, and console; and deep-pile carpeting were all also part of the T/A deal.

Buying a Challenger T/A in 1970 was not an easy task, unless you lived near Lake Michigan. Most eligible dealers were allotted one, maybe two, but the legendary Norm Kraus, of Mr. Norm's Grand-Spaulding Dodge in Chicago, got 50 for his performance-packed floor plan. Mr. Norm also advertised special treatment for his customers;

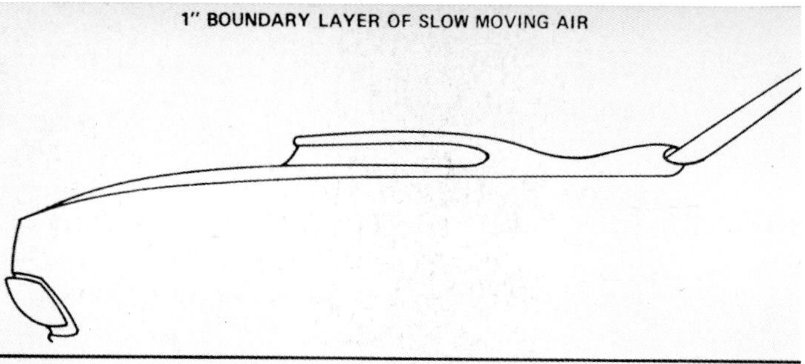

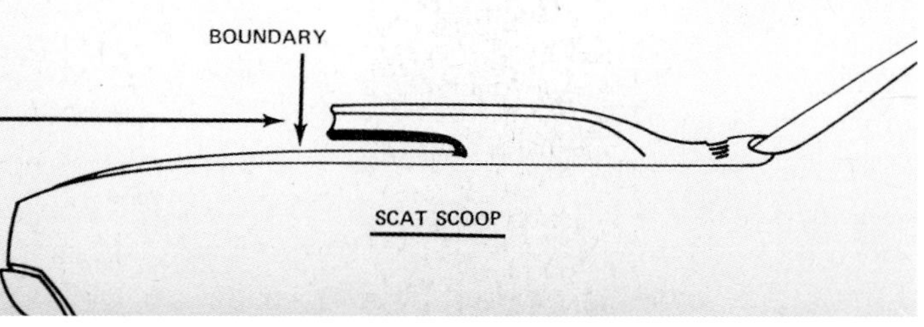

Above:
Rallye instrumentation and a sport steering wheel (with simulated wood rim) were standard inside the Challenger T/A in 1970. Both Torqueflite automatics and four-speed manuals were installed. *Mike Mueller*

Above, right:
The underside of the Challenger T/A's fiberglass hood sealed directly to the 340 Six Pack's air cleaner to allow cooler outside air a direct path into those three carburetors. *Mike Mueller*

Right:
By elevating the T/A's hood scoop slightly, designers avoided aerodynamic interference created by the boundary layer of air that naturally develops on a vehicle's surface at speed. Incoming air flowed more freely into this scoop's opening. *Chrysler LLC Corporate Historical Collection*

Left:
Three Holley two-barrel carburetors mounted on an aluminum intake helped the 340 Six Pack make 15 more horsepower compared to its four-barrel-fed counterpart. Massaged cylinder heads also contributed to the increase. *Mike Mueller*

Above:
Advertised output for the aptly named 340-cubic-inch Six Pack V-8 was 290 horsepower. Compression was 10.5:1. *Mike Mueller*

among other things, dyno-tuning and header installation while you waited. Prospective T/A buyers elsewhere weren't so lucky. Dodge equipped all 2,400 cars by dealer suggestion only, and no special orders were accepted. At dealerships other than Grand-Spaulding, it was simply a matter of taking what was on the lot or watching someone else drive off in the Challenger of your dreams.

Some who missed their opportunity in 1970 initially had high hopes for a second chance. A 1971 T/A was advertised prominently in the October 1970 issue of *Hot Rod* magazine, but it was not to be. After finishing fourth on the Trans-Am circuit, and facing changing attitudes about racing and street performance, Dodge officials decided to pull the plug on both their SCCA competition program and the Challenger T/A very late in 1970.

1971
Dodge Challenger R/T

Specifications	
Model availability	two-door hardtop
Wheelbase	110 inches
Length	192 inches
Width	76.1 inches
Height	50.9 inches
Weight	3,495 pounds
Base Price	$3,273
Track (front/rear, in inches)	59.7/60.7
Wheels	14×6
Tires	F70×14
Construction	unitized body/frame
Suspension	independent A-arms with heavy-duty torsion bars, front; solid axle with longitudinal heavy-duty leaf springs, rear
Steering	recirculating ball
Brakes	four-wheel, heavy-duty, 11-inch drums
Engine	300-horsepower, 383 Magnum V-8, standard (340, 440 Six Pack, and 426 Hemi V-8s, optional)
Bore and stroke	4.25×3.38 inches
Compression	8.5:1
Fuel delivery	single Carter four-barrel carburetor
Transmission	three-speed manual
Axle ratio	3.23:1
Production (including exports)	4,630 (3,907, domestic)

CHALLENGER T/A
End of the road for the Do-It-Yourself Kit.

This is one car where the list of standard equipment is longer than the list of options. Hey, man, this isn't the beginning of something great, it's the driving end.

Big bias-belted skins in front, bigger ones in back. The good shift, Hurst style. Power discs up front; drums, heavy-duty, in the rear. Dual exhausts with low restriction mufflers, chrome side exit megaphones.

Challenger T/A. Just the way you'd do it yourself. If you had the time. And the money. Yeah, the money. Frankly, it would probably cost you more to do it yourself. So why bother with do-it-yourself dreams? Check out this bargain for the man who'd rather be moving than building.

Check out the Standard Equipment List carefully. You'll find that everything is in order. From engine to drive train, Dodge puts it all together for you.

STANDARD EQUIPMENT

340 4-bbl. V8 □ TorqueFlite automatic transmission or 4-on-the-floor fully synchronized manual transmission □ Fiber-glass hood with Fresh Air Pack □ Hood pins □ Special Rallye Suspension (includes rear sway bar, larger front sway bar, heavy-duty shock absorbers, increased camber of rear springs) □ Rear duck tail □ Low-restriction dual side exit exhaust with megaphones □ Tires: E60x15, front; G60x15, rear; raised white letters □ 15x7.0JJ wheels □ Power front disc brakes with special semimetallic pads; 10″ rear drums □ 3.55 axle ratio—8¾ ring gear □ Vinyl front bucket seats □ Deep-pile carpeting □ Simulated wood-grained door trim inserts □ Locking flip-top gas cap □ Flush outside door handles □ T/A body side tape stripes □ Grille and deck panel blackout.

A Dodge Scat Pack magazine ad promised a second-edition Challenger T/A for 1971, but it spoke too soon. This idea failed to go from paper to production. *Chrysler LLC Corporate Historical Collection*

1971

New for 1971 were updated taillights and a revised split-grille. Grille inserts were painted silver on base models, black on R/Ts. R/T Challengers also got restyled body-side stripes and new simulated brake-cooling scoops in front of each rear wheel. The SE package didn't come back for an encore, but a low-buck model did, this time without the Deputy name. The base Challenger for 1971 was an affordable coupe fitted with fixed rear-quarter glass and the budget-conscious 198 cid slant-six backed by a three-speed manual. Dodge's 318 V-8 was again optional. A classier hardtop (offering roll-down rear windows) and sexy convertible came standard with either the 318 small-block or 225 cid six. Available at extra cost were the 340 small-block and the 383 big-block in two- and four-barrel forms.

Standard power for the R/T, available only in hardtop form in 1971, was again the 383-cubic-inch Magnum V-8, rated this time around at 300 horses due to a compression cut. Although an available 440 Magnum didn't return in 1971, the 440 Six Pack and 426 Hemi did, and they were joined on the R/T options list by the 275-horse 340. Most other options carried over from 1970, including the prominent Shaker hood.

The production breakdown by engine for the 1971 R/T was 1,078 340s, 2,509 383s, 246 440 Six Packs, and 70 Hemis. Five other Hemi Challengers were delivered in Canada.

Above:
A 1971 Challenger convertible was chosen to pace the 55th running of the Indianapolis 500. Unfortunately, local Indy Dodge dealer Eldon Palmer lost control at the end of his pace lap and crashed on pit lane, injuring various bystanders. *Chrysler LLC Corporate Historical Collection*

Left:
Base price for the V-8 Challenger convertible was $3,207 in 1971. Dodge built only 167 topless Challengers with the optional 383 Magnum V-8 that year. As in 1970, the base engine for Dodge's V-8 Challenger in 1971 was the 318 small-block. Optional V-8s included a two-barrel-fed 383 and the 383 Magnum, demonstrated here. *Mike Mueller*

Slightly revised taillights helped set the 1971 Challenger apart from its 1970 forerunner. A restyled split grille appeared up front. *Mike Mueller*

Left:
The Challenger's optional 383 Magnum big-block was downrated to 300 horsepower in 1971 thanks primarily to a compression cut to 8.5:1. *Mike Mueller*

Above:
As it did in 1970, simulated wood-grain trim adorned the Challenger's dash and door panels in 1971. The optional console, too, was complemented with a faux wood touch. *Mike Mueller*

The impressive Shaker hood scoop was a $114.20 option atop the 383 Magnum V-8 in 1971. It cost $94 atop the 340 small-block and in R/T applications that year. *Mike Mueller*

Simulated rear-quarter air scoops appeared in 1971 for the R/T, base-priced that year at $3,273. A vinyl roof was an $84.30 option. *Mike Mueller*

Blacked-out grille trim was again standard for the 1971 Challenger R/T, offered only as a hardtop. Total production was 4,630, including 3,907 domestic deliveries. *Mike Mueller*

An available small-block—the 275-horsepower, 340-cubic-inch V-8—joined the Challenger R/T options list in 1971. Production was 1,078. *Mike Mueller*

Above:
The 1971 R/T's standard stripes were restyled for maximum impact, to say the least. *Mike Mueller*

Right:
Challenger exterior shades were wild enough in 1971, with radiant choices including Top Banana, Plum Crazy, Citron Yella, Hemi Orange, and Green Go. Adding the optional cloth/vinyl bucket seats could have enhanced the eye-candy attraction even further. *Mike Mueller*

1972

A convertible Challenger never did seem to bring buyers running into Dodge dealerships. Fewer than 3,500 were delivered in the States in 1970, followed by only about 1,800 the following year. A no-brainer? You betcha. No more convertibles were built after 1971. A topless R/T also became a one-hit wonder after only 955 were sold domestically in 1970. Sadly, the R/T failed to return as well after 1971, as did the optional Hemi and 440 Six Pack. In fact, no big-blocks at all were offered for the Challenger in 1972, a clear sign that the muscle car era was all but coming to an end.

No cheesy 198-cube slant-six was used in 1972, but the strongest option was now the 340-cubic-inch small-block V-8, net-rated at 240 horses. And in place of the extinct R/T was the Challenger Rallye with its performance hood, strobe side stripes and heavy-duty suspension. Dodge's polite 318 V-8 was the Rallye's base engine. Replacing the 318 with the still-warm 340 added an extra $179 to a Rallye's bottom line. The 340 was a $245.85 option for the garden-variety 1972 Challenger.

All 1972 Challengers were hardtops with roll-up rear-quarter glass. Exterior upgrades included yet another restyled grille, this one reminding some wags of a hungry grouper trolling for its supper. New rectangular taillights, two to each side, brought up the rear. Optional goodies diminished noticeably for the third-edition Challenger indicating, in turn, that the breed itself apparently was on the wane.

Challenger Rallye production for the 1972 domestic market was 6,865. Of these, 1,853 featured the base 318 V-8. The count for the optional 340 was 5,012, of which 3,769 had automatics, 1,243 four-speeds.

1972
Dodge Challenger Rallye

Specifications

Model availability	two-door hardtop
Wheelbase	110 inches
Length	192 inches
Width	76.1 inches
Height	50.9 inches
Weight	3,225 pounds
Base Price	$3,082
Track (front/rear, in inches)	59.7/60.7
Wheels	14×6 Rallye
Tires	F70×14
Construction	unitized body/frame
Suspension	independent A-arms with heavy-duty torsion bars, front; solid axle with longitudinal heavy-duty leaf springs, rear
Steering	recirculating ball
Brakes	four-wheel drums
Engine	150-horsepower, 318-cubic-inch V-8, standard; 340 V-8, optional
Bore and stroke	3.91×3.31 inches
Compression	8.6:1
Fuel delivery	single two-barrel carburetor
Transmission	three-speed manual
Axle ratio	3.23:1
Production (including exports)	8,128 (6,865, domestic)

The Challenger Rallye replaced the R/T model for 1972. Strobe stripes and a scooped hood were standard for the 1972 Rallye. *Chrysler LLC Corporate Historical Collection*

1973 Dodge Challenger Rallye

Specifications	
Model availability	two-door hardtop
Wheelbase	110 inches
Length	199 inches
Width	77 inches
Height	50.9 inches
Weight	3,155 pounds
Base Price	Rallye package cost $145.45 with the A04 Basic Group option, $182.25 without A04
Track (front/rear, in inches)	59.7/60.7
Wheels	14×6
Tires	F70×14
Construction	unitized body/frame
Suspension	independent A-arms with heavy-duty torsion bars, front; solid axle with longitudinal heavy-duty leaf springs, rear
Steering	recirculating ball
Brakes	four-wheel drums
Engine	150-horsepower, 318-cubic-inch V-8, standard; 340 V-8, optional
Bore and stroke	3.91×3.31 inches
Compression	8.6:1
Fuel delivery	single two-barrel carburetor
Transmission	three-speed manual
Axle ratio	3.23
Production	not available

1973

Larger, safety-conscious bumper pads helped set the 1973 Challenger apart from its 1972 forerunner, and only V-8 power was offered when the slant-six was finally deep-sixed in E-body ranks. Customers in 1973 could've chosen either the standard 318 or the top-shelf 340. The Rallye model remained, as did optional hot parts like Rallye wheels, a four-speed stick (behind the 340 only), the Performance Axle Package (also 340 only), and F70 rubber.

Production surged, as mentioned, to 27,930 (all hardtops again) for 1973, up from 22,919 the previous year. But the end of the road still awaited the Challenger right around the corner.

Safety-conscious bumper pads helped identify the 1973 Challenger. The Rallye option (priced at $145.45) again was the top performance package that year. *Chrysler LLC Corporate Historical Collection*

Five-spoke road wheels were a Challenger option along with the popular Rallye rims from 1970 to 1974. The price in 1974 for the styled-steel road wheel set was $85.30. *Mike Mueller*

1974
Dodge Challenger Rallye

Specifications	
Model availability	two-door hardtop
Wheelbase	110 inches
Length	199 inches
Width	77 inches
Height	50.9 inches
Weight	3,225 pounds
Base Price	Rallye package cost $151.35 with the A04 Basic Group option, $189.55 without A04
Track (front/rear, in inches)	59.7/60.7
Wheels	14×6 vw
Tires	F70×14
Construction	unitized body/frame
Suspension	independent A-arms with heavy-duty torsion bars, front; solid axle with longitudinal heavy-duty leaf springs, rear
Steering	recirculating ball
Brakes	four-wheel drums
Engine	150-horsepower, 318-cubic-inch V-8, standard; 360 V-8, optional
Bore and stroke	3.91×3.31 inches
Compression	8.6:1
Fuel delivery	single two-barrel carburetor
Transmission	three-speed manual
Axle ratio	3.23:1
Production	not available

1974

Most notable among the last Challenger's minor upgrades were new bumpers able to withstand 5-miles-per-hour impacts, per federal mandate. The standard 318 small-block backed by a three-speed manual transmission carried over, but the ol' familiar 340 didn't return. In its place was the 360-cubic-inch A-series V-8 topped by a four-barrel carb and net-rated at 245 horsepower. This bigger small-block cost $358.85 for the base Challenger hardtop, $188.50 for the sporty, striped Rallye. Heavy-duty suspension parts were included with the 360, optional with the 318.

Power front disc brakes, a $42.55 option, were mandated when the hotter V-8 was installed, and the Performance Axle and four-speed manual options could've been combined with the 360 only. The Sure-Grip differential, a $42.70 option on its own, was included in the Performance Axle Package, itself priced at $62.85.

By 1974, the words "performance" and "compact" no longer went together, and real muscle was basically a memory in all ranks. High-powered small cars like Chrysler's E-bodies no longer seemed welcome in a rapidly reshaping market that overnight had begun refocusing on saving pennies at the pump, this due to rising gas prices inspired by the 1973 Arab oil embargo. So it was that the book on the Challenger was closed—a short story, sure, but a happy one too.

Dodge's last Challenger appeared for 1974. All models incorporated quad headlights every year from 1970 to 1974. Only V-8 models were offered in 1973 and 1974. *Mike Mueller*

Federal safety mandates led to the 1973 installation of prominent rubber bumper guards. The 1974 Challenger's bumpers could withstand 5-miles-per-hour impacts, per further orders from Washington. *Mike Mueller*

Dodge's 318-cubic-inch small-block was standard beneath the 1974 Challenger's twin-scooped hood. The only optional engine was the 360 V-8. *Mike Mueller*

Above:
Total Challenger production, including exports, was 16,437 for 1974. Base price that year was $3,109. *Mike Mueller*

Left:
The 318-cubic-inch V-8 was the Challenger's base engine for 1973 and 1974. A two-barrel carburetor fed this 150-horsepower small-block. Compression was 8.6:1. Mike *Mueller*

Index